Triumph Of Disorder
Islamic Fundamentalism, The New Face of War

Morgan Norval

• • •

McKenna Publishing Group
Indian Wells, California

Triumph of Disorder
Islamic Fundamentalism,
The New Face of War

ISBN: 0-9713659-7-0

LCCN: 2001096316

Second Edition

Contents

Dedicated to Lt. Col. James "Nick" Rowe, USA.
A man of faith, a friend, patriot, devoted family man,
noble warrior in the truest sense—
and a victim of terrorism.

Map detailing Islamic Fundamentalist activity in the United States

Introduction

Much has transpired in the two years since this book was published that reinforces its message: the destruction of our two embassies in Kenya and Tanzania; the attack on the USS Cole; and, the latest act of infamy, the coordinated destructive terrorist attacks in New York City and Washington. There are two common threads linking all of these incidents: they were carried out by militant Islamic fundamentalists and they were conceived, planned, and carried out by non-governmental organizations.

Islamic fundamentalists hate the modern world they live in and are focusing their venom on its most visible successful example, the United States. They don't want to have anything to do with the 21st Century and yearn for the glorious days of old in the feudal age. Seeing the world around them, they feel frustration and rage and their ancient puritanical mind-set becomes ever hardened and finds release in a turbo-charged war of terror against the West—especially the United States.

But they differ from their ancestors in their so-called golden era they'd like to recreate—they have access to a far superior technological menu for their war of terror than their forbearers' daggers and poisons. The destructive attacks in Africa, Ader, and the most recent ones on the World Trade Center and Pentagon, show they understand and can use modern technology to try and achieve their ancient goals.

The attacks also demonstrated the growing ability and sophistication of private non-governmental organizations to challenge the exclusive monopoly of violence claimed for itself by the nation-state. Our surveillance satellites, nuclear weapons, carrier battle groups, stealth bombers, and other Push-Button war gadgetry, failed to deter the terrorist attacks on New York City and the Pentagon. Those acts demonstrated a coordinated, well-planned effort normally associated with the military abilities of advanced nation-states. Our terrorist foes are fighting by their rules, not those of the Pentagon—and our rules of war may be outdated, as this book explains in detail.

Countering this threat will not be limited to attempts to bomb a few of bin Laden's caves into dust or accelerating Afghanistan's drive to return to the Stone Age. The military response—the politician's much touted "war on terrorism"—will resemble a counter-guerrilla war, and our Armed Forces, with the possible exception of Delta Force, Rangers, SEALS, Special Forces, and all other Special Ops units, are ill-equipped to conduct such a campaign. To win the "war on terrorism" our troops must become as ruthless, if not more so, than their will-of-the-wisp enemy. Our foes lack any scruples in conducting their mode of war, but our troops have ethics, and in the age of warfare via CNN, we will fare badly when fighting such foes. Such an endeavor will require a long line and will not be bloodless, being essentially down and dirty casualty-producing infantry combat. Will the American public put up with such a lengthy effort? Given the Vietnam experience one would be tempted to say no, but with the destruction wreaked within the US, that attitude may change. It must if the "war on terrorism" is to succeed.

While the politicians talk war, they seem to be acting like criminologists and jurists claiming they will "hunt down and bring to justice" those responsible. Hauling bin Laden, or other terrorists, before some court will not deter future acts of terrorism. Such action is akin

to treating cancer with a Band-Aid. What should we do with terrorists? My remarks to that question from a student at Washington &
Lee University during my 1998 Captive Nations lecture are just as
applicable today: "Hunt 'em down and kill 'em like rabid dogs." We
had better be prepared to do this rather than treat terrorists as criminals—a process that will neither halt, not deter terrorism.

Islamic fundamentalist terrorist organizations have not only a
vast, organized and inspired movement, but a worldwide network,
described in this book, that will preclude any quick fixes on the part
of the US. Although the theology of this movement is retrogressive
and they hate the US and the West, it is extremely adept at embracing
and using our technology for their destructive goals. They feel and
see no conflict in embracing our technology while hanging onto their
religious hatred.

The stakes are enormous and the reasons why are just as relevant today as when this book was originally written. The events on
September 11, 2001 have raised the stakes and demonstrated the seri-
ousness of the situation. In simple condensed terms, failure to successfully counter terrorism has dire consequences for the political concept of the nation-state—our major form of political organization
for the past two centuries—because the state will have failed to provide one of its most elemental functions: protection of its citizens.
When the state fails to protect its citizens, it forfeits their loyalty and
this loyalty will be transferred to whatever group or organization can
protect them. The attacks on New York City and on the Pentagon are
symptomatic of the nation-states' faltering ability to hold onto its
monopoly of violence—or, in plain words, to protect its citizen's lives
and property. Nobody knows the ultimate significance of this, but it
is likely to be eventful and very bloody.

Triumph of Disorder

The book explores and details some of these consequences and the role being played by militant Islamic fundamentalism. The events in New York City and Washington bear witness to this danger. The time between the original publication and the events on September 11, 2001, demonstrate the danger is real and growing.

Morgan Norval
September 20, 2001

Prologue

Terrorize: to dominate, coerce, or subdue
by terror, or intimidation.
Webster Reference Dictionary of The English Language,
Encyclopedic Edition.

It seemed a typical rush hour—the subway train overflowing with early morning commuters, each locked into his or her own thoughts as their bodies swayed to the rhythmic motion of the train.

But it was not a typical commute. Unnoticed by the passengers, several packages had been left under seats throughout the train by individuals already off the train. Those packages contained glass tubes, each holding chemicals dissolved in solvents, along with timing devices designed to shatter the containers, mix the chemicals and send deadly gases into the air.

Suddenly, the monotonous ride turned into a deadly nightmare—the glass tubes broke and the chemicals mixed, producing Sarin—a colorless, odorless, nerve gas twenty-six times more deadly than cyanide gas.

Panic ensued—blinded by tear-filled eyes and gasping for air, the passengers desperately tried to escape their invisible peril. All experienced tunnel vision, breathing difficulties and sore throats. Some died, many more were treated for various levels of nausea, eye irritation, and other associated injuries.

Triumph of Disorder

Many will recall that this terrorist attack occurred in Tokyo on March 20, 1995. But a similar attack could just as well take place in New York City, London, Paris, Washington, or any other city with a subway system. Only luck in the form of a stuck valve in a gas cylinder kept the Tokyo casualty count from reaching a possible 40,000 victims.

Next time, and there will be a next time somewhere in the world, lady luck might not be so generous.

• • •

"Terrorism," says Catholic University professor and terrorism expert Dr. Bard O'Neill, "is a form of warfare in which violence is directed primarily against noncombatants, usually civilians..." That's awful academic for what are apparently mindless criminal acts of violence given a political sheen.

But behind the academic jargon it is a form of warfare especially suited by the weak against the strong.

Terrorism fits in well with Islamic fundamentalism's war on both Muslim and non-Muslim alike. It is a type of warfare that is well-suited to wreak havoc in countries whose economic and political structures are fragile. The costs—financial, material and human—required to combat the terrorists threaten to overcome the meager resources of the society under siege, paving the way for a take-over by the fundamentalists. It is "war on the cheap" for the terrorists, but very costly for the society under attack.

The terrorist is fast becoming a potent weapon in today's evolving mode of warfare. The introduction of jet aircraft in the 1950s and early 1960s gave terrorists a degree of mobility and a field of operations undreamed of by their most dedicated and skillful predecessors. They could literally strike at targets of opportunity on a global basis in a matter of hours.

These sinister individuals are the ultimate hit-and-run commandos. He, or she, can attack segments of a politico-economic system without in turn being subjected to certain harm. This makes them the master of stealth warfare at a fraction of the cost of a stealth bomber.

In a democratic society, political wars are fought and won with voting power, nothing else. The democratic process allows any individual to develop a political vision for the future, convey this vision to the people and create a political organization with the aim of participating in the election. With that election the people can either accept this vision or reject it.

The Islamic fundamentalist terrorist, however, professes to support the democratic process but in reality uses it to subvert the regime and replace it with a theocratic dictatorship.

Many Islamic fundamentalists don't even bother hiding behind a democratic facade. They have little use for democracy. In fact, they hate it as well as those who practice and preach it. To them, Islamic laws are not derived from the people, but are given by Allah.

Subversion and terrorist warfare has become militant Islam's *modus operandi* in its visionary mission: to convert the world to its particular brand of Islam. The militant Islamic fundamentalist wishes to impose the rules and values of Islam's golden days. They feel that what applied to the faithful in the seventh century is just the recipe to follow in today's world. There is not a shred of doubt in their minds about that. If skeptical Muslims don't agree, they don't deserve to live, and terror is the weapon used to change their minds or cower them into obedient silence—witness the carnage in Algeria.

Militant fundamentalists, filled with religious zeal, using the tactics of terror, will not be deterred as they go forth on their messianic crusade to Islamize the world. They see themselves and the rest of the world in terms of "we" and "them." In other words, they will use the identity of their own group and its values--the tenets of Islam as perceived by themselves—to judge the worth of "them." Such an attitude leads to hostility and violence.

This has appeal to those facing an uncertain future who look for rationalizations for their plight. As the world approaches the next century, there are many dark clouds on mankind's horizon—a period of uncertainty and danger for all.

We are witnessing one of the most dangerous periods in human existence. Order is breaking down, and it's going to get a lot worse. There is a connection between the rise of terrorism, the anarchy of the former Soviet Union, the riots in Los Angeles, Islamic fundamentalists poised to take over Muslim countries, and the local thugs who threaten your life and limb.

The connection is that governments are losing their grip. They aren't what they used to be. They'd like to bring order to your neighborhood, not to mention Bosnia, Chechyna, Liberia, Sudan, Mexico and Somalia, to name a few. But they can't. As Robert Kaplan puts it, "...a medieval world coexists with a postmodern one."

The collapse of communism and the freeing of the captive nations was supposed to bring a period of world peace and expanding liberal democracy.

While hope may spring eternal, reality has a habit of smacking us in the face. The world is now more volatile, more uncertain than it was during the Cold War. It wasn't supposed to be this way. The collapse of the Soviet Union and its East Bloc allies had removed the doomsday threat of nuclear annihilation. A new era of peace was to spread over the globe.

Instead, long pent-up pressures, kept under the lid by Cold War necessities, were released and now societies are being torn asunder.

The gory results of mindless militant Islamic violence, as well as ethnic, cultural and nationalistic strife are shown regularly on nightly news television programs. Terrorists, guerrillas and drug gangs roam the world with growing impunity as traditional military responses become a more costly option.

A glance around the globe reveals a growingly unstable international environment. There are wars of succession in parts of the old Soviet empire and elsewhere; ethnic and religious conflicts in Europe, Asia, Africa and in the islands in the Pacific; tribal clashes in Africa; coups d'etat, border disputes, civil upheavals, and terrorist attacks, pushing hundreds of thousands of refugees across increasingly porous national boundaries.

The future is staring us in the face—look at Cambodia, Somalia, Liberia, "Kurdistan," or to the Balkans, Angola, Afghanistan, Sudan, Tajikistan and on and on...

• • •

She was a beauty, this eighteen-year old daughter of a shopkeeper in Lebanon. Her beauty was such that it conjured up images of Scheherazade and other princesses of Arabian lore. Such beauty attracted many suitors, for her presence as a wife would bring honor to any house. But she spurned them all, preferring instead to get an education at the American University in Beirut.

Her world changed forever one evening as she was returning home from a visit to a friend. She was surrounded by a gang of male youths—members of Hezbollah, the militant Islamic "Party of God." The young men taunted her and verbally cursed her for her desire to get an education at a western university. They jeered at her for wearing western clothing and make-up, and became more abusive and accused her of insulting the blood of the Muslim martyrs by not wearing a veil.

Finally, one of the youths threw acid on her face turning her beauty into a grotesque mask of scar tissue. As the sulfuric acid ate into her flesh, the youths screamed at her: "Allah is the greatest! Khomeini is the chief!"

Muslim fundamentalists in Bangladesh are calling for the execution of a female Bangladesh author who called for revising the Koran. The fundamentalists are accusing her of blasphemy. Her crime? She allegedly suggested in an Indian newspaper interview that the Koran should be revised thoroughly.

The woman denied the statement, saying she had called for a revision of the Islamic law, *shari'a* not the Koran. In spite of the denial, Muslim fundamentalists offered over a $5,000 reward for her assassination and the government of Bangladesh charged her with "intent to deliberately and maliciously outrage the religious feelings of Muslims." The woman fled the country in fear of her life.

Welcome to the Islamic fundamentalist's postmodern world— a frightening different world than ours.

●●●

We face a world in which many of the familiar ways we dealt with such problems have become the least likely models to follow in the future. Stubbornly clinging to these thoughts limits our options, while terrorists, drug traffickers, armed thugs and criminal syndicates skip across continents and oceans at will. All over the globe, traditional governments are fighting for their survival against these border-hoping threats.

The collapse of the Soviet Union isn't the only earth-shattering event taking place as we and the world prepare to enter the Third Millennium.

The dawn of the Information Age is remaking the world in ways that will profoundly affect how people do business, govern themselves and make war. This transformation is on a par with the other momentous transformations in human history: the transition from hunting and gathering to farming, and the transition from the farm to the factory.

In addition to revolutionizing everyday life, the computer has become a revolutionary war tool. Revolutionaries, counter-revolutionaries, extremist groups, militant Islamic fundamentalists, radical wings, separatist movements, cults and their critics, are all using the Internet—the Information Highway—for their purposes. Never before have so many people had direct access to information from every angle.

The information flow makes it possible for our interconnected world to function. Information can drive and fuel a thriving economy like the West's, or it can propel a weak economy into a stronger position.

The real-time delivery of information also aids the enemies of the West, such as terrorist groups, by allowing rapid communication and coordination between them.

The modern globalization of the world's economy, and the social changes it is creating, are separating people from familiar identities such as the nation state. Advances in communications have increased the cultural awareness of ethnic groups living within the same territory. This awareness is a two-edged sword. Not only does one become more aware of those who share the same cultural and ethnic identity, but one also becomes more aware of alien ethnic groups.

The end result is the crumbling of many of the multicultural countries of the world, as separatist movements break out in such diverse countries as Spain, Thailand, Burma, and even Ethiopia, despite its 3000-year history.

The parts are beginning to consider themselves more important than the whole. The Soviet Union has cracked up. Others will follow.

Ethnic clashes are not the only contributing factor affecting the mounting chaos throughout the world. Competition for scarce resources and demographics are others. The reality of more people striving for less resources is a sure-fire formula for conflict.

During the great secular ideological clash of the Cold War a future source of conflict was emerging from its centuries-old slumber—the religious drive of Islam. Even though resurgent Islam was second-staged by the East-West conflict, the Cold War didn't stop Islam from growing in numbers and militancy.

Militant Islam gained power in Iran in 1979, and played a major role in provoking stubborn resistance to the Soviet forces in Afghanistan, eventually forcing a Soviet withdrawal in 1988.

Islam's militant fundamentalist's brand is becoming the destabilizing force in many Muslim countries. Savage acts of violence such as car and airliner bombings, skyjackings, hostage takings, murders and other attacks of terror, committed in Islam's name have become common occurrences throughout the Islamic world.

Islamic terror acts have now spilled over into Europe, South America and the United States, as the World Trade Center bombing [all references to the World Trade Center bombing throughout this book refer to the 1993 bombing and not the events of September 11, 2001.— M.N.] and the mindless killings of workers outside the CIA has brought home to Americans who thought "it can't happen here." You could be on the wrong subway or step on the wrong plane, or simply stand on a street corner and be killed or maimed by a bomb blast from a bomb planted in a trash can. You just happened to be in the wrong place at the wrong time.

Islamic fundamentalism has since become an increasingly dangerous force outside of Iran. The coincidence of geography and geology that placed Muslim countries on top of most of the world's oil reserves will ensure a growing role in that turbulent area.

The militant Islamic fundamentalist not only threatens the stability of the oil producing regimes, but Western societies are threatened as well.

The global economy is dependent on Middle Eastern oil. Any threat to that supply is a threat of global proportions.

The threat of the terror campaign of militant Islamic extremism is potentially more dangerous. Infused with religious zealotry, self-preservation is not a significant factor in the militant Islamic terrorist's decisions. Nor does reason provide a steady hand to tell its leaders how far they can go, as caution may be against the will of Allah.

It is Allah, not political expediency, that commands the obligation of every Muslim to engage in a *jihad,* or holy war, against the enemies of Islam. That ancient obligation of Islam is still relevant today. Death has no sting for the militant, as Hamas suicide bombers have repeatedly demonstrated in Israel.

Such a concept seems inconceivable to the Western mind, steeped in the ingrained belief of the sanctity of human life. To dismiss the fanatic's desire for self-immolation is to fall into a deadly trap. It is the folly of projecting our beliefs and values on to different cultures or religious world views. It is a dangerous journey into the unreal world of self-delusion.

Terror, especially the type waged by the Islamic fundamentalist, poses difficult choices for the U.S. because of America's uniqueness among nations. Its openness, diversity, the mobility of its citizens, and their fierce hostility towards intrusions into their private lives exposes our vulnerabilities.

The terrorists are quick to exploit these. Consider: in 1996 the new head of the terrorist group, Islamic Jihad, was securely ensconced in the United States where he was a college professor at the University of Florida in Tampa. Thanks to modern technology in the form of faxes and the Internet, he and other "sleeping" Islamic terrorists have been able to stay in touch and be ready for action at a moment's notice. Upon the death of Islamic Jihad's leader by assassination in Malta in fall of 1995, the professor, Ramadan Abdullah Shallah, left his professorship and returned to Gaza to take over the reins of the terrorist group.

The good professor isn't the only radical Islamic fundamentalist living among us. All radical Islamic terrorist groups have their "sleepers," "fifth-columnists" or humanitarian front groups living within the over 4,000,000 strong Muslim community in the United States.

It was from this community, centered on a storefront mosque in Jersey City, that the planning for the World Trade Center bombing was planned and executed.

Radical militant Islamic fundamentalists have taken to terrorism with a vengeance. They are directly implicated in most terrorist attacks against the United States or its allies interests.

• • •

The sickening smell of burnt flesh hung over the downtown center of the city. Mangled bits of flesh and limbs, brains and blood, shreds of bright clothing were scattered over the street and on the buildings facing it. For the city commuters and tourists aboard a bus, the early morning ride had an unexpected, unwanted rendezvous with the grim reaper. A violent explosion had blown the bus apart. A radical Islamic extremist group claimed credit for the butchery. Once again militant Islam's war of terror had struck the innocent.

Although these bombings occur most often in Israel, they could happen anywhere, including your home town.

Terror bombings by Hamas and Hezbollah in Israel were responsible for the defeat of the Labor Party and derailing the peace process in the Middle East.

The world has seen the example of a successful Islamic fundamentalist revolution, and the terror it spawned in Iran when the Shah was toppled by Khomeini in 1979. That event is still causing shock waves throughout the world as militant Islamists are working overtime to undertake similar revolutions in Islamic countries in the Middle East and elsewhere.

One of the pressing perils of our time is that people are being cut off from their roots in cultures and community. We see this in the growing urbanization occouring throughout the world: people crammed together as a swarming, poverty-stricken rootless mass of humanity.

"The rootless are always violent," Hannah Arendt reminds us. The rootless are empty of hope and therefore they grow angry, destructive and receptive to demagoguery. In the Muslim world the rootless are the ready recruits to the banner of Islamic fundamentalism.

• • •

They huddled around the table waiting for the bomb-maker to finish his task. All eyes were focused on him as he tested the circuits for the last time before hooking the radio receiver to the bomb. A push of the button on the transmitter carried by one of those sitting at the table and more of Allah's enemies would be sent to hell.

"Remember," said the bomb-maker to those who would place the bomb in a trash can on the corner near a popular outdoor cafe, "make sure you can see the can from the alley. And wait until there's a good crowd before you set it off."

He glanced around the table at his warriors of Allah. They wore a uniform of T-shirts, jeans and scraggly beards. They were young males who should have been in school or at work, but schools and jobs were few and far between in the refugee camps stuck out in the middle of nowhere. Instead their education consisted of harangues, hate-filled lectures and sermons against Jews and Americans by the mullah at the neighboring mosque. These young males, who might otherwise have led productive lives, were instead drawn into the violent world of the terrorist striking a blow for Allah against the hated infidels.

They weren't drafted or shanghaied into this sinister world. They were willing participants in the forthcoming terror bombing that would blow innocents to bloody bits. With bomb in hand and venomous hate for their nameless, faceless victims dripping from their mouths, they set off to plant their deadly bomb and slaughter more of the guiltless.

These hard-hearted young terrorists in our bombing example were losers with minimal education, no prospects of a decent job, sullen anti-social dispositions and thus little attractiveness to women, and no future—except as warriors for Allah. All had acquired a taste for violence and killing. As long as there were mullahs and imams to urge them onward against Islam's enemies, real or imagined, they would probably not settle down to finish their schooling and be happy with the common laborer's lot.

They are unskilled, callous, rootless and have absolute contempt for life and the values we associate with Western civilization. Life is cheap, nasty, brutish and actions such as compromise, dialogue and "turning the other cheek" are viewed as deserving the utmost contempt. In the unlikely event of peace, they would not beat their spears into pruning hooks, but pursue life as violent criminals.

This phenomenon is *not* limited to the Islamic fanatic nor the Balkan or Liberian warlord. Urban gang members in the United States exhibit many of these tendencies, which doesn't bode well for future peace and tranquility in our gang-infested urban environments.

• • •

We in the United States, encouraged by the media, hold to the myth that people are naturally good and conflict, terrorism and wars by the "have nots" against the "haves" just result from misunderstandings and will be prevented by settling those differences.

That is a silly myth that should be blown away once and for all. Silly beliefs—wrong ideas—are more dangerous to our future and well-being than any atomic bomb in Iran's or Iraq's arsenals. For a large number of people on this planet, war and life in the barracks is a step up, not a step down.

Given the level of despair, poverty, and lack of opportunity endemic throughout the world including the Islamic world, to think the downtrodden mass of humanity will meekly accept their fate is dreaming. They are more likely to pick up the gun and use force to try and seize what they want. What do they have to lose?

Their current circumstances are so bad they feel they have nothing to lose. When there's nothing to lose, there's nothing to fear. The only course for the "have nots" is to grab their piece of the West's cake. Taking on the West is a no-lose option for them.

That confrontation will not be peaceful because the "haves" when pushed, will not meekly hand over their good life to the whims of the "have nots." The likely turmoil will rent asunder many existing nation states and their societies.

While we in the United States are not engaged in armed civil strife against each other, we are deeply divided and involved in rancorous political strife. With the exception of the period 1861-65, our political strife has not been waged on the battlefield. Rather, as Clausewitz reminds us, war is politics by other means. Past political controversy, while not resulting in civil war, has not been free of violence.

Riots, death and destruction of property accompanied the rise of both the labor and civil rights movements in this country. Violence lies below the surface in many of our current political controversies—on occasion violent acts have occurred in their name: environmental-ism, civil rights, welfare reform, immigration, abortion, and animal rights, to name a few. The changing nature of war, described by Martin Van Creveld, is tailor-made to take that fatal step from riots and protest to low intensity conflict—a process some feel has already happened.

The nature of war has changed—is changing—and you had better understand that evolution.

The world is becoming more and more influenced by private organizations that boast their own armies and exist outside of any law or government. You can see it in Japanese organized crime, the drug cartels of Latin America, the gangs that run much of Russia, and the radical militant Islamic fundamentalists throughout much of the Muslim world.

The rise of these powerful non-state groups is going to affect politics and events far more than the latest Washington scandal paraded on the front page of your newspaper or on the evening TV news.

Small groups, tribes, Asian triads, Islamic fundamentalists, gangsters, militias and even solitary individuals have gained increasing military effectiveness. They will exercise far more real power in the next century than they have since the middle of the 17th century.

The microchip is neutralizing the expensive modern military machines of the latter 20th century, making all-out war in the sense of WW II less profitable, and therefore less likely.

Smart shoulder held missiles, like the Stinger surface-to-air missile, effectively neutralized much of the advantage that large wealthy states formerly enjoyed in dispatching expensive air power to attack poorer, smaller groups.

This form of strife centered around non-state groups, long

thought outdated, is once more moving to center stage and influencing conflict resolution. What will be the result of this transformation? It is that wars will be fought by more and more hydra-headed gangs of terrorists, drug warlords, guerrillas or revolutionaries too decentralized, spread out and unpredictable to be targeted by cruise missiles, stealth bombers or tanks and artillery—the arsenal of our growing very expensive technological-dependent military stockpile.

Warfare is changing from pitched battles fought by armies representing nation states to conflicts carried out by non-state organizations, including Islamic terrorists.

Given the technological weapons available—deadly compact small arms and portable missiles, computers, small video cameras faxes, cellular phone, the Internet, etc., our future foes are well positioned to take advantage of the social and political openness of Western democracies.

At no time in the history of mankind have human beings been able to move so quickly, so cheaply, or so often as they can today. When you couple that mobility with the total lack of scruples of the terrorist, religious Islamic fanatic, drug lords and other players in the murky world of non-state violence, you are surrendering a whole lot of tactical flexibility to our enemies of the future. They can take advantage of new relevant technologies much quicker than the red-tape mired bureaucracies of nation states. These groups increasingly can out-spend, out-shoot, out-negotiate and out-fox nation states and their traditional ways and means for enforcing their edicts.

The spreading incidents of terror and the rise to prominence of radical Islamic fundamentalism must be viewed within the scope of these far-reaching trends. From the Third World to the former Soviet Union, to Latin America, Asia, Europe and even our southern border, these dangerous trends will affect us all.

We must examine these for they are critical to our understanding of the rising wave of terrorism and its connection with Islamic fundamentalism.

Chapter 1
Islam's Shock Troops

It is the nature of Islam to dominate, not to be dominated,
to impose its powers to the entire planet.
Shaik Hassan al;Banna, founder, Muslim Brotherhood

It was a bright day in Cairo on October 6, 1981, a good day for the parade which would celebrate the Egyptian performance in the October 1973 Yon Kippur War against Israel. The dignitaries, including President Anwar Sadat, were dressed in their immaculate uniforms, shiny medals on their chests, boots and brass polished to a high gloss. They stood on the reviewing stand waiting for the military parade to pass by in review.

It was a festive time. Yet something was wrong—four soldiers in the procession held a secret. Unlike all the other participants in the military parade, these four had live ammunition in their weapons. Led by twenty-four year-old Lieutenant Khalid Ahmed Shawki Islambouli, these four were about to send shock waves around the world.

Carrying Islambouli and his men, a military truck passed in front of the reviewing stand and came to a sudden stop. Islambouli and his three companions jumped out of the truck and fired their loaded automatic rifles at the men on the reviewing stand. Lt. Islambouli focused his attention on one man. His target was Egyptian

President Anwar Sadat. As the bullets from his AK-47 slammed into Sadat's body, he cried out: "I am Khalid al-Islambouli. I have killed Pharaoh."

The four assassins were members of Al Jihad, a clandestine Muslim fundamentalist terror clique who wanted to impose a Khomeini-style Islamic Republic in Egypt.

Twelve years later, at 12:18 P.M., a tremendous explosion erupted in the underground parking garage of the Twin Towers of the World Trade Center in the heart of New York City's business district. The black smoke from the explosion, hovering over the wintery New York skyline, announced the fact that not even the most powerful nation in the world was immune from barbaric terrorist attack.

Four months later, on June 24, 1993, FBI agents and police arrested eight suspects in a bombing plot involving three more targets in New York City: the United Nations building, the New York City Federal Building, and the Lincoln and Holland Tunnels. One of the plotters, who happened to be an FBI informant, nipped this deadly plot in the bud. It was an extremely close call.

According to the FBI, as agents rolled up to the door to enter the bomb factory, the smell of chemical fumes was over-powering. The bomb-makers were mixing the explosive concoction in 55-gallon drums. As the FBI entered the bomb factory, the five suspects were literally mixing the witches brew.

Two of the suspects in the June bomb plot were linked to the World Trade Center bombing. The perpetrators of all three incidents are Muslim fundamentalists and a common thread linked them: the blind Islamic cleric Sheik Omar Abdel-Rahman.

At the time of the New York bombing and bomb plot, he was

living and preaching in a storefront mosque in Jersey City, New Jersey. He was also a leader of Al Jihad at the time of the Sadat assassination. Rahman was arrested and charged with conspiracy by the Egyptian government but was acquitted. He subsequently fled Egypt and settled in New Jersey where he became the spiritual leader of those charged and convicted in the New York City incidents.

To understand men like Sheik Rahman, we must comprehend Islamic fundamentalism's world view. This is absolutely necessary. Americans, conditioned by history and their own hubris, tend to think of liberty, equality and opportunity as humankind's birthright. We tend to ignore or overlook the cultural differences in others. Not everyone on this planet shares our American views.

It is difficult for Americans to understand the seemingly sense-less violence of the World Trade Center bombing in New York, the bombing of the American barracks in Saudi Arabia, or the storming and seizure of the American Embassy in Teheran.

We are baffled and confused about the growing threat of ter-rorism, especially Islamic terrorism, because nobody likes to be the focus of another's hate. In our eyes at least, these are irrational and irresponsible subjects. But what may be irrational in our eyes may well be perfectly rational to people in another culture. Attacking the "great Satan" with a car bomb, revolting to us as it may seem, makes perfect sense to an Ayatollah Khomeini or a Sheik Abdel-Rahman.

To understand is to be enlightened, and, in a sense, armed and forewarned. We must explore the dark, bloody world of the Islamic fundamentalist and find answers not only to what makes them tick, but also use that knowledge to design strategies to thwart their deadly designs on Americans everywhere.

Islam's deepest tenets and dogmas are used both by the

Khomeinis and Rahmans of the Islamic fundamentalist world to justify their barbarous acts of terrorism. Yet the oldest Islamic fundamentalist state today, Saudi Arabia, is not only firmly allied to the
West, but is itself a target of militant Islamic fundamentalists.

A word of caution is required: the acts of Khomeini or Rahman
and their cohorts are no more representative of mainstream Islam
than David Koresh's acts are of Christianity. Koresh's Branch Davidians
are an anomaly.

Islam has, Khomeini and Rahman to the contrary, peaceful
tendencies. The problem that is central to Islam and makes it so vulnerable to the siren call of the violent radical is that in Islamic theory
there is no separation of the religious and the secular society.

"Islam is the religion which has most completely confounded
and intermixed the two powers," writes de Tocqueville, the author of
the celebrated book DEMOCRACY IN AMERICA, "...so that all the
acts of civil and political life are regulated more or less by religious
law."

Islam is more than a religion. It constitutes a complete social
system to be embraced by all Muslims. It is a world view that is just as
valid today as it was centuries ago. It sets standards and norms and
provides rules of conduct for its followers that touch every aspect of
life—including politics. There is no distinction between religion and
politics in Islam.

● ● ●

The man adjusted the straps of his backpack as he moved
along the crowded street at the Tournament of Roses parade in Pasa-
dena, California. He reached into the side-pocket of the pack and

grabbed one of his plastic bottles of "drinking water," unscrewed the cap and raised it towards his lips.

He did not intend to take a sip. Instead, he deliberately bumped into another parade- watching tourist, sending the bottle to the ground spilling its contents.

"Oh, excuse me," said the plain, dumpy woman he had jostled.

"No problem," replied the man. "I've got a couple more in my pack, and I should have been watching where I was going."

Ten minutes later, he repeated the incident as he walked along the parade route. Then he did it a third time in the crowded stadium holding the Rose Bowl football game.

His last bottle was "spilled" that evening in the terminal of Los Angeles International airport while on his way to board a plane for Europe and his disappearance—and for a very good reason. Each "water bottle" contained a liquid nutrient mix containing a concentration of Pulmonary Anthrax, Type E, a genetically mutated form of *Bacillus anthraxis* for which there is no known cure.

Nearly every person along the parade route and in the Rose Bowl stadium was exposed to the disease. Travellers in the airport would transport the disease to their destinations.

In over two weeks almost 200,000 people, including the transporting terrorist, would be dead—but he gloried in his coming death. He had killed in the name of Allah and the ayatollah in Iran has assured him his act would send him directly to Paradise and into the arms of scores of beautiful virgins.

• • •

Islamic fundamentalists have declared war on the infidel—

that is, you and me, using the age-old psychological ploy of demonizing the enemy. To the modern mind the enemy, by definition, is detestable. "Well, he's the enemy, isn't he?" goes the reasoning. "You couldn't kill them if you thought he was just like you." This apparently self-evident truth—that man can't kill an enemy understood to be honorable and like himself—is something all cultures seem to share, even the Muslim world.

The enemy must then, in some way, be dehumanized, degraded to less than full human status. The infidel—those who aren't Muslims—fit the bill for the militant Islamic fundamentalist. In the minds of the radical fundamentalist, if one isn't enlightened enough to see the righteousness of Islam, that person is a subhuman being. The infidel is pictured as evil and loathsome, deserving to be killed as an enemy of God.

Similar thinking on a secular level has resulted in Nazi Germany's gas chambers and the Soviet Union's Gulag death camps, the Chinese Communist's extermination policies, and the killing fields of the Khymer Rouge in Cambodia

While warring on the infidel, the faithful must also be cleansed of corruption. This corruption according to Khomeini and the fundamentalists, was caused by the evil influence of the West. The West beguiled the imagination of large sections of Muslim and corrupted them. That corrupting influence was far more disastrous for Islam than any loss of territory. Far graver, claimed Khomeini, is the loss of the hearts and minds of large sections of Islam's youth to Western ideology, dress, music and food.

Because of this corrupting influence, the infidels had no reason to attack Islamic states with their armies. Islam was defeated from within by its own rulers, who ignored Islamic holy law in the name of

Western-style secularism. These evil influence must be rooted out by all means possible—so goes the justification of the reign of terror in post-revolutionary Iran.

As far as the Ayatollahs and their fundamentalist followers are concerned, every single lock of hair or bit of feminine flesh that shows from beneath a chador carelessly worn is like a dagger aimed at the heart of Islam.

Such an attitude goes far to explain the fundamentalist's attitude towards women. It can be best descried as old fashion segregation based on sex instead of race or color—in short, gender apartheid. The fundamentalist theory of feminism is the condescending one that women are vulnerable, fragile and subject to temptations. They must be protected from themselves by the guiding hand of men. This chauvinistic attitude is bolstered by quoting the Koran, the holy book of Islam: "Men are managers of the affairs of women: for that God has preferred in bounty one of them over another..."

The laws of sacred Islam do not permit women to be combatants, even though many Islamic terror groups such as the PLO had females terrorists. Yet their employment goes against Khomeini-inspired Shi'ite theology. To have used women in typical suicide bombings like those that destroyed the Marine barracks in Lebanon would have undermined their character. This position is made quite clear by a decree by Hezbollah's Shaykh Abd al-Karim Ubayd:

"One of the nationalist women asked me, 'does Islam permit a woman to join in military operations of the resistance to the occupation, and would she go to paradise if she were martyred?' The *jihad* in Islam is forbidden to women except in self-defense and in the absence of menfolk...My answer to this women was that her *jihad* was impermissible regardless of motive or reason...."

A woman's place, therefore, is in the home, where she is to raise the children and make the home environment conducive to Islam. This is all part and parcel of the fundamentalist's goal to make the social environment such that it won't lead the believer into temptation.

Saudi Arabia provides a good example of this attitude towards women, Muslim as well as non-Muslim. The *muttawin,* which means "enforcers of obedience" in Arabic, are the religious police, and are the kingdom's defenders of morals. They have the power to compel shops to close at prayer time, arbitrarily destroy goods they consider idolatrous, raid homes suspected of having alcoholic beverages, and beat the exposed calves of European women who dare to wear western fashions.

Women are not allowed to drive automobiles. They even risk arrest for being in a vehicle driven by a man who is not an employee or relative. Being in a car with a man, not so categorized, implies a lack of morals on her part.

Some Saudi's are against any contact with the West. Sheik Abdul-Aziz bin Baz, who heads the Council of Senior Islamic Scholars in the kingdom, warns parents not to send their children abroad to study or live with foreign families to learn a Western language.

He said this was part of a plot by the enemies of Islam to corrupt young Muslims.

Many Saudi's routinely go abroad during the oppressively hot summer months, but even this is suspect to the sheik. He calls travel brochures a "great evil" whose purpose is to seduce Muslims into debauchery by providing opportunities to sin.

This hard-line attitude exists in a country that is supposed to be a friend of the West. It is informative in that it does point out the strong undercurrents of Islamic fundamentalism that exist even in pro-Western Muslim states. Given the right circumstance this attitude could mushroom and become a serious threat to the stability of moderate Islamic regimes. If they fall into the hands of the fundamentalists, at the minimum, you can imagine how much you'll pay for a gallon of gasoline at the local gas station.

One of the key duties and obligations of the militant fundamentalist is to increase the number of believers and reduce the number of infidels. The ends justify the means in carrying out this obligation to spread the faith. What is important to the militant zealot is his motive.

The existence of the infidel violates what is right in the eyes of the fundamentalist—namely that everybody should be a follower of Islam. The more the infidel resists the conversion the angrier the fundamentalist gets because that resistance is seen as a violation of God's will that the whole world be converted to Islam.

Therefore, the faithful are justified to use any method that will advance that goal. Nothing is off limits in the service of Islam, as long as ones motives are pure. Hijacking hostages, blowing up airliners, placing truck bombs in parking garages in New York City or outside barracks in Saudi Arabia, for example, are all acceptable because these acts either further the spread of the faith across the globe, or eliminate enemies of Islam.

This idea was given religious sanction by Khomeini. Its convoluted reasoning goes something like this: If one allows the infidels to continue playing their roles as corruptors on earth, their eventual moral punishment when they face their day of judgement will be that much harsher. Thus, if Muslims kill the infidel in order to put a stop to their corrupting activities, Muslims have indeed done them a service. For to allow the infidel to stay alive means to let them do more corrupting activities. By killing them now, the Muslim is lessening their punishment on their day of judgement. It is the "we had to destroy the village in order to save it," mentality with a religious sanction.

Further, the Islamic fundamentalist does not view war against the non-believer as evil. After all, they claim, it was Allah himself who commands men to wage war and to kill. The Koran commands: "Wage war until all corruption and all disobedience (of divine law) are wiped out!" Muslims are under the obligation of Allah to wage war, and this war is a good war. It is good because it is a holy war that purifies the earth. This is the reasoning of the militant Islamic fundamentalist and it justifies the atrocities they inflict on all they consider their enemies. It is an attitude that elevates the practice of terrorism to a sacred calling. A true follower of the faith slays his enemy.

In the act of pure violence there is a double act of liberation: the victim has been freed from his false role, the victor has freed his own spirit for authentic service to Allah.

The clouds of black smoke that poured out of the World Trade Center that wintery day in New York City showed the fundamentalists are putting their convictions into action.

The rise of radical Islamic fundamentalism is part of a centuries-old drama that continues to unfold: the dogged march of militant Islam throughout the globe. Names such as Hezbollah, Hamas, Islamic Jihad, and the *mujahideen* are already gracing the pages of our newspapers. They will be joined by the new groups springing up bent on either imposing their view of Islam on another country, or carrying out violent terrorist attacks on the "Great Satan"—the United States.

The World Trade Center and Saudi Arabian bombings, more than any other incidents, have brought the violent nature of Islamic fundamentalism and its reliance on terrorism into the American conscience. We are witnessing the dawn of a new era, one which will see nationalistic and ethnic clashes rise to the forefront. Terrorism and subversion will become common denominators of this new era. Blood may well run in the streets.

We are entering a period, not of peaceful economic competition, but of warfare between ethnic, cultural and nationalistic groups. Given that, it is not surprising that religious attitudes, beliefs, and fanaticism of the warring groups will play a larger role in the motivation of armed conflicts than it has since the counter-reformation three-hundred years ago.

At the present time, the fastest growing religion in the world is Islam. While there are many reasons for this, one facet of Islam's appeal may be its very militancy—its willingness to fight for its beliefs. After all, most people in the world are not pacifists and people in many parts of the world—including downtrodden groups in the developed world—are finding Islam attractive precisely because it is prepared to fight.

If the growing militancy of one religion continues, it almost certainly will compel others to follow suit. People will be driven to defend their ideals and way of life, as well as their physical existence, and they will be able to do so only under the banner of some great and powerful idea. Thus Muhammed's recent revival may yet bring on that of the Christian Lord, and He will not be the Lord of love but of battle.

This point is bolstered by the English historian Paul Johnson, who stated in his book *Modern Times: From the Twenties to the Nineties:* "The fundamentalist spirit of Islam, gathering force in the third quarter of the twentieth century, became a powerful, popular and, to many, frightening phenomenon in the 1980s. It affected all the great religions...Thus the revival of Islamic extremism, which began in the 1950s and by the early 1980s had spread to most of the Muslim world, provoked violent reactions. In India, for example, the Hindu-based Janata Dal Party had, by the end of the 1980s, been goaded into forms of religious extremism by Islamic pressure, and early in 1991 there was widespread violence in northern India as Hindus fought to reclaim the shrines of their gods where mosques had been built...."

Iran is the unquestioned leader in spreading the hard core brand of Islamic fundamentalism throughout the world. Ayatollah Khomeini adopted terrorism as Iranian national policy in October 1979 after a 12-man Islamic Council issued a *fatwa,* a religious decree, that gave him the right to resort to terrorism if he saw fit. From that moment down to the present, crimes and barbaric acts committed by Islamic terrorists to spread the Islamic revolution were given religious sanction.

Action followed swiftly. The following month the American Embassy was seized and the Iranians set up a structured chain of command, under the Bureau of Aid for World Liberation, to oversee the campaign of terror. The Bureau plans and directs acts of terror sanctioned by the Islamic Council.

The goal of Iran's hard liners is to create a universal Islamic republic based on the one they established in Iran. Over a billion Muslims already inhabit the Da al-Islam—the world of Islam, and it is these who are the primary target of the Iranians. But the non-Muslim world was also targeted. After all, how could a universal republic be established unless the *entire* world was converted to Islam?

To carry out this ambitious project, a world wide network was required. Using mosques—even brand new ones, Islamic culture centers and Iranian embassies, a network was in fact established. In many instances, the mosques and cultural centers were financed by Iran. This network is the key to spread the Islamic revolution to unseat moderate Muslim regimes, attack the West—particularly the United States— and spread their fundamentalist faith.

This was a system the Iranians knew intimately. It worked extremely well for them in their campaign to overthrow the Shah. It was fueled by the tape recordings of the Ayatollah Khomeini's harangues, recorded in France and smuggled into Iran. Once inside the country, the mosques became distribution centers for these cassette recordings.

The Shi'ite of Iran aren't the only ones to use tape cassettes to spread their message of Islamic fundamentalism. Their Islamic rivals, the Sunni fundamentalists, also use tape recordings to whip the faithful into a frenzy bent on overthrowing moderate Sunni Islamic regimes. The Muslim Brotherhood and the Jamiaat-e Islam in Egypt spread their revolutionary message by the extensive use of taped sermons of their spiritual leaders.

The power of the mosque has never been appreciated in America, with its tolerant view of religion, but they are being built in ever increasing numbers throughout Europe and the United States, in addition to those in the Muslim world. Given the "open borders" policy of the European Community and the loose border controls in the United States, there is no way of keeping fundamentalist Islam out of these regions.

Living in the West, and in particular in the United States, has provided Islamic fundamentalist terror groups with freedoms and maneuverability they never experienced in their native lands. Here they are free to disseminate their extremist propaganda calling for death and violence. They can raise money for their terror organizations and direct from America terrorist operations back home, and exploit other freedoms of American society.

Yet this freedom hasn't moderated their ideological hatred for the U.S., for its support of friendly countries in the Middle East, and for the institutional concepts of secularism, democracy, and western culture. The bombing of the World Trade Center was a deliberate act of political terrorism designed to "punish" the United States for its democracy and Western ideals—in other words its existence.

Every mosque built in non-Muslim countries becomes a potential focal point for spreading the faith. Some, but not all, will be spreading the hard line message of the fundamentalists. Over a thousand mosques have been built in France and new ones are going up at the rate of two a month. Their movement into Europe has not been altogether smooth. They are causing growing concern in France, Germany and England. France alone has over five million Muslims. They come from former French North African colonies, and the bulk are from Algeria. Many of these Muslims have no desire to assimilate into French society.

In 1989, Catholic, Islamic and Jewish religious leaders of France, the Prime Minister, and others got embroiled in a dress-code incident involving three Muslim girls in French schools. The three girls insisted on wearing chadors, the traditional Islamic robe-like dress for females designed to hide their feminine figure. The principal of the school barred the chadors, on the grounds that the wearing of religious clothing to school broke French law which insists its public schools be religiously neutral. All hell broke loose. Agitated by local Muslim clerics, a wave of religious hysteria of wearing chadors spread across schools where classes were heavily laden with Muslim students but where there had been no previous trouble. Egged-on by the imams, Islamization of the French school system was carried on by defiant girls wearing chadors and abusing and threatening those of the faith who wanted only to pursue their studies. One embittered French politician commented, "if they don't want to abide by French laws, let them go home."

Muslim emigrants in Germany, especially those from Turkey, are attacked by neonazi groups.

In 1991, militant Muslims formed their own Muslim parliament in England. Its leader, Kalim Siddiqui, said, in essence, that Muslims in Britain will oppose, and if necessary defy, any legislation that is regarded as un-Muslim. The imposition of un-Muslim law by the will of the majority, dressed up as democracy, is totally unacceptable to these extremists.

The guiding hand behind the Muslim Parliament in England is the pro-Iranian Muslim Institute which claims extraterritoriality for its decrees and teaches that Western civilization is the sick man of the world.

Similar parliaments are planned for other Western countries when their Muslim populations are deemed large enough. In such countries there will be two legal codes, the normal law of the land and the Islamic law the faithful will follow. In the view of the faithful, their's is the only one that counts.

The Serbian ethnic cleansing campaign against the Bosnians is a very sordid affair that is overloading an already brimming cup of hatred. Bosnia's Muslims have no ethnic relationship to the Arabs or the Iranians. Their ancestors were converted by the Turks when they were part of the Ottoman Empire. Now the Bosnians are solidly in the Muslim camp and the Islamic fundamentalists are taking advantage of the situation.

Some European analysts now speak of the prospect of an Islamic state with Bosnia as its nucleus, which would incorporate the predominantly Muslim Serbian province of Kosovo and possibly be joined by Albania.

Iran has sent arms, equipment and four-hundred Revolutionary Guards to organize and radicalize the Muslims in the region. The Iranians are organizing Bosnian terrorist groups loyal to Iran and its brand of fundamentalist Islam.

The presence of the Iranian Revolutionary Guards has heightened the concerns of Western governments over the growing influence of Iran in the Balkans. The Iranians see the Bosnian situation as a way to get at the soft underbelly of Europe.

Bosnian muslims have also been trained not only by Iran, but by our NATO allies Turkey. Starting in 1995, a few hundred Bosnian muslims and some Arab *mujahedin* recruited in Bosnia, were selected by Turkish Intelligence (MIT) and sent to a base in Northern Cyprus for training. After training, many of the Bosnians were deployed in Chechyna, Afghanistan, Kashmir, and northern Iraq against the Kurds.

Turkey plans to use these clandestine terrorist/agents for long-term penetration throughout the Middle East and Central asia.

The Middle east and Central Asia aren't their only destinations. In the spring of 1996, an Islamic terrorist support network was exposed in Western Europe. They were smuggling arms, money and explosives to Islamic fundamentalist terror groups in Algeria and other

North African countries. Many key figures in this network were Bosnian muslims who had received training from the Turks. These networks were also on the verge of launching violent terror attacks in France, Belgium and other European countries, but were thwarted when the networks were "rolled up" in the nick of time by Western police and intelligence agencies.

There are over ten million Muslims in Europe and Islam has become the second largest religion in many non-Muslim countries. There are about five million Muslims in North America and Islam is the second largest religion in both the United States and Canada. Over 500 Islamic centers have been built in the United States. Two-thirds of American Muslims are of Arab decent, while one-third belong to the various Black Muslim sects. One of these, the Nation of Islam, led by Louis Farrakhan, harbor intense racial hatred for whites and Jews.

During the next half-century, the world's population will double. Although some experts feel new technological advances and spreading free market economics will cope with this population explosion, others aren't so optimistic. Robert Kaplan points out a major stumbling block to this confident outlook in a thought provoking February 1994 article in *The Atlantic Monthly.* These optimists "...fail to note that as the National Academy of Sciences has pointed out, 95 percent of the population increase will be in the poorest regions of the world, where governments now—just look at Africa—show little ability to function, let alone to implement even marginal improvements."

Thus, almost all of the world's peoples, by the middle of the 21st century, will face bleak circumstances: living in shantytowns where attempts to rise above poverty, cultural chaos and ethnic strife will doom them to a precarious, violent struggle for existence. Their choices will be limited: life under totalitarianism such as Saddam Hussein's Iraq; fascist mini-states such as Bosnia; or, warlord societies such as Liberia or Somalia.

The population explosion will coincide with ,and add to, a great migration of peoples. The migration will be, within existing borders, as rural dwellers move into the cities, or across borders, as people flee strife, famine, resource depletion and disease, seeking a better life. As Albert Sauvy, a French demographer succinctly put it, "If wealth does not go where people are, the people naturally go where wealth is."

This migration foreshadows another Islamic invasion of Europe. Demographers project the Middle East alone (including Iran) could reach a population of three-hundred to four-hundred million by 2030. That population would be considerably higher than the expected number of people of European decent living in what is now the European community.

If large numbers of Middle Eastern and African migrants swarm into Europe in the 2000s and beyond, the result will not only be a migration of individuals, it will be a migration of Islam. The great majority would be Muslims originating in the Mediterranean crescent running from Marrakesh to Istanbul.

Europe won't be the only place Muslim refugees will flock to. Many will cross the Atlantic Ocean to join the estimated five to six million Muslims already in the United States. They will tend to flock to the cities, which are already suffering many sights of societal decay.

We have many violent enemies and too many open doors. One

of the founding ideals of the United States, that of arms open wide, to accept those from other countries, allows terrorists to slip in under the cloak of this benevolence and be in a position to cause us great harm.

Many of our inner cities are approaching a state of anarchy. The arrival of large numbers of people will increase the competition for fewer jobs and dwindling public services. It can't help but elevate an already tense situation.

It was in storefront mosques in Brooklyn, New York and Jersey City, New Jersey, where the plot was cooked up by Islamic fundamentalists to bomb the World Trade Center. Waves of immigrants fleeing from crumbling Muslim countries will wash more, not less, Sheik Abdel-Rahmans upon our shores.

A billion Muslims make up the world of Islam. While not all of them subscribe to the violent views of the fundamentalists, a growing number of them do. It is well to remember the dictum of Mao Tse Tung regarding the relationship of the terrorist and guerrilla to the people. Mao has aptly compared the terrorist and guerrilla to the fish and the people to the water they swim in. If the political temperature is right, the fish, however few in number, will thrive and proliferate.

The political temperature is heating up all over the globe and it bodes well for both the future of terrorism and the fortunes of Islamic fundamentalism. It is time we turned our attention to this.

Chapter 2
Frightening New World

They shall fight every one against his brother; and every one against his neighbor; city against city, and kingdom against kingdom.
Isaiah 19:2

World Trade Center, Oklahoma City, Olympic Park, Atlanta, Dharhan, Saudi Arabia, London, Tokyo subway system, Paris subway system, Lockerby, Scotland, terrorist bombings in Argentina, Moscow and Israel, and on and on and on, are more than headline stories in the news. This is the frightful new world we now face.

The world is not treading the path predicted by the experts.

Following the break-up of the Soviet Union, after Eastern Europe was free, after the Chinese Communists adopted capitalism, a new, long period of peace and tranquility—the New World Order—was to descend upon the world, or so the experts said.

It's not happening that way. Instead, these countries have become unglued. Replacing them is a new climate of violence, a strange brand of criminal anarchy. These nations aren't alone. The same sort of malevolent disease is infecting the wealthy West, including the United States.

Outlaw groups, with their own armies, are becoming more of a factor throughout the world. From West Africa to, Latin America, Central Asia, Russia, and the Muslim world, these gangs of thugs, radical Islamic terrorists, or warlords are challenging the existing order.

There is underway a world wide showdown between two ancient enemies, the Muslim world and the Christian West. This struggle is underway at the same time the world is going through a major historical transformation from the Industrial Age to the so-called Information Age.

The mainstream press reflects only a dim awareness that this confrontation is going on. They report wars in Chechnya and Bosnia. But they don't see the connections and give no useful advice.

Slavic peoples (including Serbs and Russians) are facing militant Islamic peoples along a three thousand mile front from Bosnia to Afghanistan. Chechnya is merely the midpoint in this confrontation.

The atrocities and outrages carried out by these powerful armed non-state groups will influence events far more than the items you read on the front page of your newspaper or watch on the evening news. With their increasing military effectiveness, they will exercise far more real power in the next century than they have since the Thirty Years War in Europe during the 17th century.

Computer chip technology is revolutionizing warfare, making smaller, deadlier, weapons readily available to the 21st century warrior.
Smart shoulder-held weapons, like the Stinger surface-to-air missile and the Javelin anti-tank missile, give the new world disorder warrior and terrorist a means of fighting the armed forces of the large, wealthy states.

Radical Islamic fundamentalist groups, one of these transnational non-state groups, are armed and dangerous. They are waging wars of terror throughout the Muslim as well as the non-Muslim world.

What's more, we in the West have had our own confrontation with Islam. It turned into a hot war in the Persian Gulf and has made the United States a target for Islamic terrorists as the World Trade Center and Saudi Arabian bombings graphically demonstrated.

Iran and Iraq are powerful Islamic countries with huge oil reserves. For all practical purposes, they are at war with the U.S. At any time, Iraq may make another attempt to seize the Gulf Kingdom of Kuwait, Saudi Arabia, and the Emirates. The United States military, becoming bogged-down in the Bosnian morass where they are vulnerable to terror attacks by Islamic fundamentalists, may be too preoccupied to mount another Desert Storm.

Even though they fought each other in a bitter eight-year war, there are indications the two are exploring the possibility of a loose, tacit alliance. Iran helped Iraq evade the UN embargo and sell its oil. A marriage of convenience makes sense. They could humiliate the West, backed up by the blackmail threat of nuclear or biological warfare purchased on the international arms black market, and seize most of the world's oil. Militant radical Islam would then be in the driver's seat. Japan and Europe would cut any kind of deal to keep the oil coming.

The United States would quickly fall in line with Japan and Europe. Why? The answer is simple: it would require a nasty, bloody war to reverse the situation. Kicking Iran and Iraq out of the conquered Gulf states would *not* be a repeat of Desert Storm.

People in the West don't like war. We'll do anything to avoid it and keep our children out of it. Even when vital interests are at stake it's extremely hard to get the Western public to go to war. And then the war had better be short, with very few casualties.

For most Americans the big issues are things like Social Security benefits, or the fortunes of their favorite professional athletic team, or the availability of the latest technological gadgets of the dawning Information Age. Profits, jobs, leisure time and economic activity, not geopolitics, are uppermost in the minds of the American people. The Information Age, however, will immeasurably effect history and geopolitics.

The technologies of this new era of mankind are shattering the power of national governments. The movers and shakers, the trendsetters, the new Information Age elites are quickly setting themselves free of the politicians. These people are capable of moving trillions of dollars to all corners of the globe each and every day. They have closer ties and loyalties to their trading partners around the Pacific Rim than to the bureaucrats and politicians in Washington.

Politicians can't hold computer assets hostage to their demands. That's quite a monumental change from their influence during the Industrial Age of steel mills, coal mines and factories, which can't be moved when legislators decide to tax or regulate them. Computerized assets can be transmitted by modem at the speed of light anywhere in the world. The Information Age elites won't hang around anymore to be ripped off by the politicians.

The birth of world wide computer and communications networks is remaking global societies in a way that is far more profound than many think. Global communications systems make it possible for our interconnected world to function. They enable information to be transmitted back and forth all over the world instantaneously. Information can drive and sustain a thriving economy, or it can propel a weak economy into a stronger position. This instantaneous delivery of information fuels the economies of the West, enabling them to gain a standard of living out of reach by three-quarters of the world's population.

This interconnectedness, however, does have a big risk: a failure in one part can spread like wild fire to the rest of the connected parts. For example, a collapse of the financial system of one of the major world economic powers—Japan, Germany, the United States, take your pick—could bring down the world economy like a house of cards.

• • •

The Iranian was hunched over the keyboard of his computer in the back room of the store-front mosque in Dearborn, Michigan. His fingers danced across the keyboard, stroking the keys with the self-confidence of a concert pianist. Unlike a pianist, the man's fingers were not playing a melodious concerto, they were tapping out an act of war against New York City.

The man, a member of a radical Islamic terror group, the Avengers of Allah, was taking advantage of the global communications system to attack one of the financial, business, and cultural hubs of the United States.

The terrorist was going to attack the soft under belly of the city. He was going to take out New York City's electrical system. Computers, phones, subways, lights, indeed our modern economy, is dependent upon electrical power. By depriving New York City of its electrical power, the Avenger of Allah terrorist group was going to throw the city into chaos.

Other members of the Avengers were waiting in New York for the lights to go out and they would add to the chaos with fire-bombings and satchel-bombings of pre-selected targets.

The success of the plan depended upon the Dearborn terrorist turning off the electricity to New York City. It wouldn't be that difficult a task.

Our mythical terrorist would shut off the electricity with an attack on New York's main power grid operated by Consolidated Edison. The attack would be in the form of a massive power surge which would cause the grid to shut down. The weapon would be the laptop computer of the terrorist, his modem and a telephone.

What our terrorist in Dearborn was doing with his computer was simple: he was penetrating the communications center of ConEd and tricking ConEd's monitoring sensing equipment into thinking there was a massive power surge in the grid.

The terrorist, miles away in Michigan, with modem, phone and a common piece of underground hacker's software, maneuvered his way through the Internet with purloined access codes that allowed him illicit entry into Consolidated Edison's computers. Once inside the company's computer, our techno-terrorist's job was relatively simple: fool ConEd's computers into thinking they were getting hit with a power surge and the company's fail-safe devices would automatically kick in to prevent the "surge" from causing major damage to the sensitive electrical system.

A fluctuation above or below the sixty-cycles-per-second normal synchronized electrical pulse will cause the system's protective devices to automatically go to work not knowing whether the signals they received are true or false. It really doesn't matter for the result is the same: shutting down the electrical power going into New York City.

Without electricity, the city ceases to function. Without spilling a drop of blood, the Avengers of Allah would bring New York to a screeching halt.

It is now possible for a terrorist to do more damage with a computer terminal than that caused by the World Trade Center bombing. Although our mythical terrorist operated out of Dearborn, Michigan, he could just as easily been sitting thousands of miles away in Baghdad, Damascus, or Tehran.

Computers in Crisis, a report of the National Research Council warns: "Tomorrow's terrorist may be able to do more damage with a keyboard than with a bomb."

Neither government nor industry has the means to protect the nation against computer attacks that could shut down communications and power grids. General Robert T. Marsh, chairman of the Commission on Critical Infrastructure Protection points outs: "While a catastrophic cyber attack has not occurred, we have enough isolated incidents to know that the potential for disaster is real."

Our mythical terrorist used a laptop computer to wreak havoc in New York City. This is not the only use terrorists, guerrillas, or criminals can make of technology in their war on their enemies. Modern technology provides a new vista of strategies and techniques to advance their cause. The magnitude and variety of advanced electronics, surveillance equipment, and access to media outlets with their real-time dissemination capability, are tools that will be used by militant religious insurgents, as well as their secular cousins, when conducting revolutionary terrorist warfare in the dawning Information Age.

• • •

Societies are rapidly moving towards increased dependence

upon four critical interrelated infrastructures which are vulnerable to sabotage.

The power grid that distributes electricity is the basis of today's modern society. With it gone, or severely damaged, not much else can happen.

The communications infrastructure—land, sea, air and satellites are extremely critical. Ninety-five percent of the military and one-hundred percent of all financial and industrial communications go over the open, vulnerable public networks.

The global financial structure depends upon the first two infrastructures, and is perhaps the most vulnerable to theft and denial attack by computer hackers or computer wise terrorists. Ninety-nine percent of all "wealth" is digital—what happens when it evaporates?

Transportation systems rely upon the other three. The air traffic system, for example, requires both power and communication to manage the thousands of airplanes in the sky. What happens to them if air traffic control across an entire country goes down?

Without all of these infrastructures properly and reliably functioning, neither the private nor public sector can function. No heat, no air conditioning, no food distribution, no light, no radio or TV, no Internet. These are all at the mercy of a terrorists using a computer instead of a bomb.

The global financial system is just one of many complex systems that enable modern society to function smoothly. There is, however, a down side: the more complex a system is, the easier it is for glitches to develop in the system, and these glitches have a tendency to cause major disruptions in the scheme.

Consider the two famous power outages in the Western United States during the summer of 1996. The whopper, caused by the failure of a surge protector, shut down electrical power in eleven Western states plus parts of Canada and Mexico. The other, caused by a tree limb falling on a transmission line, while not as extensive, still blacked-out large portions of the West.

The electrical power grid, both in the U.S. and in its interconnectedness with Canada and Mexico, is a very complex system designed to provide a continuous smooth flow of electricity to its customers. But, as the two examples show, it didn't take much to disrupt it with some serious consequences.

In the mid-1980s a computer at The Bank of New York went on a tear and began overwriting data on government securities transactions. Before the glitch was discovered, the bank owed the Federal Reserve $32 billion without knowing who had bought what securities. The problem was eventually rectified by the bank at a huge cost. The bank had to float a loan from the Fed by pledging all the bank's assets as collateral. The bank also lost $5 million in interest in the bailout deal.

A two-week June 1997 Pentagon war game, "Operation Eligible Receiver" brought home just how vulnerable our computers are to hacker attacks.

Using software obtained easily from hacker-sites on the Internet, the participants in the war game could have shut down the U.S. electric power grid within days and rendered useless command-and-control elements of the U.S. Pacific Command.

"The most telling thing for the Department of Defense," said a defense official involved in the game, "when all was said and done, is that basically for a two-week period the command-and-control capability in the Pacific theater would have been denied by the 'infowar' attacks, and that was the period of the exercise."

The attackers also foiled virtually all efforts to trace them, which will give continuing headaches to officials in our computer-dependent military.

Crashes of intricate computer-run transportation distribution systems have tied up passenger and freight trains in Western states and it parts of Europe.

In short, the more God-like power we have appropriated for ourselves, the more confused and complex our world has become—and the more opportunities for it to collapse.

An unnamed U.S. intelligence official has boasted that with $1 billion and 20 capable hackers, he could shut down America. The intelligence official is exaggerating: it won't take that much money or that many hackers. What he could achieve, a terrorist could too.

In February 1998, the Pentagon, concerned over a series of hacking incidents involving sensitive computers, notified the White House that an Iraqi electronic attack might be underway under cover of the hacking incidents. A flurry of attacks were occurring at the same time U.S. military preparations were in progress for large scale air and missile attacks on Iraq. These attacks were to be in response to Iraqi refusal to permit U.N. weapons inspectors from suspected weapons sites.

Only weeks later did the Pentagon learn that Iraq wasn't involved, but it shows how vulnerable to attack, be it by hackers or terrorists, are our Information Age computers networks.

Chapter 3
The Troubled World of Babel

Man is born into trouble, as the sparks fly upward.
Job 5:7

The modern globalization of the world's economy, and the social changes it is creating are separating people from familiar identities such as the nation state. Religion can, and has, stepped in to give people a new sense of identity. This is specially true of Islam. The identification with a religion transcends national boundaries and can unite societies. It may somewhat dampen the centrifugal forces tearing apart existing societies, but these forces may even overwhelm religion's unifying efforts.

A society is also a cultural entity wherein a people share common ingredients such as language, history, religion, and institutions. Benedict Anderson, in a fascinating book, *Imagined Communities,* defined a national community—a nation state if you will—as an "imagined community." It is imagined because members of even the smallest nation will never know most of their fellow-members, meet them, or even hear of them, yet in the minds of each lives the image of their communion. Neither language, nor ethnicity nor religion, Anderson argues, are sufficiently held in common to explain what a nation really is.

Today this imagination is fading and people are seeking identity with the component parts of their societies. Call it multiculturalism, ethnic awareness or a return to one's roots, but it is an inescapable conclusion that the bonds that have held people to the most visible form of modern society, the nation state, have loosened. The global communications network has played a major role in this occurrence.

Global interconnectedness has introduced a negative force that separates and sharpens the tensions among the parts of today's crumbling societies. The parts are beginning to consider themselves more important than the whole. The Soviet Union has cracked up. Others will follow, including China, Pakistan and India.

Advances in communications have increased the cultural awareness of ethnic groups living within the same territory. This awareness is a two-edged sword. Not only does one become more aware of those who share his cultural and ethnic identity, but he also becomes more aware of alien ethnic groups.

The end result of these processes is the crumbling of many of the multicultural countries of the world as separatist movements break out in such diverse countries as Spain, Thailand and even Ethiopia, despite its three-thousand-year history.

Thanks to world wide television coverage, people in different parts of the world can actually see, in real time, how other people are living and dying. This instantaneous viewing has a dark side as it arouses feelings of envy, hatred and desire among the different peoples of the world. These are strong, often destructive emotions which will increase the destabilization in the new world disorder.

It's ironic that the same global communications system that drive the economies of the West also allows the "have nots" of the world to see how the "haves" of the West live. The grass, they can see, *is* greener on the other side of the fence and they want a piece of the action. More and more, they are willing to pay any price to get it, including the use of force.

This is contrary to the myth, encouraged by the press, that people are naturally good and wars by the "have nots" against the "haves' just result from misunderstandings and will be prevented by settling those differences. However much we may wish to believe human behavior should be subject to the rule of law, human history, unfortunately, shows clearly that many people "play by the rules" only when it suits them.   Individuals and groups can either produce, and thus create wealth, or seize the wealth created by others.

Given the level of despair, poverty, and lack of opportunity endemic in the areas populated by the "have nots," to think this down-trodden mass of humanity won't pick up the gun is carrying myth-making to dangerous lengths of self-delusion. It is a myth that should be blow away once and for all. Wrong ideas are more dangerous to our future and well being than any atomic bomb in Iran's or Iraq's arsenal. For a large number of people on this planet, war and life in the bar-racks is a step up, not a step down.

Throughout history, for every person who has had a horror of war, there is another who found it the most marvelous experience of his life. Richard Heckler speaks of this attitude in his book *In Search of the Warrior Spirit:*

> "This urgent calling of nature longs to be tested, seeks to be challenged beyond itself. The warrior within beseeches Mars, the god of War, to deliver us to that crucial battlefield that will redeem us into the terrifying immediacy of the moment...We long for the encounter that will ultimately empower us with dignity and honor...Be not mistaken, the longing is there and it's loving and terrible and beautiful and tragic."

In places like Serbia, the Middle East, Liberia, and Somalia, to name just a few, people find liberation in violence. The radical Islamic fundamentalist revels in the violence he can inflict upon others.

When there is nothing to lose, there's nothing to fear. The only course for the "have nots" is to go grab their piece of the West's cake. Confronting the West is a no-lose option for them.

That confrontation will not be peaceful because the "haves," when pushed, will not meekly hand over their good life to the whims of the "have nots." The resulting turmoil will likely rent asunder many existing nation states and their societies.

We in the West will find ourselves increasingly under siege by new demands. One of these challengers is Islam, and its challenge is unlikely to be peaceful. Islam is expanding from its traditional heartland to the four corners of the earth: south into Africa; north into Europe, east into Asia; and, west to the United States where the fastest growing religion is Islam.

Islam is on the march into Europe. France already has over four million Muslims and is fearful of an Islamic wave arriving on their shores if France's former North African colonies fall into the hands of militant Islamic fundamentalists. North African immigrants are arriving in Spain in droves.

The current situation in Bosnia is reviving the old Islamic dream of a drive into the heartland of Europe by way of the Danube. Muslim aid, both in weaponry and members of the Islamic foreign legion funded by Iran and Saudi Arabia, is pouring into Bosnia. The Bosnian Muslim enclaves will become the advance base for future militant Islamic intrigue in Europe.

Russia, which considers itself a European nation, is under Islamic assault along its entire southern flank, from the Black Sea to Vladivostok. European culture, from the Atlantic to the Pacific is under assault by militant Islamic fundamentalism.

Militant Islamic fundamentalism's biggest danger to the world lies in its totalitarian nature and willingness to use mindless violence to achieve its goals. The militant Islamist seeks power, not just to rule fellow Muslims or convert non-believers, but to change them, to impose Islamic fundamentalism's vision of an Islamic utopia.

Like all totalitarians throughout history, the militant Islamic extremist seeks to control every aspect of life in their utopia. Nothing is innocent, nothing is private, and nothing is outside the all-seeing eyes and always listening ears of the fundamentalist theocracy.

It is Allah's will, the militant fundamentalist believes, that they have the answers to fix the Muslim's lot in the world. The Islamic militant, furthermore, believes with fervent certainty that in any given circumstance Islam is the absolute code of right and wrong, that this code has been revealed from God to the Prophet.

His modern apostles, the militant Islamic extremists, have the absolute duty to enforce the Prophet's code on themselves and the rest of the world. In the fundamentalist's mind, he is the true believer of the faith, there are no shades of gray and a thought can be as evil as a deed. And Western thought is among the most evil the faithful can be exposed to and become ensnared in.

The militant Islamic fundamentalist, like his secular brothers the Leninist, Maoist and Nazi, have no use for pragmatism. A pragmatist, by nature, is a compromiser, and there is no compromising of the true faith. Pragmatism is among the greatest of sins and evils to every true believer.

The militant Islamic true believer, like the good totalitarian, would rather cut off his nose to spite his face, or pluck out his eye if it offends Allah, than compromise his belief. He would rather fight and die for the faith than compromise one bit of Allah's truth. What the West sees as murder or terrorism, the militant Islamic fundamentalist sees as the ultimate act of devotion, and is willing to die to spread the faith and prove his devotion.

It is this willingness, often eagerness, to die that makes Islamic fundamentalism's followers so dangerous: they have nothing to lose, and no fear of death. Indeed, to some death is a liberating experience. It removes them from this corrupt and sinful world into paradise, populated by beautiful virgins waiting to serve the heroic martyred faithful. It is a reward not a tribulation.

There will be no bothersome and uncertain process of appearing before Allah's tribunal on judgement day for him. His service for Allah in fighting and killing unbelievers and dying in the process exempts him from such a fearsome ordeal.

The militant Islamic extremist, like his secular totalitarian cousin, has nothing but contempt and hatred for the middle-of-the-roaders. His world is stark and simple: there are only two classes of people, and those who aren't with him are against him. The militant Islamic fundamentalist demands the bodies and souls of his followers and, with the fundamentalist leading his flock, is embarked upon a crusade that will end in victory for the faithful or death.

Given the fact that there is no separation of the sacred and secular in Islam, the siren song of Islamic fundamentalism's totalitarian nature and excesses make it a ready political vehicle for radical Islamic demagogues. It is particularly attractive to Muslim youth because of the woes buffeting the Muslim world: poverty, lack of jobs for the educated and uneducated alike, oppressive, inefficient, unresponsive government, and a strong feeling of alienation with a rapidly changing world.

The way promised by the Khomeinis, Hezbollah imams, Hamas leaders, and other militant Islamic fundamentalists is tailor-made for these angry youth. It gives them a justification for violently striking out at their enemies, real or imagined. Islamic fundamentalism also gives them a blueprint for a better life. Catharsis and salvation, all under one violent theological tent, are the two strong appealing motivations that lure zealous followers to the banner of Islamic fundamentalism.

Violent Islamic fundamentalism, however, will not sweep the world in the manner of Islam's early years, in spite of the fantasies of Islamic fundamentalism's more fevered proponents. Unlike the Soviet Union, the holy shrine of communism, fundamentalist Islam is not headquartered in a superpower. Given the world trend towards decentralization and the enormous expense involved, few Islamic countries can realistically become superpowers. This severely constrains fundamentalist Islam's ability to build political empires. Nor does it, as yet, possess either nuclear weapons or a superpower's military ability to use them. Iran, Iraq, Libya and Pakistan are all working overtime to develop a nuclear capability (in fact Pakistan has already nuclear devices), but the effort may well bankrupt them. All, however, face serious internal problems that complicate and hinder their ability to spend the enormous sums needed to acquire sufficient nuclear weapons for their arsenals.

Building atomic weaponry is no simple task. Fissionable nuclear material is not in abundant supply, and is under monitoring by a U.N. international group. Only governments can legally produce it, so that tracing those aiding nuclear terrorists is a routine task. A caveat, however: proliferation monitoring can easily overlook a more primitive nuclear weapon—non-bomb grade radioactive material that can be deadly in the hands of a terrorist. Iran has been known to have tried to buy such material originating in the former Soviet Union.

A cheaper, and just as deadly, option is the development and use, or threat to use, chemical and biological weapons of mass destruction. Iran, Iraq, and Libya all have amassed these non-nuclear weapons of mass destruction and it is only a matter of time before terrorists begin using them against their enemies.

Islamic fundamentalism and its violent agenda will hurt America's interests because it defines itself culturally as anti-Western and politically as anti-American.

During the half-century since World War II, only North Vietnam has succeeded in using war to move an international border by as much as a single inch, although Iraq tried twice against Iran and Kuwait. During the same period of time, terrorism, subversion, guerrilla warfare—non-state war if you please—has produced some momentous changes. The entire shape of the globe has been transformed: from France and Britain, to the former Soviet Union, the mightiest empires that ever existed have crumbled into dust. In the process, hundreds of millions, if not billions, of people have come to live under political regimes different from the ones they were accustomed to—all without a single major war between nation states.

The continuous weakening, or even disappearance, of the authority of the nation state will unleash a resurgence of ancient tribal and cultural affinities. In country after country—from the Balkans to Africa, India to Quebec, old values and the will to enforce them with coercion that were the cement of the nation state are being eroded or tossed away. People are deciding that it is better to fight and die in the name of the tribe or group than in the name of a discredited and disappearing national entity. It is safer to be among your kith and kin as a majority in a small enclave than to be a minority in a political entity ruled by your enemy.

It is also safer and makes more sense in the gloomy future ahead for the minority tribe or group to flee or fight and, if necessary to exterminate, their foes than to coexist with them. Bosnia, Rwanda and Liberia are graphic bloody examples of this ancient barbaric tribalization.

There is much more to existence than political identification. The chief idea being the promotion of security for specified groups of people in a defined scope of territory.

The Western intellectual tradition, hung-up on the normative aspects of the nation state, is ill-equipped to handle "ethnicity" in its modern-day manifestations. The West's dismal record in coping with non-state war illustrates not only its failure, but the growing danger it faces.

Today, terrorism is being driven by ethnic hatred or religious fanaticism. It is a type of warfare that lends itself to atrocity, because you dehumanize your opponent. It results in massacres and the concept of ethnic cleansing or genocide. As the World Trade Center and Dharhan bombings showed, terror tactics are now calculated to kill in quantity. It is a trend that is fraught with sinister global consequences.

The elements are in place for a destructive re-tribalization of the Muslim Arab world. Seventeen out of twenty-two Arab states have a declining Gross National Product (GNP). Seventy percent of their population is under the age of twenty-five. The future for these kids is bleak; they aren't going to get an MBA or go to medical school. They are rootless, frustrated, ready and eager to pick up the gun to give meaning to their life. In short, they are ready recruits for the terror fraternity of the radical Islamic fundamentalists.

Meanwhile, the population is expected to double in the next twenty years. These fundamental trends *are* going to effect our way of life as we know it.

They have already made their appearance in two widely separated Western countries, South Africa and the United States.

Armed Muslim vigilantes have killed drug dealers and clashed with police in Cape Town, South Africa. The vigilantes have vowed to eradicate drug dealing by local gangs. The marchers were heading for the home of a drug lord to kill him when the police and army moved in and halted the march.

Even though the Muslim vigilantes were concentrating on criminals, it shows they are more than willing to take the law into their own hands in pursuit of their cause of the moment. They have received paramilitary training at a training camp near Cape Town. While the vigilantes profess to be defending their neighborhoods from crime, the South African government fears they may be moving towards a future challenge for power.

In fact, at least two members of the South African Islamic vigilante group, People Against Gangsterism and Drugs (PAGAD), received terrorist training in Iran. The training arrangement was probably set up when Iranian President Rafsanjani visited South Africa in September 1996. Two members of his entourage, actually members of the Iranian Intelligence Service, remained behind after his departure, presumably with the connivance of the South African immigration department. The Iranian intelligence officials made contact with PAGAD and agreed to fund their activities in return for "intelligence," and when the time is ripe, action. It doesn't require much imagination to fathom what type of targets will attract the attention of PAGAD acting for Iran: Western and Israeli business and personnel.

It is also thought that PAGAD has made contact with Hezbollah and Hamas. Although the thought that PAGAD aims to turn South Africa into an Islamic state borders on the realm of fantasy, they have the potential to cause a great deal of trouble.

We are not talking about a few angry people either. PAGAD mobilized over 5,000, mostly young men, for their August 11, 1996 Cape Town march.

The Nation of Islam is also advocating violence in the United States as part of their quest for a separate Black Nation within the existing borders of America. Speaking at an April 27, 1996 youth gang meeting in the Watts section of Los Angeles, Tony Muhammad, the West Coast representative of the Nation of Islam, urged the gangs to unite in a common armed struggle against the white society.

"When we come together as one army, we can take Watts, we can take South-Central, we can take Los Angeles and then the West coast...," Muhammad told the over 500 representatives of black and Latino gangs at the meeting.

Muhammad's boss, Louis Farrakhan, delivered a similar message during his October 1995 Washington, D.C. "Million Man March." He told white Americans, "I know you call (some Hispanics) 'illegal aliens,' but hell, you took Texas from them...And now they're coming back across the border to what is northern Mexico: Texas, Arizona, New Mexico, and California. They don't see themselves as illegal aliens; I think they might see you as an illegal alien."

Farrakhan has been promised aid and support from Libya. At a January 1996 meeting in Tripoli, Libya's leader, Col. Muammar Quadaffi offered to donate a billion dollars to the Nation of Islam. According to Jana, the official Libyan news agency, they agreed to mobilize the "oppressed" minorities in the US— that is blacks, Arabs,

Muslims and American Indians.

Quadaffi called for the creation in America of a separate black state with its own army manned by black soldiers from the US armed forces. This echoes Farrakhan's own calls for white Americans to hand over eight or ten states to black Americans for their exclusive use, to make amends for slavery.

The relationship between Quadaffi and Farrakhan dates back to 1985 when Quadaffi lent the Nation of Islam five million dollars for business projects. He also offered arms to the Nation of Islam so they could overthrow the whites in an armed struggle.

Farrakhan also visited Iran and the Sudan, both Islamic fundamentalist states who have a history of supporting terrorism. If they and the Nation of Islam become allies, dangerous days may loom ahead in our inner cities where the Nation of Islam has a presence and a growing appeal.

The Islamic fundamentalists are a menace. Their "us against them" attitude and fatalistic philosophy of having nothing to lose is an explosive combination. It will ensure conflict, within the world of Islam where they must purify the faith, and in the West, where they live in Muslim enclaves surrounded by the hated infidels.

From these Muslim enclaves they are positioned to rally forth and strike out at "corrupt Muslim collaborators" and infidels alike. They will use the violent terrorist tools and methods of the bomb, bullet and knife. Their bloody deeds will be the headlines on the nightly TV news. It will be the Hobbsean nightmare of every man for himself. Life will be solitary, nasty, brutish and short. It will be an age that only a Viking or barbarian could love.

Chapter 4
Man's Oldest Enemy

*The Lord shall smite thee with a consumption, and with a fever, and with an
inflammation, and with an extreme burning, and with the sword, and with
blasting, and with mildew; and they shall pursue thee until thou perish.*
Deuteronomy 28:23

The world is faced with a threat from mankind's oldest, smallest and dangerous enemy: bacteria and their diseases. They haven't
gone away just because science has developed "miracle" drugs and
vaccines. Nor have they disappeared from the world as the West has
cleaned up its cities and towns. Deadly diseases are still with us and
pose a serious threat to collapsing societies and nations—the breeding ground of terrorists who will bring their toxins with them wherever they go.

The world has become much more vulnerable to the outbreak
and spread of both new and long-thought cured infectious diseases.
The shrinking of the global village and the ease of travel is driving
this new danger. An infected person travelling on a jet airliner can
arrive at his destination and be miles away before disease symptoms
appear in his fellow passengers. Each of these passengers, in turn, can
carry and spread the disease to others.

The disease doesn't have to rely on human vectors to get to
the four corners of the earth. The jet plane, and its cargo, can carry
insects bringing infections into new ecological environments.

Triumph of Disorder

Modern medicine has given modern society a false sense of security. Diseases have been mankind's enemy since the dawn of humanity and these microbes have proven to be very adaptable and resilient. All diseases need is a means to get to their intended host. The victim provides a friendly environment where the disease can thrive and spread.

The new world disorder, with its societal breakdowns will provide excellent opportunities for diseases to work their deadly ways on *Homo Sapiens.* The teeming masses, often in over-crowded urban slums, can easily pass the disease to others in many different ways during the course of everyday activity. Diseases can be passed as people breathe on each other, touch their fellow man, handle food, discharge their human wastes into water, etc. Cities, especially those lacking good infrastructures such as water treatment and sewage disposal, are great havens for diseases.

Modern medicine is finding that miracle drugs haven't vanquished the germs. The germs are fighting back, using plasmids, jumping genes, mobile DNA, mutation and sharing of resistance factors to overcome whatever drugs doctors are using against them. By 1993, nearly every common pathogenic bacterial species had developed some significant resistance to drugs. At least two dozen of these microbial enemies' new strains pose potential life-threatening crisis to humanity, having successfully countered most available antibiotic treatments.

The changing nature of war, arising out of the social anarchy of collapsing societies, has enhanced the ability of diseases to spread and wreak their deadly effects. The violent guerrilla wars, the mindless violence of criminal gangs or terrorists, and the spread of drugs have devastated societies. They have caused homelessness, refugee migrations, and the destruction of basic infrastructures.

The outbreak of non-state war on a global scale has created golden opportunities for old diseases to reappear on history's stage. As a result, diseases such as typhus, cholera, tuberculosis, and measles are flourishing. These diseases are spreading on their own in the friendly environment of war-torn regions of the world.

Even more ominous, these diseases can spread by deliberate acts of man. They can become the "poor man's" weapon of mass destruction.

Genetic engineering and other biological research has made biological warfare an attractive option for terrorists. Virologist Karl Johnson says, "It's only a matter of months—years, at most—before people nail down the genes for virulence and airborne transmission. And then any crackpot with a few thousand dollar's worth of equipment and a college biology education under his belt could manufacture bugs that would make Ebola look like a walk around the park."

That view isn't far-fetched. The Japanese Aum Shinrikyo cult that released Sarin nerve gas into the Tokyo subway system wasn't limiting its arsenal to nerve gas. They also developed biological war agents to use in future terror attacks. US official have also arrested several would-be home grown American terrorists for acquiring and plotting the use of deadly anthrax agents.

We are, unfortunately, ill-prepared to cope with a biological terror attack.

"Are we ready," asked Michael Osterholm, the state epidemiologist at Minnesota's Department of Health?

"Absolutely not," was his answer at an April 14, 1998 news conference organized by the National Foundation for Infectious Diseases.

One of the main reasons why a biological weapon will become more attractive to terrorists is the weapon's delayed action. A small five-pound box of smallpox virus would contain about a million doses, and could be triggered to release the virus silently over a two-week period. No one would know until long after the terrorist had disappeared.

Or consider a frightening World Health Organization (WHO) scenario where one-hundred pounds of anthrax would be dispersed just a mile upwind from our nation's capital. Washington, D.C. has a population slightly over a half-million and in just a short time this amount of anthrax released by our terrorist could kill or incapacitate almost half of them.

Such an attack would overwhelm existing health care facilities and even if these were well-stocked with vaccines and antibiotics that can be used against anthrax, they are useless once the victims show symptoms of the disease.

Imagine that a new drug-resistant form of influenza sweeps the globe. Whether the disease is natural or man-made the effect will be the same. Millions will die in the Third World from lack of medical care. The effects will also be catastrophic in Europe and the United States. The population in both areas are aging and susceptible to disease. As the influenza sweeps through this aging population it will overtax our overburdened heath care facilities leading to a huge death toll.

Is such an epidemic likely, or is it just a scenario best left to science fiction?

Today, at the dawn of the new millennium, we live in a world where tuberculosis and malaria kill over one-hundred million people a year. AIDS has killed two million while infecting almost twenty-five million more. Diseases considered vanquished by modern medicine are making a deadly comeback; most in forms resistent to common anti-biotics. These pestilences will have a profound impact on the world, especially in those areas where the process of collapse is well underway. We in the West can take no comfort from their potential deadly effects.

Consider the past to get an idea of the potential magnitude of the problem: the Bubonic Plague killed at least one-third of Europe's population in the 14th century, tuberculosis took huge numbers in the 19th century, and the 1918 influenza outbreak killed over twenty-five million world wide.

Many of the trends contributing to the breakdown of societies also enhance the spread of deadly diseases.

The population increase and its growing urbanization mean a lot of people living close to one another. Over two-hundred million people live in fifteen megacities, mostly in the Third World. The tightly-packed masses of these slum-infested cities are perfect sites for deadly epidemics to break out. The sickness would be far beyond the control of modern medicine. Medical facilities in most of these megacities are rudimentary at best for the vast number of their poverty-stricken residents.

The raw sewage that flows in the streets attracting flies, mos-quitos, rats and other vermin, aids both the germination and spread of these diseases. The insects and vermin become disease vectors and spread their microbial parasites to man. These megacity slums are disease epidemics waiting to happen.

Poverty is endemic in the Third World and is increasing in First World societies as well. It will help, not hinder, the spread of new possible drug-resistant diseases—whether natural or genetically engineered by man.

This shouldn't surprise anyone. The poor don't eat as often, nor as well as the non-poor. They live in horrendous squalor with virtually no sewage treatment facilities and no clean drinking water. In the West many of the poor are also drug addicts. These addicts share dirty needles with other addicts, aiding in the spread of diseases. All of this—poverty, poor sanitation, polluted drinking water, and drug addiction—creates a huge world wide population with depressed immune systems—enticing targets for a wide variety of deadly, infectious organisms.

The majority of these populations live in societies populated by corrupt officials, pursuing unrealistic economic policies, and often down right neglect. People are fleeing these depressed circumstances in droves. They are also bringing with them swarms of deadly microbes swimming in their bloodstreams.

Swift, cheap, available transportation makes travel easy for those fleeing misery at home. Consider air travel figures from 1990: 280 million people travelled the globe on international flights; 424 million flew on U.S. domestic flights. All these people were jammed together in airplanes breathing the same air, which often fails to meet basic health standards for U.S. work places. These flights are perfect places for transmitting airborne diseases. In one instance, a flight attendant passed tuberculosis to 23 crew members.

Modern transportation systems are also bringing new deadly disease vectors along with the goods and people travelling the world's highways, sea lanes and airways.

One traveler who has found a new home in the United States is a deadly winged immigrant from Asia, the Tiger mosquito. It arrived in the U.S. in 1985 via a shipload of water-logged tires from Japan. The mosquito is especially nasty and aggressive and isn't choosey where it sucks its blood—rats, man, pigs, fowl, any warm-blooded creature seems to suffice. This insect will spread its germs from one animal to another, or from animal to human, or from one human to another.

The mosquito also brought some deadly baggage with it from Asia: Yellow Fever and Dengue Fever numbers 1, 2, and 3. The Tiger took Dengue Fever number 2 to Havana, Cuba, infecting almost 350,000 people in three months.

The Tiger mosquito is now spreading through the United States. Its current territory extends from Puerto Rico, where Dengue Fever is now endemic, to Chicago, encompassing seventeen states in all. Is it a growing problem? The Center for Disease Control thinks it is: "The presence of *A. albopictus* (Tiger mosquito) dramatically increases the probability that exotic viruses will be brought into the urban human environments of America."

As the world's population grows, and social disorders keep pace or accelerate, the opportunities for germs—man-made or otherwise—to do their deadly deeds will multiply. In 1978, health officials throughout the world boldly predicted that by the dawn of the 21st century all of humanity would be immunized and infectious diseases would be under control.

Instead of control, disease-carrying microbes are adapting to changes by mutating, or undergoing high-speed natural selection. They threaten to overwhelm our immune systems and a coming plague of global proportions is not out of the question.

We are, as the poet Matthew Arnold put it, "Wandering between two worlds/One dead, the other unable to be born."

Chapter 5
War's New Face

...The cold, brutal fact is that much present day military power is simply irrelevant as instrument for extending or defending political interests over most of the globe.

Martin Van Creveld

The new world disorder will create a new political landscape: an increasing number of mini-states as existing states split apart along clan, tribal, ethnic, or regional lines. Most of this division will take place in the Third World but even the West will not be immune from the effects of dissolution as events in Russia and former Yugoslavia demonstrate.

As the new world disorder spreads, the international arena will become an amalgam of many small and weaker political entities, and some surviving larger ones. These larger ones, like the United States, will try to maintain the status quo, but it will be a dangerous, costly, often futile, effort.

It will be futile because many of these new political entities will be states in name only. Policing such an international melange will be dangerous, bloody and expensive as our experiences in Somalia and Bosnia show. The growing political crisis in the U.S. over mounting debt and entitlement reform may even cripple the U.S.'s ability to be the world's policeman.

Terrorist war—a war in which there are no uniforms or borders—will escalate. It is the war of the future and it will be difficult to defeat.

The Israeli historian, Martin Van Creveld, brings us face-to-face with this new era in his book, *The Transformation of War*. It is a brilliant, vivid description of war in the future which challenges our current assumptions on the subject. This type of war is waged by small bands of combatants, not large masses of manpower.

Small-scale military eruptions around the globe are showing the deadly power of these new forms of warfare with a different cast of characters—guerrillas, terrorists and criminals—pursuing various goals by violent means, employing a range of weaponry which varies from the most primitive to the most sophisticated. This type of conflict challenges existing distinctions between civilian and soldier, individual crime and organized violence, terrorism and war.

The advent of nuclear weapons has led to a decline in the ability of states to engage in large conflicts unless they wish to commit suicide. But this hasn't stuffed the war genie back into his bottle. The number of wars waged by organizations other than states has increased. In 1996 alone, out of approximately 60 wars fought all over the world, not a single one was fought by states—at least not on both sides. It is within this phenomenon that the terrorist campaigns promised by the Khomeinis, the narco-terrorists, mafias, and warlords will be carried out.

In the last half of the twentieth century, this growing conflict has been *much* more bloody than wars between states. Compared to Algeria—300,000 to 1,000,000 dead, Vietnam—at least 1,000,000 dead, Afghanistan—another 1,000,000, Rwanda—a half-million so far, and countless others, the majority of wars between states during the same period produced piddling deaths by comparison.

Triumph of Disorder

It is possible that no more than 25,000 to 35,000 Iraqi soldiers died in the Gulf War. That figure pales in comparison to some of the bloody non-state conflicts we witness today. Not even the largest interstate war in the last half century—Korea or Vietnam, take your pick—came close to the horrors of the Nigerian civil war. In that non-state war, two to three million are said to have died.

This bloody trend will continue its march into the Third Millennium, and it is going to be with us for a long time to come. It will be vicious, violent, and it will likely touch many, whether here, in Europe, Russia, Asia, or some backwater segment of the Third World.

Major Ralph Peters, writing in *Parameters,* the Army War College journal, said, "...we confront *today,* creatively organized enemies employing behaviors and technologies ranging from those of the stone-age to those at the imagination's edge...At present, we are preparing for the war we want to fight someday, not for the conflicts we cannot avoid."

To the American soldier, inoculated by liberal democracy's moral and behavioral codes, the vicious, unscrupulous enemy of the future—rebels, warlord warriors, gangsters, guerrillas, terrorists—are formidable enemies. American and other Western soldiers in general learn a highly stylized form of warfare, with both written and customary rules. We are at our best fighting organized soldiers who attempt a symmetrical response.

But the non-state warrior doesn't fight according to our rules of engagement. The ambush of U.S. Army Rangers in Mogadishu by Somali warlords looks like a modern version of Braddock's defeat of the French and Indian War of the 18th century. Russian regulars recently were wiped out like General Custer at the Little Big Horn by Tajikistan tribesmen who slipped across the Afghan border.

The United States should brace for a bloody, no-holds-barred type of combat, quite alien to our way of doing battle.

• • •

The gang of armed men worked their way down the meandering streets of the shanty-town slum towards their target, a small crumbling mud and wattle building surrounded by an adobe wall topped with a few strands of badly rusting barbed wire. The building was a local police post which was the only visible sign of the government's existence in this part of the sprawling shanty-town. Inside, policemen sat, afraid to go out after dark.

The armed men moved slowly, trying to avoid the fetid pools of waste and water collecting in the ruts of the dirt path that posed as a street. They crept forward between the rows of lean-to's of corrugated zinc roofing sheets, cardboard, and green plastic sheeting.

Fearful eyes and tight lips followed the armed men's slow progress, for sleeping was often difficult when one's stomach was wreaked with hunger pangs and a warning shout would turn the attention of the armed team upon oneself. As the wretched slum dwellers watched the slow procession of the men, cradling AK-47s and RPG-7 rocket launchers, they unconsciously drew further back into the dark recesses of their miserable shacks, hoping to become invisible to the armed men. Fifty meters out, the leader of the team waved his hands first to one side, and then to the other. Following his directions, the two dozen men with him spread out in a rough crescent formation facing the police post. When the leader thought his men were in position, he shouldered his assault rifle and squeezed off a burst at the sentry, dozing off in a chair inside the locked wire gate of the compound. The rest of the men followed suit, and the silence of the slum was shattered by the rattle of gunfire and the whoosh-bang of the RPG-7s, as bullets and rocket-grenades slammed into the police post.

Was this another guerrilla attack on government forces in some Third World new world disorder civil war? It well could have been, or it could have been something else. The incident could have been a criminal gang's spat with the police for infringing on the gang's turf. Police corruption is rife in the Third World. As the government's authority becomes weaker and weaker, their security forces turn to crime and become a law unto themselves. They become no different than the non-state predatory groups they are fighting in the name of their crumbling society. This hypothetical incident, however, typifies the nasty, close-quarter nature of conflict the world now faces.

• • •

Islamic fundamentalism's heavy involvement in terrorism as its main instrument of waging war provides a vivid example of the type of conflict that will plague the new world disorder. It is an ideal weapon for them to use because it is done clandestinely. Unlike the conventional soldier on the battlefield, a terrorist can attack his targets, military or civilian, without in turn being subjected to certain harm. Fighting this ghost-like foe will be difficult, bloody and expensive.

Furthermore, the terrorist, and his other non-state compatriots, operate with fewer constrains than nation-states. They don't study the Geneva Convention on prisoner of war—they seldom take prisoners. Nor do they take special care to keep civilians out of the battle—

on the contrary, civilians are their most likely targets.

They do not have a rigid hierarchical command structure, and are quite capable of assembling a terrorist team from various parts of the world for a single specific mission. Once the mission is over, they scatter to the four corners of the earth.

Nor do they have vast bureaucracies planning budgets, strategies, designing weapons, and shuffling papers. If they need weapons they buy them from the black market or get them from a supplier state such as Iran or Libya. If they need money they rob a bank, sell some drugs, or use funds gained in some other criminal enterprise. No begging, hat-in-hand to a miserly legislative body.

In short, not only do these groups operate with less constraints, but they cooperate with one another far better than the U.N. and NATO managed in the Bosnian crisis.

There was close cooperation among five different Islamic fundamentalist terror groups that coalesced in the World Trade Center bombing and related terrorist plots in New York City. They were: 1) Sheik Omar Abdul Rahman's Gamm'at Islam of Egypt; 2) Sudan's National Islamic Front (members of the Sudanese Mission to the United Nations and five Sudanese arrested for a planned series of bomb attacks in New York; 3) Hamas (Mohammad Saleh, owner of a Yonkers gas station who was to supply the fuel to make the bombs in the other planned NYC attacks and who was also a key figure for Hamas in arranging Hamas terrorist training in the Sudan; 4) Islamic Jihad (its head, Abdel Aziz-Odeh was an unindicted co-conspirator but was believed by law enforcement officials to have known about the bomb plots in New York; and, 5) ul-Fuqra (a militant black militant-Pakistani organization with followers in Colorado, New York, Canada and Pakistan).

Triumph of Disorder

As terrorists step up their attacks on targeted societies, a loss of confidence will spread among the citizens in the ability of the authorities to function and react to the threat. A vicious cycle will ensue: loss of confidence in the authorities leads to an escalation of terror acts, which create even greater losses of confidence among the citizenry until the possibility of a total collapse of order becomes reality.

For most people faced with a climate of collapse, personal and family survival becomes paramount. People will rally behind those who can restore order. In the future this may well be the terrorist, who only has to stop his terror campaign in order to bring a degree of peace. Or, it will be the tyrant who can muster enough force to impose tyranny on all.

We can also expect the state's fading monopoly on coercive violence to help its nearest competitor—organized crime. Organized crime, after all, provides the main competition to the nation state in employing violence for coercive purposes. It is no coincidence that drug cartels, gangs, mafias and triads of various sorts are springing up like toadstools around the world. As the nation state gets weaker, these groups are getting stronger and bolder.

With a society permeated by a basic lack of trust, protection becomes essential. The criminal gang, terrorist, or warlord provides the protection—a phenomenon on-going in Columbia, Liberia, Somalia, and parts of the old Soviet Union.

Because of the weakening of the nation state, terrorism will become more widespread in the future. From these secret, tightly-knit terror cells will evolve local and regional warlords who will create a political climate akin to that of the feudal era or China in the 1920s.

In the West, terrorist acts are viewed as morally repugnant. This form of war, with its reliance on indiscriminate killing of soldier, policeman and civilian alike, is seen at best as dishonorable, at worst as criminal. It is the antithesis of the Western way of waging war, a subject we will explore shortly.

Such moral sentiments do not concern the militant Islamic fundamentalist. He overcomes the part of him that says he is a murderer of women and children. He denies this guilt by convincing himself that his victims are less than animals, that they are evil vermin who deserve to die. His guilt is also overcome because of the sanction given by the theological musings of his Islamic imams.

The imam gives the terrorist a religious reason for the killing of his victims, who, he is told, are Islam's enemies. How they are killed is of little concern to both the terrorist and the imam. They *are* Islam's enemies and deserve to die. The ends justify the means and pose no moral dilemma for the militant Islamist. Such an attitude is difficult to fight in terms of modern rules of engagements because we fall into our self-designed trap of assuming our foes share our values. They don't.

The futile attempt by the United Nations at "nation-building" in Somalia bears that out. The U.N had at its beck and call the military might of the United States, flush from its success in the Gulf War. The United States could impose neither its, or the United Nation's will upon the warring clans and could not reconstitute the imagined Somalia state. The warring clans *are* the state in the areas of Somalia under their control.

The United States has the biggest and most efficient coercive apparatus in the existing international order—its military forces, funded by the economic strength of the American economy. The collapse of the Soviet Union, and the U.S. victory in the Gulf War, has left the U.S. as the world's only mature superpower.

This may be a mixed blessing. No one is quarrelling with the necessity for military forces in an increasingly dangerous world. And the U.S. is the leader in developing and equipping its military with the high-tech weaponry the planners feel will dominate the battlefield of the future. But what if they are wrong? What if these weapons are being designed for the wrong battlefield? What if these high-tech weapons are useless against the terrorist?

During the Gulf War, the apparent invincibility of American forces was only too vivid. Future terror tyrants will take to heart the lesson of the Gulf War: a force massed for a conventional war of maneuver or attrition is a sitting-duck to a high-tech modern military.

The U.S. will soon face a different operational environment than it did during either the Cold War or Desert Storm. While Third World threats may seem manageable today, future Saddam Husseins, and even international criminal cartels in partnership with rogue states will have both the incentive and, because of the rapid diffusion of advanced military technology, the means to mount far more serious operational challenges to the American military than they faced from Iraq in 1991.

U.S., European, and Latin American intelligence and law enforcement officials are aware that Russian organized criminal groups, flush with dollars, are forming alliances with Colombian drug traffickers and are bartering weapons for cocaine. Attempts by the Russian crime syndicates to sell a submarine, helicopters, and surface-to-air missiles to the Colombian drug lords have already been detected.

Access to surface-to-air missiles would provide an effective method of attacking anti-drug forces targeting hard to reach jungle drug facilities. Helicopters, especially armored ones, would give the drug cartels a more secure means of transporting drugs and thwarting raids.

Acquiring such advanced weapons makes the drug gang, war-lord, terrorist or guerrilla group more effective and dangerous. The ability to confront their enemies increases dramatically.

Forward bases, they key to America's ability to project power throughout the world, will soon become potential liabilities, instead of precious strategic assets. The reason is simple: as rogue states, or international terrorist organizations for that matter, get their hands on an ever increasing number of available ranged-fire systems (ballistic and low-altitude cruise missiles), more effective munitions (precision-guided missiles and nuclear, chemical, and biological munitions), and more sophisticated communications, navigational and imaging sys-tems—many of a commercial nature—forward bases will become highly vulnerable, immovable targets.

The 1996 truck bombing of an American Air Base in Saudi Arabia demonstrates this vulnerability. The truck bomb was not of the caliber or as sophisticated as the much deadlier weapons that are now available to terrorists. Such bases, far from deterring potential enemies, will have the paradoxical effect of lessening deterrence. These bases will become fixed-targeted hostages to groups possessing long-range strike weapons.

Such a situation will likely force the U.S. into more reliance on its naval forces as its major force-projection instrument. This isn't an outlandish consideration when almost 75% of the world's population lives within 100 miles of a seacoast. But, U.S. military operations in these littoral areas will become increasingly dangerous and costly.

Many of these conflicts may evolve around control of vital sea choke points. Choke points occur where sea-lane restrictions lead to a concentration of shipping within a limited area. Most of these restrictions occur where sea-lanes converge around peninsulas and promontories. Other factors controlling choke point location are adverse currents, storms and other climatic events.

Choke points are significant for both economic and military reasons. Halting merchant shipping or making its passage through a choke point highly dangerous obviously has economic costs to maritime trade. Shutting down the flow of oil to the West, the enemies of Islamic fundamentalism, would be striking a blow for Allah by disrupting non-Muslim societies dependent on oil.

Choke points are also important for military reasons. They facilitate surveillance and provide the best opportunity along the sea-lanes for attacking shipping during hostilities. Targets are plentiful and concentrated in confined areas.

Choke point control is of vital importance in war. Whoever controls the choke point controls the traffic through it. Control of these vital geographic features is threatened by instability and/or hostility in the riparian states encompassing the choke point. Another aspect of control is the characteristic of its geography, including its length, width and depth.

Taking these factors into account, the most important choke points in the world are: Bab el-Mandeb, Dover Straits, the Dardanelles, the Strait of Gibraltar, the Strait of Hormuz and the Strait of Malacca.

Passage through the Bab el-Mandeb is divided by Perim Island. The larger of the two passages measures 9 nautical miles. It provides the southern entrance to the Suez Canal and lies within the territorial waters of North and South Yemen, Djibouti, and Ethiopia. Three of these countries are Muslim and have internal unrest. If any of these fall into the hands of radical Islamic fundamentalists they would be well-positioned to close the Suez Canal and pose a significant risk to Western shipping.

The Strait of Hormuz is 96 nautical miles long and 21 nautical miles wide. Passage from the Indian Ocean moves through Omani territorial waters into the Persian Gulf. Shipping then continues through Iranian territorial waters. The Strait of Hormuz is the only sea outlet for most of the oil-producing Gulf States and is the world's most vital oil choke point. Its importance cannot be overstated.

The Strait of Hormuz is also surrounded by Muslim states, including Iran, the godfather of Islamic fundamentalism. Instability is rife in the region, much of it inspired and supported by Tehran. If most of the riparian states fall into militant Islamic hands, the potential for serious mischief is huge. They would be in a position to subject Western nations dependant on their oil to radical Islamic blackmail.

The Strait of Gibraltar is 36 nautical miles long, varying in width from 27 to 8 nautical miles. It separates Europe from Africa at the western end of the Mediterranean Sea. If Morocco, on the southern side of the strait, fell into Islamic fundamentalists' hands the potential for interdiction of this important choke point increases.

The Dardanelles, the waterway to the Black Sea, is bordered on both sides by Turkey, an Islamic state in which a fundamentalist political party is part of the Turkish government coalition.

The Dover Strait between England and France is the least susceptible to militant Islam's possible interdiction, although suicide terrorist attacks can't be ruled out.

The Strait of Malacca is one of the most important in the world, linking the Indian and Pacific Oceans. Including the Singapore Strait, it is 600 nautical miles long and varies in width from 8.4 nautical miles at the southern end to 140 nautical miles at the northern end. Islands and shoals in the southern end limit large vessels to a channel only two nautical miles in width.   In addition to being surrounded by Muslim countries, the Strait of Malacca is also afflicted with a growing problem of piracy.

Choke points are becoming increasingly vulnerable from land attack, especially with low-cost sophisticated cruise missiles.

• • •

Given the huge amount of cash involved in the drug trade, narco-terror rogue states, and their non-state criminal or terrorist partners can afford some very lethal weapons systems. Submarines, sophisticated mines, low-altitude cruise missiles, are just three such systems. These systems can create exclusion zones not only along sea route choke points and off the immediate coast, but perhaps several hundred miles out to sea. To penetrate these, American naval forces would face conditions that pose a high risk to their survival.

The weapons required to establish these exclusion zones of sea denial will be smaller, different and less costly than those the U.S. would need to gain control of the sea and be able to send the Marines ashore. Should the fleet move into this dangerous area, it may require nothing more than saturating the fleet's defenses with a large number of relatively cheap anti-ship missiles. For example, assuming a $400,000 price tag for a low-altitude cruise missile (the cost may be considerably less), an enemy could fire over 10,000 such missiles at our fleet and still not equal the cost of a single aircraft carrier.

One of these missiles for sale on the open market is the Russian 3M-60 URAN cruise missile. URAN coastal batteries have been aggressively marketed by the Russians. It can be deployed as a shore-to-ship missile for coastal defense, or to engage surface combatants on their passage through straits or between islands, or rain missiles down on a beach invasion formation.

The basic configuration of the battery is four launchers, four transporter-reloaders, and two command, control and communications posts. The growing proliferation and deployment of the URAN poses a potentially growing threat to U.S. Naval surface ships and Marine Corps Expeditionary Units.

The URAN isn't the only weapons system posing a serious threat to U.S. naval power projection in the 21st century. The Russian diesel-electric KILO submarine is another. While it is doubtful even drug gangs flush with cash will purchase, at $250 million, and man a KILO, they are being purchased by potential enemies such as China, Iran, Libya and Syria.

The KILO is renown to be the quietest diesel-electric submarine in the world. The ship is designed to replicate the background undersea noise of the littoral sea. This makes sonar detection of the sub difficult at best.

The KILO is capable of being equipped with three primary weapons systems: 1) surface-to-air missiles, 2) anti-ship and anti-submarine torpedoes, and 3) shallow-water mines.

Iran's deployment of two KILOs in the Strait of Hormuz, in addition to advanced Russian and Chinese coastal batteries of anti-ship cruise missiles, such as the URAN, could close that choke point. How serious a threat would that be? It was through this choke point that 94% of all logistic support for the Gulf War passed. Don't forget a major portion of the oil shipped by tanker to Europe, Asia, and the United States must transit the Straits of Hormuz.

KILOs have been exported to several Third World countries, many of them not friendly to the United States. The subs have been sold to China, Iran, India, Algeria, Poland, Romania, North Korea, Libya, Syria,and, possibly Iraq. In addition, T-53 wake-homing torpedoes have been sold to at least 15 countries, including North Korean, Iraq, China, and Libya.

With weapons like this in unscrupulous hands, will the U.S. military be able to bully the dictators and tyrants populating the world of the future into doing what the U.S. wants?

Not likely. Instead of providing targets for high-tech weaponry, the West's enemies will fight differently. They will use small widely dispersed unconventional military forces to fight a non-conventional war. The tactics will not be a war of maneuver, but raids, subversion, terror, and guerrilla war.

Terrorist-manned small missile equipped vessels can inflict severe damage with little risk. In June 1971, for example, Palestinian guerrillas firing rockets from a small motorboat behind Perim Island in the Strait of Bab el-Mandeb sank the tanker *Coral Sea,* which was heading through the Strait of Tiran for Eilat, Israel.

Effective action against shipping in choke points take place at a low cost and the attackers can be difficult to detect. Remember the Red Sea mining incident in the 1980s? In spite of several strong suggestions, the identity of those who laid the mines is still not clear.

Piracy is on the rise according to the UN's International Maritime Bureau, which reported 79 attacks during the first six months of 1997. The modern pirate is a career criminal or terrorist with a Kalashnikov assault rifle and a speedboat.

Piracy is also once again raising its ugly head in the Mediterranean, after an almost 200-year absence. The waters off Sicily, Malta,

Italy, and especially the Corfu Channel off Albania are now infested with a new breed of pirates. Their prey is private yachts. These pirates often murder the yacht's owners and passengers and use the stolen craft to smuggle narcotics or commit other acts of piracy.

These forms of organized violence are difficult, if not impossible, to counter by cruise missiles and smart bombs targeted from space. The new enemy forces of the future will not be conventional powers like the old Soviet Union, nor tin-pot dictators like Saddam Hussein.

Instead, they will be armed bands from political entities of small "states," or fragments of existing countries, ruled by bands of terrorists, religious fanatics, drug lords, or criminal gangs. They will not be deterred by the West's high-tech arsenal of missiles, nuclear navies, and expensive ponderous formations of tanks and armored personnel carriers. These forces will fight by their own rules, not those of the West—and the West's rules of warfare may be outdated.

God will not be, as Voltaire said, "on the side of bigger battalions." Instead, his favor will have shifted to smaller groups of armed men.

The American way of war epitomizes how the West wages war: it involves nation states battling each other with their conventional armies, navies, and air forces. Central to the American way of war, demonstrated spectacularly in the Gulf War, is the idea of annihilating the enemy using firepower and mass to apply overwhelming force on the battlefield.

The Western way of war is waged within the theoretical framework of Karl von Clausewitz, a long-dead Prussian officer who fought in the Napoleonic Wars almost two centuries ago. He laid out the theoretical framework in his celebrated book, *On War.*

Triumph of Disorder

Clausewitz has dominated Western military thinking to this day. Unfortunately, his framework may be the wrong guide to follow in dealing with war in the new world disorder.

Warfare, however, existed long before Clausewitz and his holy trinity appeared on history's stage. Compared with man's long history, trinitarian war is just a short epoch in mankind's bloody fascination with warfare.

For most of history war was waged by families, clans tribes, villages, cities, religions, and even commercial enterprises, (the Great Catalan Company in the fourteenth century, and the British and Dutch East India Companies, to name just three.) Warfare was just as bloody, indeed, as University of Illinois at Chicago anthropology professor Lawrence H. Keeley demonstrates in his book, *War Before Civilzation: The Myth of the Peaceful Savage*, there is mounting evidence that warfare in prehistoric societies was in fact more deadly, more frequent, and more ruthless than modern war.

War was fought for many reasons other than reasons of state—hardly surprising since the nation state hadn't been invented—loot, crops or grazing lands, slaves, women (Helen of Troy—the face that launched a thousand ships and a ten-year war), religious reasons (The Old Testament is full of accounts of the religious wars of the Jews in the ancient Middle East.), and for the sacrificial victims demanded by the pagan Aztec gods. Non-trinitarian warfare has been the steady companion of man for most of his history.

Ancient tribal and family-based clan societies warred on one another, without the benefit of the Clausewitz trinity. There was no nation state, just other tribal societies.

A slightly more sophisticated system was the war-making process in the ancient Greek city states. Even though the city state was a highly organized government, when it came time for war the leader in charge raised the force. He either took volunteers or selected those who hadn't fulfilled their obligatory war duties. When they fought, they fought for themselves. Honor and glory in war was heaped on the skill of individual fighters, not on the corporate body of the particular city state.

Early republican Rome conducted its wars in a similar manner. It was only when Rome's economic fortunes rose could it afford to pay for a permanent standing army and a glimpse of the Clausewitzian trinity emerged.

During the Roman Empire the idea of the nation state existing apart from the rulers of Rome was non-existent. The Roman emperors were the state, and their rule was based upon their ability to command loyal military forces to enforce their will.

The rise and expansion of Islam does not fit the Clausewitz universe.

Islam was spread by the nomadic raiding warriors of the Arabian peninsula. They were not a nation state but a collection of feudal clans. Even united under the Prophet and his successors, the crusading warriors of Islam resembled not so much an army, but a marauding horde. There was no nation state. It was a theological empire ruled by the Prophet and his successors.

Nor was there any division of the army and the people. All Muslims are duty bound by the tenets of Islam to spread the faith, by the sword if necessary—an obligation today's Islamic fundamentalists are carrying out with a vengeance.

It was only years after the Islamic empire was established and the Ottomans were its rulers that it began showing Clausewitzian characteristics, mainly because it borrowed ideas freely from the more powerful European states. The Ottomans established a permanent standing army and there was a distinct division between it and the people. The people, however, were actually the downtrodden subjects of the despotic Ottoman rulers and were not involved in the political or war making decision of the empire. They were ruled, and war was waged, on the whims of the rulers.

By the tenth century Europe was coming out of the Dark Ages, with the advent of feudalism. The feudal military system was based upon the armored knight. These fighters required expensive equipment—horses, armor, battle axes and heavy lances. Mastering the fighting tactics of carrying a heavy lance, or wielding a battle ax, while wearing heavy armor atop a galloping horse, required years of practice. In short, it required a professional warrior. This professionalism, along with the costs of equipping and maintaining knights, assured only a small fraction of the feudal males would be warriors.

The constraints of feudalism on the length of military service led directly to the formation and hiring of private armies, mercenaries if you will. By the eighteenth century, well after the birth of the modern state, all major European armies relied on mercenaries: one-half the Prussian army; one-third of the French army; and almost a third of the British army were mercenaries. England used 18,000 mercenaries during the American War of Independence.

The effects of using private armies by European rulers was two-fold: wars were fought by comparatively small armies of professional soldiers; and war was not an affair of the people, it concerned only the rulers spats among themselves.

That changed with the French Revolution and the Napoleonic Wars. Between 1793 and 1815, a new form of war arose. War now became a matter of the nation in arms as the French, infused with revolutionary ardor and under the brilliant leadership of Napoleon, fought and bled Europe dry.

These wars caused thinkers to evaluate war: how it was fought, who fought it, and for whom was it fought—the holy trinity of Clausewitz—the state, the army, and the people.

Clausewitz is the most influential military theorist in the world today. His theories were accepted by both the Communists and the West during the Cold War. The United States military establishment is still thoroughly steeped in Clausewitzian thinking and U.S. military doctrine is still grounded on the dead Prussian's ideas.

Unfortunately, Clausewitz's trinitarian war will not be the major mode of conflict in the coming new world disorder. That period will weaken and even remove one of the three legs of the Clausewitz trinity—the nation state. If there is no state to organize and direct the fighting, that war has become non-trinitarian.

Even where the state remains it is likely to be a much weaker entity. It may become so weak it will be unable to eradicate the organized violence of non-state groups within its borders, as in places like Liberia. It will lose its monopoly on war. As a result, it will also lose the loyalty of its citizens in growing numbers throughout the world.

It will lose this support because the state is failing to provide one of its most elemental functions: the protection of its citizens. When the state fails to protect its citizens, it forfeits their loyalty. This loyalty will be transferred to whatever group or organization can protect them. The growing rampant violent crime in the major urban areas of the U.S., the violent societal collapse in the Third World, and the violent criminal anarchy in the former Soviet Union show graphically the growing failure of the nation state to protect many of its citizens.

Triumph of Disorder

In much of the world the nation state, a creature of the West, doesn't have strong ties with its citizens. The people's major loyalties are to their clan, tribe or religious grouping. The resurrection of cultural, tribal and ethnic nationalities throughout the world provides stark examples of this trend against the nation state. This rising nationalism is often accompanied by violence.

...

Populations are migrating to cities seeking employment, social support, and a better way of life. A century ago there were no predominantly urban countries. In 1920 England was the only nation with over 50 percent of its population in cities or towns over 20,000. In 1970, 12 percent of the world population lived in cities of 500,000 or more. Estimate are that nearly 45 percent of the world's population will live in urban areas by the year 2000.

Urban centers include the political institutions for nations, states or provinces, regions and municipalities, as well as the economic base of industry, banking, and commerce. Cities are increasingly important to the control of a nations wealth and power. Consequently, cities are becoming inviting targets for destabilizing military or paramilitary operation.

As people seek the cities for the security they appear to offer, governments' difficulties increase. Large squatter settlements and areas of poverty exist in and around most, if not all, of the world's large cities. As people overcrowd cities and resources become overtaxed, the socio-political environments grow ripe for dissent, social unrest, and humanitarian aid.

We are seeing greater emphasis upon military operations located in the urban areas. Insurgencies such as *Sendaro Luminoso* (Shining Path) have forsaken rural terrain in favor of urban terrain because that is where greatest unrest is found—where the people and resources are located, and it is easier to move undetected in the large urban sprawls.

The future will require U.S. military forces to operate in urban centers. The opponents will be Martin Van Creveld's cast of non-state fighters: from warlord-led gangs, terrorists and religious fanatics, to criminal cartels, to militias, to techno-bandits.

The political importance of the urban centers must be thoroughly understood. The U.S. cannot destroy or significantly damage the infrastructure of a foreign urban center in pursuit of military goals and expect the local population to remain friendly to either U.S. forces or those we may be supporting. Nor can we indiscriminately use force in precise ways that cause unnecessary noncombatant casualties without political or financial penalty.

Our experience in Somalia illustrates the problems. Our mission in Somalia was nebulous: secure the peace and get out without casualties. As a result the rules of engagement (ROE) were confusing. In fact the Somalis had the ROE figured out before U.S. troops, and used it to their advantage.

Somalia also heightened the perception of the U.S. reluctance to use force. Our enemies don't doubt our capacity, graphically demonstrated in the Gulf War. They doubt our will. They are fully aware of America's Achilles Heel: the U.S. unwillingness to take casualties.

Fighting in the urban environment will cause casualties as it will require a large number of infantry. In urban combat, the attacker may need to outnumber the defender by ratios of between 6 to 1 and 10 to 1. And the defender will extract a bloody price—casualties up to 40% according to the U.S. Marine Corps War Fighting Labs.

Third World urban fighting will be more likely than any repeats of the Gulf War, or what our military prepared for during the long Cold War.

Warfare in the new world disorder will become increasingly non-trinitarian, and traditional Clausewitzian-steeped forces will be ineffectual against it.

Chapter 6
Iran: Creating the Islamic Paradise

Islam is not Christianity...Islam is the religion of agitation,
revolution, blood, liberation and martyrdom.

Shaikh Morteza Motahari

It was November 1979, and on television screens across the country people watched angry Iranian mobs jostling blindfolded American hostages seized in the Iranian takeover of the United States Embassy. It was this event, more than any other, that launched a Western hatred towards Iran.

The vilification heaped upon the West, especially the United States, further fanned the flames of this animosity. The Ayatollah Khomeini termed the United States the "Great Satan," and blamed her for all the evils of the world. The Iranian people, it seemed, had turned into barbaric savages. Almost two decades later, little has changed. America is still Iran's bitter enemy.

Americans responded with uncommon rancor, harassing Iranian students and painting Khomeini's dour features on dart boards and toilet bowls. Iranians provoked more American venom than any other foreign people since the hostility shown towards the Japanese during World War II.

Even though relations with Iran had been friendly, the actions of Khomeini, his mobs and his support of terrorism stripped away the thin veneer of civility between the two nations. The world watched in amazement as bearded clerics assumed control in what was thought to be a bastion of stability in the turbulent Middle East. Militant Islamic fundamentalism had succeeded in overthrowing the Peacock Throne.

That event shocked the world because, on the surface, the Shah's regime appeared strong. Its military was armed with modern American and British weapons, and was considered by the West as a stabilizing influence in the Persian Gulf. The ancient institution of the throne had deep roots in the history of the country. It was a unifying force in a country which was a collection of different racial, religious, cultural and linguistic peoples, most of whom hated one another. The Peacock throne was seen by most of these diverse groups as the only protection they had from the depredations of their enemies. The country appeared stable and strong. Yet revolution came to Iran.

In the final analysis, the Shah was not toppled because he was pro-West, or a capitalist, or corrupt or cruel—those qualities are endemic to most Middle Eastern rulers. He destroyed himself by succumbing to the fatal temptation of modern times: the lure of social engineering. The Shah's policies sowed the seeds of his own destruction by creating a growing wave of discontent fostered by his ego and the harsh methods used to satisfy his growing vanity.

In January 1963, he launched his revolution from above to transform Iran into a strong modern day society. Called the White Revolution, it included agrarian reform, forced nationalization, industrial development, voting rights for women, and the eradication of illiteracy. The White Revolutionary restructuring of Iran was to be completed during the Shah's lifetime and involved social engineering on a massive scale. It was a program certain to provoke controversy, especially among the conservative radical Shi'ite clergy. It especially offended Khomeini.

Shortly after the Shah launched his program, Khomeini began voicing his vehement opposition. He used a religious ceremony to open his venomous war of words against the Shah: "You miserable wretch...isn't it time for you to think and reflect a little, to ponder where all this is leading you...?"

This diatribe not only elevated Khomeini to the forefront in the growing opposition to the Shah's White Revolution, but led to his incarceration. His arrest touched-off violent riots which were eventually put down with much loss of life. A year of further denunciations by Khomeini led to his exile from Iran, where he remained until his triumphant return after the Shah's departure in 1979.

Khomeini's opposition, even in exile, did not slow the Shah's White Revolution. The monarch lavished ever increasing sums on his various projects: $2.7 billion from 1963-68, $10 billion, 1968-72; $70 billion, 1973-78. These vast sums were spent on all manner of projects from building roads and schools, to restoring the ancient Persian capital of Persopolis. You name it, the Shah and his planners tried to do it. In the process they exhibited all the arrogance, greed and incompetence of a Soviet bureaucrat and, in so doing, stirred-up growing resentment and opposition to the monarchy throughout Iran.

It didn't matter, the Shah was determined to change Iranian society overnight and transform it into a model for the Middle East. There was, however, little popular demand for such a change within Iran, except from the courtiers and hangers-on of the Shah and his cronies. They were quite happy with the White Revolution as they were enriching themselves from the huge amounts of money being squandered on the pet projects of the moment.

Triumph of Disorder

The Shah plunged full-speed ahead, boasting that his White Revolution combined the principles of capitalism with socialism, even communism. The whole structure of Iran was being turned upside down.

Unlike the sorcerer's apprentice, whose experiments got out of hand, the Shah didn't have a teacher to rescue him. His massive program of collectivization and social engineering couldn't be reversed by waving a magic wand. It required a major reversal of his beloved White Revolution and the Shah's ego wouldn't permit that—so he pressed on.

The Shah's program alienated many of his traditional supporters. The nationwide collectivization of agriculture angered the rural peasants. Roaring inflation, fueled by his extravagant spending, had ruinous effects upon merchants and small businessmen. Many were driven out of business or into the black market and into the arms of the growing opposition to the Shah.

The corruption in the country grew as the Shah and his friends enriched themselves at the expense of the people. The corruption had ruinous effects on the urban middle class whose businesses were destroyed by the Shah's cronies. They were being pushed to the wall and in desperation they began allying themselves with Khomeini and supported his efforts to overthrow the throne.

Through his megalomaniacal zeal to transform Iran by socialistic central planing schemes, the Shah created a revolutionary climate of growing dissent and rapidly vanishing support for his regime. It led to his downfall.

There were many in Iran who wanted to see the Shah go but only Khomeini had the statute and the following to transform the dissent into effective action.

Iran's revolution did *not* follow the classic patterns laid out by Mao or Lenin. Most of the Iranian activities never got out of the "organizational" stage of classic revolutionary war theory. In fact most of the terrorism and guerrilla war incidents were done by Khomeini's ineffectual rivals, the *Mojahedin-e-Khalq*, a Marxist-oriented guerrilla force, and the Iranian Communist Party.

These rivals posed a potential problem for the campaign to oust the Shah. If they could be maneuvered into fighting each other, it would take a lot of pressure off the Shah. Divide and conquer is as sound a counterrevolutionary strategy as it is for the basis of a foreign policy. Often rivals spend as much time fighting each other as they do trying to overthrow their common enemy. This fratricidal infighting helps the government's counterrevolutionary program by providing it the opportunity to infiltrate the revolutionary ranks and play one group off against the other.

Successful revolutions are well organized affairs. They don't erupt out of the blue. All revolutions are carefully planned and organized. It requires coordinated action of many people pooling their efforts towards a common goal. Both Lenin's and Mao's revolutionary movements were highly organized, and both succeeded. Guevara's seat-of-the-pants effort in Bolivia was a fiasco and demonstrated the fatal folly of trying to carry out a revolution with no organization and little planning to back it up.

The internal leaders of Khomeini's rivals inside Iran lacked both the widespread organization and the leadership ability available to Khomeini. The fact that they were in Iran while Khomeini was in exile in France wasn't much of an advantage.

In spite of this handicap, Khomeini was able to preside and direct his campaign to topple the throne by using his extensive network of contacts within Iran's thousands of mosques. They were the key to his success.

There were over 180,000 members of the Shi'ite clergy in Iran and many of them were devoted followers of Khomeini. They formed a tremendous revolutionary network waiting to be energized in the campaign to overthrow the Shah. Khomeini didn't hesitate to use it.

He used his position and prestige as Iran's Shi'ite religious authority to attack the government as un-Islamic and under the control and influence of the hated infidel—the United States. As a religious teacher he had a large number of former students who were now mullahs throughout Iran. These former students revered Khomeini and became his contacts and supporters inside Iran during his long period in exile. Simple, cheap modern technology was skillfully used in facilitating revolution inside Iran. It was almost impossible for the Shah's secret police to stop the spread of his messages attacking and undermining the monarchy.

Khomeini's words were recorded week after week on tape cassettes and smuggled into Iran, where they were eagerly snapped up, reproduced and distributed throughout his nationwide network centered around the thousands of mosques in Iran.

The Iranian revolution started in the mosques. His tape messages were played there for the masses who had come to pray. They were suffering under the Shah's policies and were receptive to the recorded harangues. Khomeini's recordings provided inspiration and instructions to the faithful that jammed the mosques to hear them. His words carried weight all over Iran.

Khomeini was first and foremost a theologian, not a politician or professional revolutionary. But he recognized the real potential in the deteriorating situation in Iran and was shrewd in capitalizing on it. He blended nationalism and religion in his campaign to overthrow the Shah.

Using this mixture, he created and encouraged the growing anti-monarchical militancy in Iran. Khomeini's spartan lifestyle also won him a widespread following among the people who were sick of the corrupt, luxury-loving politicians. The fact that he was a man of god gave him both the spiritual and temporal authority which the Shah and his government lacked. He used them to organize demonstrations, strikes, and mass mobilization campaigns of riots and protest in Iran.

Khomeini never organized guerrilla units, nor did he plan on a protracted war to bring down the Shah. His campaign was geared to removing the legitimacy of the Shah and undermining the military, the power behind the throne.

Unlike post-revolutionary Iran, terror did not play a major role in Khomeini's drive for power. He knew that guerrilla attacks, by their very nature, would involve attacks on isolated police and military units. Such attacks would invite reprisals and tend to unify the military against those responsible for the attacks. Bloodshed, he reasoned, would rally the army behind the Shah.

Instead, he waged a masterful cold-blooded psychological war against the military and fought it on moral grounds using tactics that struck a responsive chord in the psyche of Shi'ite Iranians—the martyr complex that permeates Shi'ite Islamic history. We must fight from within the soldiers' hearts, was his message. Let the army kill as many as it wants, until the soldiers are shaken to their hearts by the massacres they have committed. Then the army will collapse and you will have disarmed the army.

A close associate of Khomeini, Dr. Ibrahim Yazdi, said Khomeini used his religious authority to urge all members of the armed forces to follow and obey their religious obligations and join the revolutionaries by leaving their posts, disobeying their commanders' orders and becoming servants of the popular revolution. In the end it worked because Khomeini, as a Grand Ayatollah, had tremendous authority in Iran and he used it to mobilize Iranians against the Shah.

One especially effective mass mobilization tactic was to use traditional religious holidays, funerals and mourning processions as protest rallies against the Shah. Rioters or demonstrators killed in clashes with the security forces were treated as heroes and martyrs. Khomeini's lieutenants, the mullahs, used the traditional fortieth day of mourning for those killed and turned it into agitation, propaganda demonstrations and provocations against the Shah. The oratory on these occasions was often interspersed with playing recorded speeches of Khomeini to stir up the passions of the mourners.

If, as often happened, the activities got out of hand and were fired upon by the Shah's loyal security troops, the revolution was provided with a new bunch of martyrs, and more opportunities to organize other anti-Shah demonstrations in the guise of traditional mourning observances. Nor were Khomeini's lieutenants inside Iran above using agitators to provoke an armed confrontation with the sole purpose of provoking a shoot-out in order to provide enough funerals to keep the masses stirred up against the government.

These acts were the stage props for Khomeini's simple and direct message: abolish the Iranian monarchy. He used this simple goal to unite the differing groups within Iran into a solid front of opposition to the regime. His prestige was such that he was able to rally the people behind an anti-Shah coalition because he capitalized on the growing dissent and a "throw-the-bums-out" mood in the country.

The mass mobilization campaign cleverly orchestrated by Khomeini was not about some striving for democracy or the creation of an Islamic republic, it was simple opposition to the Shah. Khomeini was very quiet and kept to himself, while the riots and demonstrations were going on, as to what would replace the Shah. He knew what he wanted, as did his closest associates—the creation of a strict Islamic theocratic state—but he kept his thoughts to himself.

This silence was interpreted by the different faction uniting under his banner as silent assent for their particular point of view. They read into his silence what they, not Khomeini, had in mind for Iran's future.

The Shah's response to the Khomeini threat was tepid. Under pressure from the Carter Administration for human rights abuses, the Shah vacillated between periods of halfhearted liberalization and crackdowns. He released political prisoners, returned Iran to the Islamic calendar, abolished his puppet political party, launched an anti-corruption campaign and restored a degree of freedom of the press.

Instead of defusing the situation these measures had the opposite effect. Each concession brought further demands from his opponents. The Shah was reluctant to be too brutal in his periodic crackdown and this reluctance quickly spread to the military. This hesitation compromised the counterrevolutionary program. It takes massive organization, dedication, sacrifice and time to defeat a revolutionary movement. The government under assault must decide early if it is willing to pay the price, and it will be high. Half-measures lead only to protracted, costly defeats.

The Shah was reluctant to pay the price and it cost him his

throne. His program of collectivism, which he refused to abandon, was impossible to impose without terror. He hadn't the heart to do it to the degree necessary to cower his opposition. Although he felt betrayed by the United States, in the end he lacked the will and power so necessary to maintain his regime.

The Shah's utopian dream of transforming tradition-bound Shi'ite Iran into a modern collectivized state faded rapidly. A utopia is a mental concept founded on a single idea and grounded in deep-rooted faith of that idea. Remove the faith and the utopian dream collapses like a house of cards, as reality is seen for what it is.

Reality for the Shah was howling mobs surging through the streets of Iranian cities demanding his scalp. His utopian idea for his new Iran was drowning in the mob's chants: "Death to the Shah!"

This lack of will played right into the hands of the Khomeini's campaign to undermine the morale of the army. If your leader isn't willing to use the force available, reasoned the army, then why should they stick their necks out? They didn't and that sealed the Shah's fate.

The loss of will by the Iranian military was summed up in the observation of the French military attache in Tehran: "...No army could confront its own people for an extended period. If the Iranian revolution was something of a few months duration, the army could have resisted, but by now it was too late to expect it to do so."

The departure of the Shah on January 16, 1979 left Khomeini free to impose his Islamic republic on Iran. Terror and youth were important ingredients in his success. He killed, imprisoned or caused his opponents to flee Iran in fear of their lives. Even those that fled were often pursued and killed by hit teams of youthful terrorist fanatics trained by the new Iranian theocratic state.

The elimination of dissidents and opponents of the Iranian

Islamic Republic has been one of its constant, long-standing policies. Opponents living in exile have been hunted down and murdered by Iranian intelligence agents using logistical support from local terror cells. More than sixty Iranian expatriates have been murdered abroad by Tehran's hit squads.

The youth of Iran were an extremely valuable part of Khomeini's overall strategy. They were the frontline soldiers on the battlefield in the revolutionary war. It has been said that war is a job for the young and Khomeini used them skillfully. In spite of the general contempt for human life that permeates Khomeini's brand of revolutionary Islamic fundamentalism, youth are more than just cannon fodder. They are the future of his revolution. It is the youth who will be faced with the actual task of creating a truly Islamic society both in and outside of Iran.

Khomeini's view of the value of youth was based on theological grounds: they weren't as "corrupt" as adults. Being less "corrupt" they were more open to the true tenets of Islam as perceived by the Islamic fundamentalists. In addition, so reasoned Khomeini and the fundamentalists, it was the corrupt West that invented the system that divides human life into artificial categories. Within these created structures children are expected and made to act childishly. In the process, they become corrupted, by playing games, etc., instead of serving Islam by cutting down the forces of evil on the battlefield.

Khomeini particularly hates the United States because he views American society and its liberal democracy as corrupt and a corrosive influence on Muslims. Therefore, it must be destroyed.

Youth are very malleable. If they haven't reached maturity, they often are not able to conceptualize the difference between right and wrong. Because of this, young people between the ages of ten and eighteen can kill and hate without showing the same remorse their elders would. This was a trait the Iranian revolution exploited to its advantage.

To help Khomeini consolidate his revolution and impose a strict Islamic fundamentalist regime in Iran, the Iranian youth were organized into Revolutionary Komitehs. They became the shock troops of Khomeini in ways reminiscent of the Red Guards of Mao's Chinese Cultural revolution. They organized and directed the mobs that roamed, like packs of hungry wolves, through the streets of Iran's cities demanding the ousting of the Shah. They provoked incidents with the police and loyal security forces that resulted in bloodshed and further chaos. After the Shah left the country, the Komitehs took over the administrative and police powers and through these helped Khomeini consolidate his power.

His Islamic republic was an oppressive totalitarian society given religious sanction. The justification is grounded in Shi'ite theology whereby the individual's desires are repressed in favor of those of the community. The individual is assimilated into the community, thus losing his individuality.

By losing his individuality, the one becomes a member of a society which will be united with his Creator. But that can only happen if the faithful are living in accordance with the law of the Koran.

Given the fallen nature of man, every moment of his existence must be regulated, or guided, by the religious authority. Left to his own devices, man will quickly succumb to the temptations of the Devil. This is totalitarianism with a religious dressing.

A true believer must not allow his thoughts to be diverted for a single moment from the worship of Allah and the performance of his duties under divine law. The idea is to fill every second with thoughts of Allah, thus preventing "other thoughts" from invading one's mind.

"A man who thinks is sending signals to Satan," is the view of the Islamic purist. Thinking is deemed not only dangerous but unnecessary since all the answers to all imaginable questions can be found in the Koran and the Hadith. If the faithful aren't sure, then the theologians of the day are there precisely to clarify every issue and to guide the faithful in all aspects of life.

Such an attitude seems too incredible to comprehend to the Western mind steeped in rationalism, individual freedom and initiative.

This world view and resulting regimentation of society in Iran has been going on for almost two decades and was enforced at its inception by Iran's Red Guards. Thousands of teenagers, wearing the headbands of the Khomeini-formed Volunteers for Martyrdom, were patrolling Iran to help root out corruption and "satanic" activity. These zealots were said to have broken into a total of seventy-nine thousand private homes in five years, seizing enormous quantities of objects of sin such as tape recorders, playing cards, chess and backgammon sets, musical instruments, records, lipsticks, perfumes, and indecent clothes. Also seized were un-Islamic literature and paintings or sculptures that might induce viewers to have "wrong" thoughts.

Estimates put the number of Iranians who have been imprisoned since the revolution on charges of "un-Islamic behavior" at over a million, or one in forty of the population. At least two thousand have been executed for "crimes" such as adultery, homosexuality, and even for organizing "mixed" parties of men and women.

It was the youth of the Komitehs that plotted and seized the American Embassy in Tehran and held the diplomatic personnel hostage for 444 days.

The revolution was a success and the country was in the hands of a priesthood which had little or no training or experience in exercising political power. The result was a barbarous totalitarian terror exercised by a small group of fundamentalist despots, acting in the name of Islam. It was a model Khomeini wanted to impose on all of the world.

Iran sees itself as the leader of the charge within the Muslim world against the "corrupt" West. An emerging strategy can be detected: dominate the Persian Gulf and choke off the West's biggest source of oil. Time, the mullahs of Iran feel, is on their side. The Americans, the world's remaining superpower, are impatient and are like a storm: although threatening, they leave the scene quickly. All Iran has to do is weather the storm and, after it passes, it will be business as usual. And that business is to expand Iran's influence in the Middle East and elsewhere.

Iran, at present, has to play a careful and clandestine game to counter U.S. influence in the Middle East in the face of the threat of superior American military power. But they have no intention of abandoning their vehement anti-American policy. They are biding their time, while improving their ability to eventually interdict the flow of oil through the Strait of Hormuz, and develop weapons of mass destruction: nuclear, chemical and biological.

Iran also looks north and sees opportunity in the Muslim republics of the former Soviet union. It views strife in Bosnia as opening up the possibility of Islamic rule in Europe. To further this ambition, Iranian leaders had long urged Muslims countries to provide help in Bosnia, in violation of the U.N. arms embargo. Iran put her money where her mouth was by supplying weapons and men to help the Bosnians. By the time of the Dayton Accords, up to 4,000 Muslims from over two dozen Islamic countries were said to be fighting in Bosnia. NATO denials to the contrary, many of them remain to this day.

Iran's economy is in shambles. Its military was devastated by the purges of the Khomeini regime and the long Iran-Iraq War. That hasn't deterred her from her self-appointed mission.

Iran has had some incredible luck in her efforts. To an uncanny degree, Iran has benefitted from virtually all the cataclysmic events that have rocked the world in the last few years. Operation Desert Storm crippled its biggest enemy. Then, just as Iran embarked on rearmament, the collapse of the Soviet Union and the Warsaw Pact opened up a vast new arms bazaar in which cash-starved Soviet-Bloc nations are eager to sell weapons cheaply. Thanks to these low prices, as low as $50,000 for a modern T-72 main battle tank, the Iranian arms buildup is fast making it the dominant military in the Middle East.

Though they are strengthening their military, terrorism is still the main tool Iran is using to fight its enemies and spread its militant brand of Islamic fundamentalism throughout the world.

Chapter 7
Iran: Islamic Fundamentalism's Godfather

...When I hear an Iranian leader described as a moderate,
it reminds me of the definition that an Iranian moderate
"is a mullah that has run out of ammunition."

Edward V. Badaloto, Executive Director, International
Association for Counterterrorism & Security Professionals

Once he had consolidated his power in Iran, Khomeini turned his attention to exporting his brand of Islamic fundamentalism. It became one of the corner stones of Iranian foreign policy and terrorist violence was its key tool.

First of all, Iran sees itself as the only true defender of Islam's holy sites because they are occupied by "corrupt" and hostile forces such as Saudi Arabia, Israel, and Iraq.

Iran feels it can spread its Islamic revolution and remove the "corrupt" occupiers with fundamentalist Islamic republics. Iran sees it as their duty to support and work with fundamentalist terror movements such as Hezbollah, Hamas, Islamic Jihad, and the Jama al-Islamiyah, to name a few.

An old Arab saying, *"din Muhammad bi' l-Saif,"* (Muhammad's divine law can be implemented only by the sword,) could well be the motto of the Iranian mullahs and their Islamic fundamentalist allies.

The Iranian government's pursuit of weapons of mass destruction is part of its commitment to lead the Muslim world against the infidel West. Iran views Islam as the successor to communism in the effort to topple the Judeo-Christian led new world order. A Reuters wire-service report from Tehran in October 1991 reinforces this long-standing view: "After the fall of Marxism, Islam replaced it, and as long as Islam exists, U.S. hostility exists, and as long as U.S. hostility exists, the struggle exists."

The impact of Iran's campaign to export its revolution extends beyond Iran. Embassies throughout the Middle East have been fortified and strategic facilities in the United States, including the White House, the Pentagon, the U.S. Capitol, and the State Department, were secured behind massive concrete blocks to prevent another suicide attack like the one that destroyed the Marine barracks in Lebanon in 1983.

Khomeini, his successors, and their fellow Islamic fundamentalist allies are capitalizing on a modern Muslim dilemma. When Muslim leaders reject Western political, economic and social values for their countries, the West brands them as reactionary. Western aid either dries up or, as in the case of Pakistan and Saudi Arabia, is severely limited.

But when Muslim leaders compromise, or are accused of compromising their own Islamic values, they suffer varying degrees of internal turmoil and are often violently rejected by their own people. Such was the fate of Egyptian President Anwar Sadat and the Shah of Iran.

The Iranian government and fellow travelers constantly use this dilemma for their own ends by means of terror and subversion.

Iran's subversive activities have escalated throughout the world.

In Africa, Iran-controlled Hezbollah bases in the Sudan are assisting Islamic movements in Egypt, Tunis and Algeria. Iranian advisors in Nigeria are guiding fundamentalist groups and are active in Eritrea and Ethiopia as well. They are also active in Kuala Lumpur, the capital of Muslim Malaysia and the headquarters of the revolutionary Muslim Movement of the Moros in the Philippines and the Thai Islamic guerrillas. Their message is the gospel of violent Islamic fundamentalism. Their goal is to produce clones of Iran throughout the Moslem world.

The Moslem population of the former Soviet Union is also a target of Iranian subversion and intrigue. Both the U.S. and the Russian government are aware that Iran, Iraq and Pakistan are trying to buy conventional and weapons of mass destruction from Kazakhstan and other Moslem republics.

According to the CIA, Iran hopes to lead the Moslem world and will allocate $10 billion in the next four years to buy missiles, airplanes, offensive submarines and tanks. Iran financed North Korea's development program for the SCUD C missile. Not only did Iran finance its development, but also agreed to buy 100 of them.

CIA Director, George Tenet, told Congress in 1998 that Iran will seek the increased use of terrorism and the development of weapons of mass destruction "in order to subvert or intimidate our allies, undermine the confidence of our friends and allies in our military presence, and eventually expel us from the region." He noted that Iran "is building its capabilities to produce and deliver weapons of mass destruction—chemical, biological and nuclear," and, "Iran sees terrorism as a useful tool."

This effort is directed at making Iran the major power in the Middle East. Possessing weapons of mass destruction, the mullahs feel, will deter the U.S. from attacking Iran. With this deterrence in place, the Iranians will have a free hand to use their favorite weapons of terror and subversion to spread their brand of Islamic fundamentalism throughout the world.

The Iranian regime sanctions this terrorism in the name of religion. Tehran gives religious sanction to acts of terror calling them divine duties and promising the perpetrators a place in heaven. Shedding innocent blood is justified as a necessary price of spreading the faith.

The World Trade Center bombing is an example of Islamic fundamentalism's lashing out at innocents close to the heart of the West. This act of terror well illustrates the callous, contemptuous attitude of Islamic fundamentalists.

Iran, and its Islamic republic clone in the Sudan, consider international terrorism an indispensable instrument of state policy. They are determined to gain, through the use of terror, what they could not achieve through conventional means.

The May 23, 1997 election of Mohammad Khatami, an alleged Iranian moderate, to the office of President of Iran is not likely to change Iran's role in sponsoring terrorism. Although Khatami promised more personal freedom and greater democracy, the Iranian clerics can check any such tendencies, or any attempt to stop using terrorism as an instrument of state policy. Under the country's complex religious constitution they can override any law or executive order of the land they deem to be "un-Islamic."

Given this checking power and the fact that the Iranian Parliament is still in the hands of supporters of Iran's supreme leader, Ayatollah Khameini, the chosen successor of Khomeini, Iran will continue along its path of supporting Islamic terrorism throughout the world.

At present, the clerical leaders in Tehran and Khartoum are convinced they must prevent, at all costs, the emergence of a post-Cold War order in which the U.S. is the sole superpower and Western democratic values dominate.

Given the weakening of the nation state and its effects on the international order, the radical Islamists are betting that time is on their side. The future of Islam, they are convinced, rides on the success of their campaign to scotch the emergence of this new world order. They have organized and allocated immense resources to this long-term struggle ensuring dangerous years ahead.

● ● ●

The morning winter chill hung in the air that January 25, 1993 morning as a long line of commuters were sitting in their cars at a red light on Dolly Madison Boulevard outside Washington, D.C. They were waiting to turn left into the Central Intelligence Agency, Langley, Virginia headquarters.

This normal everyday monotonous rush hour scene was abruptly shattered as a lone gunman calmly walked down the line of cars and randomly shot five of the motorists, killing two and wounding three.

The killer, a Pakistani national, Mir Amail Kansi, then jumped into a brown van, drove to his apartment and hid the murder weapon under a couch. Kansi grabbed an overnight bag, caught a plane, and within a day of the shooting, was back in Pakistan where he promptly vanished.

The official U.S. government line on the shooting was that

Kansi was unhappy about the treatment of Muslims in Bosnia and he wanted to "make a big statement" by shooting up the CIA, the White House, or Israeli Embassy.

FBI agents were quickly sent to Pakistan to help Pakistani authorities track down, capture, and return Kansi to the United States.

The agents returned empty-handed as not a trace of Kansi could be found in Pakistan. Little wonder, the FBI was looking in the wrong place. They should have looked in Iran, for Kansi was part of Iran's vast international terror network.

The Iranian's terror network and supporting organization basically operates on three levels: in states where the chances of installing an Islamic republic are good; where there is an outside chance of installing an Islamic republic; and, where there is little or no chance of installing an Islamic republic. Iran's terror network is capable of making mischief in all of these situations.

Iran's subversive activity is directed from the highest levels of the Iranian government by the Council for the Islamic Revolution. The Council was established by Khomeini as a policy coordinating body to facilitate the exporting of the Iranian brand of militant Islamic fundamentalism.

Operational control is in the hands of specially trained, fiercely loyal Revolutionary Guards operating out of Iranian Embassies. The Revolutionary Guards do their clandestine work through civilian front groups. These front groups, called Muslim Islamic Groups (MIG), are set up in the targeted country and have a variety of ostensible legal functions; one front may be a Muslim cultural group formed to assist cultural activities in "solidarity with their Muslim brothers," another may be religious groups formed to expound Khomeini's view of Islam and how it applies in the targeted country; or, it may be simply a group formed to assist pilgrims in visiting the holy sites of Islam.

The most effective MIGs are those that do charitable works and provide assistance in cases of natural disasters such as typhoons, earthquakes or famine relief. More often than not, these Iranian-controlled charitable groups deliver help and assistance long before the government relief assistance arrives on the scene.

When that happens the grateful victims are open and more receptive to the message being spread by these groups. Getting the word out is the bottom line for all MIGs: spread the militant Islamic message and build up a base of support among the people in the targeted country for further action geared towards imposing a militant Islamic regime.

As the fronts' activities expand, they keep branching out and spread throughout the country. The ideal progression of the fronts expansion is from the major cities down to the neighborhood, be it rural or urban.

The final objective is to replace the existing governmental structure with one controlled by the Islamic militants. They are following classic revolutionary strategy as practiced by Lenin, Mao, and others.

As the MIGs become more extensive and spread their tentacles throughout the country down to the local level, they become a "shadow government" in the targeted country.

On a parallel track with the establishment of MIGs, the Revolutionary Guards establish a clandestine cell-structured terror organization. The terror organization's sole function is to carry out terror acts deemed necessary by the Revolutionary Guard leader in the country.

This shadowy terror group is totally under the iron-grip control of the Revolutionary Guards.

The MIGs have absolutely no knowledge, or anything to do with this deep-cover terror group. They have no contacts and often no direct knowledge of its existence. The MIGs have no input into the recruitment of terrorists, one of the prime missions of the deep-cover group.

The MIGs' tasks are to pursue only the goals and activities for which they were organized. Such strict adherence to its purpose is not only good security, but also allows the MIGs to deny any connection with the terrorist activity of the secret clandestine terror group controlled by the Revolutionary Guards.

By means of its tight grip on the activities of the various fronts, however, the Revolutionary Guards can spot and recruit potential terrorists who are members of any particular MIG front.

It was by means of this Iranian network that Kansi and the CIA had their fatal encounter. It is clear he was an Iranian agent, not simply a disgruntled "lone gunman."

Kansi's Pushtan tribe has long been active in the drug and arms smuggling trade in and out of Afghanistan during the Soviet occupation of that country. Iranian intelligence often helped the Pushtans in this trade.

Kansi grew up amid this atmosphere of intrigue and daring adventure, and no doubt, caught the eye of the Iranians.

Kansi further came to the attention of the Iranians through the activities of their various fronts at Pakistani universities. Kansi was a student at Quetta College, where he was a member of the Pushtan Student Association.

There was a rival group at Quetta college, the Baluchi Student

Association. The Baluchi tribes had long been agitating for their own Baluchi state, most of which would be carved out of Pakistan.

Kansi did something very strange: he suddenly dropped out of the Pushtan Student Association and joined the Baluchi Student Association. What made this act so unusual was that Kansi was a member of a noble Pushtan family with impeccable Pushtan credentials. He had a bright and respectable future in Pushtan tribal politics.

He quickly became very active in anti-Pakistan demonstrations, strange activity for a noble son of a rival group.

Yet it wasn't so strange after all. Pakistani sources claim his pro-Baluchi activity was merely a cover for getting into the United States as part of Iran's terror network. That reasoning seems right on the money because Kansi cited fears of political persecution because of his pro-Baluchi activities in his request for political asylum on March 3, 1991.

Once in the United States, his actions suggested a previously directed motive: he went out of his way to get work that would put him in contact with the CIA—a job with a courier company that delivered to the CIA. What better cover could an agent want to become familiar with the routine of his target without arousing suspicion.

Kansi used the information to plan the hit and his elaborate get away. He slipped out of the U.S., made it to Pakistan, where he disappeared for four years. This sequence of events leads one to the conclusion he had a lot of skilled, professional help. He was finally betrayed as a result of a $2 million reward and kidnapped by the FBI in Pakistan and returned to the U.S. where he was tried, convicted and sentenced to death.

The help Kansi received came from the Iranian world wide terror network set up in order to export the Iranian revolution.

Militant Islamic activity has increased in Pakistan to the point were the country's then leader, Prime Minister Benazir Bhutto reinstated the *shari'a* Islamic law. The outspoken western-educated Bhutto has an extremely liberal view of Islam and politics. She obviously had to walk a narrow strict path as the militant fundamentalists were pushing her away from her prior liberal tendencies towards the hard Islamic line.

Survival, both political and personal, guide her political life. The Islamic extremists wouldn't have the slightest qualms in killing her for her liberal views of Islam. The Iranians are also operating in other Muslim countries, such as Bangladesh, where Tehran feels there is only an outside chance of establishing an Islamic republic. As could be expected, the Iranian terror network organization is on a much lower and more unobtrusive scale.

Iran's efforts are again under the tight control of the Revolutionary Guards. The Guards establish cover groups in the form of MIGs like they did in Pakistan, though their purposes are different.

Since the Iranians feel a country like Bangladesh is unlikely to be receptive to Tehran's subversion and propaganda efforts, the front groups have a different role. They exist to cover the clandestine terror cells that will be set up to carry out selected terrorist acts in Bangladesh, or in the adjacent Benghali region of India.

The Muslim Islamic Groups will do some of their normal front activities—cultural, charitable, or what have you—but the activity is only window-dressing to camouflage the existence and activity of the deep-cover subversive cells.

If, however, circumstances within the targeted country change and the fundamentalist's efforts appear to be bearing fruit, the Iranian terror network can rapidly adapt. If this were to happen, say in

Bangladesh, the Revolutionary Guard Control efforts would mimic those in Pakistan.

Iran's three-leveled approach to organizing and exporting terror gives it a large degree of flexibility. Iran is capable of stirring up trouble at all three levels.

Bangladesh furnishes a recent example of that flexibility. A feminist Bangladesh author had said in a news interview that some changes should be made in the Koran to reflect modern feminism. Her remarks gave the militant fundamentalists an opportunity to raise a real ruckus. Militants organized demonstrations and took to the streets of Dhaka, the capital of Bangladesh. The zealots called for the arrest and execution of the feminist author, Dr. Taslim Nasrin. The militants then turned up the heat. They put a growing bounty on her head, and finally forced Nasrin to flee Bangladesh and seek asylum in Sweden.

On the surface, Bangladesh, a poverty-stricken land of rivers and rice, has yet to turn into an Islamic fundamentalist state. It does provide a warning: the fundamentalists are well prepared to take advantage of any situation to advance their cause. An incident we in the West would consider a free speech issue is viewed by the Islamic extremists as a public blasphemy issue.

That issue can quickly become a national or international cause for Islamic militants. The presence of an Islamic organization, especially one part of the Iranian terror network, can capitalize and maximize the impact of a Nasrin-type incident. Each success brings the goal of an Islamic republic one step forward.

The road to that goal may long, but the militant activists in Bangladesh foresee a day when they will succeed and Allah will reign supreme.

Given the abject poverty and exploding birthrate in Bangladesh, social stability will almost surely deteriorate. Discontent and unrest will grow as the government tries to cope with a situation that seems unsolvable.

Immersed in this sea of discontent, waiting to take advantage of the situation, the militant Islamic fundamentalists prepares for battle. Lurking in the shadows, ready to wade into the tempest, is the Iranian international terror network.

Iran's well-organized world wide terror network is well suited to begin terror campaigns even in countries where Muslims are a minority of the population. Even though the terror masters in Tehran don't think they have a chance at setting up an Islamic republic, they will still set up their clandestine terror network.

They are alive and well in almost all countries where Iran has an embassy or consulate. The absence of either is no handicap because they are flexible enough to work in countries where they fund mosques, student associations, and Muslim cultural centers and schools.

The main goals of these efforts are to recruit potential local terrorists and help them establish their own local militant Islamic revolutionary terror cells owing loyalty and obedience to Iran.

Financed by Tehran from its special fund to export the revolution, propaganda materials such as pamphlets, books, video and audio cassettes are distributed throughout the Muslim community. Speakers are provided for lectures touting the fundamentalist's line.

Local Muslims who seem more receptive to the militant's message are approached and invited to Iran for further study and recruitment. The vast majority of these "students" travelling to Iran may never become terrorists on their return home. Many, however, if not most, are bound to be more sympathetic to militant Islam's message than before.

Those who are exceptionally zealous and pass further scrutiny may be invited to attend one of the many terrorist training facilities in Iran. Numerous training camps have been established in Iran to handle, train and prepare terrorists for Khomeini's grand scheme of exporting his brand of Islamic extremism. Thousands, Iranians as well as non-Iranians, have passed through these camps where they learned the deadly arts of terrorism—murder, intimidation and religious zealotry.

While undergoing training, the instructors keep their eyes out for those recruits who show exceptional zeal. The overly zealous are approached and screened by the camp's religious leaders to see if they would be willing to volunteer for suicide missions. The few trainees that pass that test are then sent to special camps that train them and form them into elite bands of fanatical terrorists willing to kill and die in the name of Khomeini and the cause of Islam.

Ayatollah Mahalati, Khomeini's man in charge of creating elite bands of fanatical terrorists, told his pupils: "Our aim here is to break you. For you have been shaped by this earthly life for the purpose of performing ordinary deeds. We mean to put you back together again in a totally new form, so that you can serve your Creator and be fit for entry into Paradise."

In addition to the mandatory five daily prayers required of all the faithful, the trainees were given numerous daily short recitations from the Koran to stimulate and enhance the student's religious fervor. Evenings were taken up with more discussions of Islamic history, law, or other points of Islamic obligations. These discussions were led by the camp's religious mullahs, or by guest speakers who were often close associates of Khomeini or his successor.

Physical training and formal classes in terrorist tactics and weapons use occupied the students' remaining daylight hours.

After a few weeks of this intensive training, various students were encouraged to get further on-the-job-training with elite specialized units of the Revolutionary Guards. These units performed varied tasks: raids behind enemy lines during the Iran-Iraq War; raids inside Iran on suspected regime opponents; serving as bodyguards for high-ranking ayatollahs; and, having the students carry out executions of condemned opponents of the regime.

All of these had a single purpose: to find those students who were fanatically dedicated to Khomeini and his successor, and were eager to kill and die in his name.

By such training methods, indoctrination and bloodying their hands, the trainees bound themselves to the ideals of Khomeini's Islamic revolution and overcame their natural self-preservation tendencies. The "blessed ones" were now death-dealing fanatics ready to kill or be killed for the cause of Khomeini-style Islamic fundamentalism.

Upon graduation from these terror schools, they are ready to return and become part of Iran's deep-cover clandestine terror network, run by Iran's Revolutionary Guards.

The terror network is there prowling deep in the background behind the screen of the on-going cultural and propaganda effort. It is controlled by the Revolutionary Guards who run a network of clandestine cells consisting of no more than nine people per cell.

Each cell is completely unaware of the existence of other terror cells in the network and there is no contact between cells. The only contact the individual cells have is with their Revolutionary Guards contact, or one of his cut-out surrogates.

The network also has parallel clandestine groups whose function is to assist the terror cells. They provide the terror cells with their weapons, funds, safe-houses and other needed logistic and intelligence.

Although most of the cell members have been recruited from activities such as the student associations or the mosques, their activity is tightly controlled by the Revolutionary guards terror structure. The cell members association with their fellow students or mosques is just enough to maintain cover.

It is extremely important for the terror network that their old associates and fellow worshippers at the mosque are unaware of the existence of these terror cells. They are tightly compartmentalized which makes it hard for local security forces to penetrate this super-secret terror network lurking in their midst.

The United States is not fertile ground for the spread of Islamic fundamentalism. The possibility of converting the largely Christian American population to Islam and then imposing a radical Islamic regime is extremely remote. Given such an unhealthy climate for Islamic extremism, one could assume Islamic extremists wouldn't waste resources on a war of terror where the odds of success are so low.

Banish such thoughts. Islam *is* waging, and *will* continue to wage, a war of terror in places like the U.S. and Europe where Islam is both a minority religion and there exists an underlying hostility to the message of Muhammad.

Militant Islam has reasons, other than converting its enemies, for waging a war of terror. The use of terror may be the only feasible weapon in militant Islam's arsenal. It will use that weapon to strike blows against the infidel West.

Having witnessed what the United States did to Iraq, Iran will avoid a direct confrontation with the U.S. Instead, they will use a deniable and indirect form of war—terrorism.

Iran's terror network is alive and well in the United States. Although the Iranians lack an embassy in Washington where the Revolutionary Guards would normally control the network, there are other avenues for Iran to direct their secret terror cells.

The office of Iran's permanent United Nations representative in New York and the Iranian embassies in Canada and Cuba are used to coordinate and supervise terror activity in the United States. From these centers, the Iranians can easily direct the terror cells, many of them hiding among the thousands of Iranian students living and studying in American universities. The March 6, 1989 issue of US News & World Report said that from among the 30,000 Iranian student population, Iran could count on some 1,000 militants to conduct terrorist acts.

A network of support facilities operates through legal societies, student associations, foundations and the old Islamic staple—the mosque. This network provides a steady and safe flow of funds and communication with the Taleghani Center in Tehran, the nerve center for foreign based Iranian subversive activities.

Other militant Islamic revolutionary terror groups, beside those controlled by Iran, also have terror networks in the United States. Operating out of New Jersey, Chicago and Texas, radical Islamists have conducted military exercises at training camps, raised money, organized, recruited and trained would-be terrorists for operations on American soil. The World Trade Center bombers, for example, trained at a rifle range in Connecticut.

The U.S is a source of a lot of money used to finance terror acts in the Middle East. Hamas, for example, raises the bulk of its funds through alleged charitable activities. A former head of the FBI's counterterrorism unit told the November 13, 1994 CBS news show "60 Minutes," that Hamas "collects money, produces propaganda, films, videos, recruits, and even engages in paramilitary training in the U.S."

The World Trade Center bombing and the failed terror attempts on the United Nations building and Hudson River tunnels in New York City show militant Islamic terrorism is a real threat to the United States.

The threat is real. They have succeeded in establishing deep-cover, terror cells on American turf. These cells and supporting networks are tailored to carry out acts of terror against the United States—militant Islam's "Great Satan." We haven't seen the last of militant Islam's terror activity on our shores.

Terrorism will be able to flourish in the United States because it is a free society. A free society is full of the blood on which a militant Islamic fundamentalist can leech: easy access to money, freedom of movement, good communications, a free press and a liberal judiciary. The militant Islamic terrorist takes advantage of our strengths as a people in order to wage their war of terror on a non-Muslim society.

Chapter 8
Hezbollah:
Iran's Surrogate

*Islam says: whatever good there is exists thanks to the sword and in
the shadow of the sword! People cannot be made obedient except
with the sword. The sword is the key to Paradise,
which can be opened only for Holy Warriors!*
Ayatollah Ruhollah Khomeini

The grey wintry calm of July 18, 1994 in Buenos Aires was
shattered when a car bomb exploded in the street outside the building
housing Argentina's largest Jewish cultural center.

The cultural center, on Pasteur Street, was located in the traditional Jewish neighborhood of Once, adjacent to downtown Buenos
Aires. It was the hub of Jewish cultural activities not only in Argentina, but for the rest of South American Jews. For fifty years, the
building had been the nerve center for the western hemisphere's second largest Jewish population. The quarter-million Jews of Argentina
were second in size only to the Jewish population of the United States.
Now it lay in ruins, a hundred torn bodies mingled with the rubble.

The cultural center bombing came a little over two years after
a similar attack on the Israeli Embassy in Buenos Aires, killing twenty-
nine and injuring two-hundred-forty.

The Lebanon-based radical Islamic fundamentalist terror
group, Hezbollah, claimed responsibility for both incidents. The ter-

rorists, however, weren't finished with their bloody work. The next day a bomb caused the crash of a Panamanian commuter plane, flight HP 1202, killing twenty-one people. Twelve of the nineteen passengers were Jewish and four were Israeli citizens.

Eight days after the Buenos Aires blast, the terrorists struck again thousands of miles away from Argentina. A car bomb destroyed a two-story brick annex of the Israeli embassy in the Kensington district of London, injuring fourteen people.

Hours later, they struck again eight miles away in the Finchley area of London. This time the target was a building housing Israeli and Jewish organizations, including the Joint Israel Appeal, a charity that supported Jewish causes in England and Israel.

Although Hezbollah didn't claim credit for the bombings in London, the *Times* of London, quoted a senior British official as saying the Lebanon-based terrorist group was believed responsible for both London attacks.

The bombings follow the pattern of Hezbollah action in the past. The Panamanian plane bombing was the work of a Hezbollah suicide bomber. U.S. and British counterintelligence officials initially doubted a terrorist role in the Panamanian crash but became convinced of foul play. They speculated the bomber carried the device on board and died in the crash. Intelligence sources in Washington said all but one of the bodies from the Panamanian plane had been claimed. The unclaimed passenger has been identified as a young Lebanese traveling under the name of Lyal Jamal. He lost his hands and face in the explosion. Such injuries indicate the bomber set off the bomb concealed in a camera, radio, or in a briefcase carried with him on the plane.

The plot thickens. The unclaimed dead Lebanese was travelling on a false U.S. passport. Both Western intelligence sources and Lebanese authorities believe the dead man was from the Bekaa Valley in Lebanon. That infamous place houses Hezbollah training camps staffed with Iranian Revolutionary Guard trainers.

Who, and what, is Hezbollah and how did it extend its tentacles of terror around the globe?

Hezbollah means the Party of God. It was founded in the Iranian holy city of Qom in 1973 by Ayatollah Muhammad Ghaffari. Its aim was to oppose the reign of the Shah and return Iran to the true Islam of the past. Ayatollah Ghaffari died in prison but his son, Hadi, has picked-up the torch. Under Hadi's guidance, the Party of God boasts over a million members in Iran and has branches all over the world, including the United States.

The Detroit area is the center of Hezbollah activities in the U.S. Activists sell calendars, among other items, to raise money for Hezbollah's military wing, and in nearby Dearborn, where many Lebanese live, cable channel 23 regularly rebroadcasts programs from Beirut's al-Mansur TV, which is owned by Hezbollah.

Hezbollah's philosophy can be summed up as "us against them." The world is divided between the world of the True Believer— the Party of Allah supporters, and everybody else who are, by Hezbollah's reasoning, the supporters of Satan. Their ultimate spiritual leader was, and continues to be, the late Ayatollah Khomeini. "We have no leader or source but the Imam; we shall follow him," is the rallying cry of Hezbollah.

Hezbollah's scope encompasses the whole world as they consider every Muslim to be a member of Hezbollah, although most Muslim's aren't aware of it. Hezbollah is, in many ways, unique in that it is not structured like other political or revolutionary organizations.

The Party of Allah, according to *Our Path,* one of its theoretical pamphlets, is not a political organization in the classical style. It represents a way of life. As such, it can also be likened to a semi-secret fraternity. Hezbollah is Allah's recruiting station on earth, and thus functions as a clearing house for mankind, where those who will be admitted into Paradise are separated from those destined for Hell.

Although the original Hezbollah was founded in Iran, its most vicious offshoot was formed in Lebanon. Its founding father was an Iraqi-born Shi'ite who eventually became known as the Imam of Lebanon—Mussa Sadr. In his career as a Muslim cleric, Sadr eventually became a follower of Khomeini. His mission, as he saw it, was to organize and minister to the Shi'ite community in southern Lebanon. They had the bad luck of being on the bottom rung of the socio-political ladder and were discriminated against by everybody else in Lebanon.

In the early 1970s, he formed a Shi'ite militia. Its main function was to protect the Shi'ite community from the depredations of Palestinian guerrillas that had established bases in southern Lebanon for terror attacks on Israel. Sadr was a very clever, charismatic individual and had no hesitation in accepting Israeli aid to further his twin goals of driving the Palestinians out of Shi'ite areas of Lebanon, and building up Shi'ite strength to stand up to the Christians in Lebanon.

Because of Sadr's leadership, Hezbollah got support from almost every foreign power interested in Lebanon—from Israel to Syria. Sadr wanted to drive the Palestinians out of southern Lebanon and away from the Israeli borders. The Syrians saw in Sadr a leader capable of counterbalancing the influence of pro-Egyptian Sunni Muslims in Lebanon.

Given the changing and intercine nature of Middle East politics, Sadr also cultivated ties with Quadaffi in Libya. That attempt, however, proved fatal for Sadr as he was killed during a 1978 visit to Libya. As a result, he became a mythological figure for Lebanese Shi'ites.

By the time of Sadr's death, the Lebanese Shi'ites had become heavily influenced by Khomeini's brand of revolutionary Islam. They began to see themselves as an important participant in an Islamic revolution that would sweep the world and impose the true Faith. From Sadr's militia came the main Lebanese terror groups— Amal and Hezbollah. Although both had similar roots, Hezbollah soon eclipsed Amal on the international terror stage. The world has felt the sting of Hezbollah's attacks for years.

Hezbollah's power base was assured by the presence of Iranian Revolutionary Guard Corps personnel in Lebanon. Dispatched from Teheran, the Guards provide training and support for Hezbollah terrorists and are part of the late Ayatollah Khomeini and his successors' strategy of exporting the Iranian Shi'ite Islamic Revolution. The presence of a large Shi'ite community in Lebanon, coupled with the on-going chaos in that war-torn land, was a golden opportunity for Teheran mischief making.

Hezbollah has four regional headquarters: Baalbek (training); Beirut (operational planning and Administration); Nabatiyah (southern region); and, Tehran (international headquarters). Over these regional groups rules Hezbollah's Central Committee, a 17-man Supreme Islamic Council, which decides administrative, political, judicial and military matters, and reports directly to Iran.

Any doubt about Hezbollah's ties to Iran were settled in a March 1, 1992 press conference by Sheikh Hassan Nassrallah, appointed Hezbollah secretary to replace Sheikh Abbas Musawi who was killed in a 1992 Israeli air raid. He said: "As for any connection between the Hezbollah and the Islamic Revolutionary Guards Corps, we consider ourselves part of the Islamic revolution of Iran and there is no secrecy about it."

Hezbollah's troops are local Lebanese Shi'ite and number around 5,000, including 2,000 trained terrorists operating out of camps in the northern Bekaa Valley. The rest of their forces live in their own villages in southern Lebanon and provide assistance for Hezbollah's operations against Israel and her Lebanese Christian allies.

Hezbollah's arms and supplies are furnished by Iran, delivered by way of Syria. They have a wide variety of modern weapons in their arsenal, including artillery, Sagger anti-tank missiles, and Katyuska rockets and launchers used to bombard villages in northern Israel. They have armored personnel carriers needed for supporting semi-conventional assaults and even have high-speed attack boats and other naval equipment.

While Iran foots the bill for this equipment, it is the Syrian army that actually hauls the material to the terrorists and provides additional logistical support.

Hezbollah military camps are located in the northern Bekaa Valley in an area controlled by the Syrian military and they work closely with the Syrians. Hezbollah uses the same operations room that the Syrians use—where attacks against Israel and their Christian militia allies in southern Lebanon are planned and coordinated.

Hezbollah is known to have training camps in Afghanistan, Iran, Lebanon, and the Sudan. It has extensive terrorist cells throughout the world including those in the United States, Canada, Europe, Scandinavia, and on the jungle border of Argentina, Brazil, and Paraguay.

The terror group has received a steady supply of advanced explosives and detonation devices which has enabled it to create what has become their trademark: the car bomb. Never was this capacity more evident than the infamous 1983 attack on the U.S. Marine barracks in Beirut. The resulting explosion killed hundreds.

Hezbollah functions as a valuable deniable surrogate for Iran's export of its radical brand of Islam by means of terrorism. Hezbollah's goals are Iran's goals. Yet, when convenient, as in the bombings in Buenos Aires, Panama, and London, Iran can smugly distance itself, claiming the Lebanon group has no connection to Tehran. They denied any involvement, claiming it was being fingered because it was opposed to the Middle East peace process.

Hezbollah receives an estimated $100 million per year in aid and support from Iran—a sizeable amount. Does the old saying "he who pays the piper calls the tune" apply? The evidence, although circumstantial, is compelling that it does.

Consider the three bomb attacks in a little over a week— Buenos Aires, Panama and London. These blasts all occurred around the time when peace was seeming to break out between Israel and two of her enemies—Jordan and the Palestinians. Coincidence? Iran is bitterly opposed to any peaceful situation involving the state of Israel. To sign peace accords with Israel means granting them legitimacy, something Iran rejects out of hand. Anything that disrupts the peace process has the blessing of Iran, if not its active behind the scenes participation.

These three incidents involved a high degree of planning, coordination, good intelligence and logistical preparation all coming together to successfully carry out three covert operations in three widely-separated places within a short period of time. It was not the work of amateurs that characterized the World trade Center bombings.

It would be fruitful to point out some of the hurdles that had to be overcome and the effort involved in carrying out these three incidents.

First of all, consider the intelligence needed for the Buenos Aires bombings: the terrorists had to know the location of the target; the layout of the neighborhood; the traffic pattern and frequency of police activity in the area of the target. This was essential so the bombers could be assured of a parking place where the bomb would do the most damage and be free of police interference.

They also had to know a lot about the working and visiting routine, which would provide information when the building was most likely to be occupied and have plenty of victims. This, and a myriad of other details, would have been checked out and taken into account in planning the incident. This, and other intelligence, was gathered without apparently arousing suspicion.

Some of the intelligence and assistance may have been provided by Argentinians. Martin Edwin Anderson, author of a critical book about Argentina's former military dictators, suggests the terrorists may have been given logistic help by local anti-Semites. That help may have come from once-purged neo-Nazis within the military that Argentine President Menem had restored to government service.

Adding to this atmosphere of complicity is the fact that a similar bomb attack against the Israeli embassy two years earlier in Buenos Aires was never fully investigated, suggesting that someone in the Menem government protected or helped the terrorists.

Other ominous signs are found in the Argentine President's family ties. Mr. Menem is the son of Shi'ite Muslim parents from

Syria. He converted to the Roman Catholic faith, a political must in Argentina. Menem and his estranged wife Zulema, a Syrian Alawite Muslim, have close ties to important members of narco-dictator Hafez Assad's anti-Israel Ba'ath party.

In 1982, Menem visited Moammar Quadaffi's Libya. In 1986, following the aerial bombing of Quadaffi's Tripoli headquarters, Menem called for the expulsion from Buenos Aires of U. S. Ambassador Frank Ortiz.

Even if Anderson's charges are true, it does not detract from the cold professionalism of the recent terror attacks. Anderson's speculations would have made the terror attacks easier and would have enabled the planners to devote more time and resources to the other terror incidents they had in mind—Panama and London. But the terrorist would still have had to develop their contacts and who to trust in the Argentine government. And that required good intelligence which, more than likely came from Iranian sources.

That shouldn't surprise anyone. The Iranian regime's hatred for Israel and Jews in general and its support of terrorism is well known. These three incidents, in a short interval of time in the summer of 1994, show Islamic terrorism, despite its appearance of irrationality, is actually the result of cold calculation, planning, support and encouragement of sponsoring states like Iran.

Iran uses its intelligence service extensively to facilitate and carry out terrorist attacks. Intelligence officers in Iranian embassies use the diplomatic pouch for smuggling weapons and money for terrorist groups. Throughout the world, including the U.S., Iranian embassies and consulates are forward outposts for terrorist operations. Intelligence specialists have noted an increase in activity of Iranian "attaches" coming and going in the weeks prior to and following bombings and assassinations carried out by Iranian surrogates such as Hezbollah.

Their terrorism is carried out purposefully, in a cold-blooded, calculated manner. Their hand in the 1994 Buenos Aires bombing was suspected by all. Actual proof was, apparently, not that hard for the Argentines to find, if they had so desired.

Consider also the technical expertise involved in the bombings. The Panamanian bombing required a compact explosive device powerful enough to blow the plane up. Yet it had to be camouflaged so the bomb could pass security checks at the airport and be carried aboard the plane. Making such a device requires a high degree of sophisticated technical knowledge.

There is also more to a making car bomb than just stuffing it full of explosives and blowing it up. Explosives must be chosen and placed in such a manner so most of the explosive force is directed toward the target and not dissipated away from it.

The car bomb used in the 1992 Israeli embassy attack in Buenos Aires was made by explosives experts using military-grade explosives. The car bomb, according to experts, was constructed in accordance with the proven principles of shaped charges used by Iranian and Syrian controlled terrorists since the bombings in Beirut.

Over 100 kilograms of high explosives, with a 55-60 kilogram charge of hexogene reinforced by other solid plastique elements to enhance blast and fragmentation, as well as fats or wax to ensure the contours of the shaped charge, were used in the bomb. The bomb was built to have the maximum force of the explosion directed at its target. The device was activated by an electronic detonator.

The collection of the material, the construction of the bomb and the method of its utilization all point to professionals. The bomber, or bombers, had either military or terrorist training in explosives. Most likely, they had both and it would be a safe wager that they learned their vicious deadly skills in the terrorist training camps in the Middle East. Hezbollah terrorists have received such training from Iranian Revolutionary Guards, and other terror instructors, in their camps in the Bekaa valley.

The car bomb is becoming the tool of the trade of the militant Islamic fundamentalist terrorist, especially those associated with Iran.

In addition to its terrorist activities, Hezbollah also undertakes governmental and social functions among the Shi'ite community. These activities are straight out of any classic revolutionary textbook. This activity enables Hezbollah to sink its roots deep into Lebanese Shi'ite society. This allows them to solidify their growing support and helps them to withstand any possible future shifts of political alliances in the Middle East.

Hezbollah has created an Islamic welfare state for the poor in significant parts of the southern suburbs and Bekaa Valley. It has opened its own hospitals and runs clinics and pharmacies. It has opened cooperatives which sell basic foodstuffs at subsidized prices, and at times there have been free food distribution campaigns. Hezbollah has opened a number of small factories and has virtually taken over the government school system in much of southern Lebanon.

When you consider that anarchy reigns in southern Lebanon, this activity takes on a significant importance. The cities and towns have stopped functioning. The existing Lebanese government operates neither hospitals nor medical clinics. Health care is done on a "find it where you can" basis furnished by private individuals or private organizations. Hezbollah has filled this vacuum with its social and political program. It has become the de facto government in the areas under its control. It is classic terrorist revolutionary war theory put into practice.

Building support among the people is a cardinal principle of the successful 20th century revolutions. Hezbollah's revolutionary activism, even if in the name of religion instead of some secular ideology, is like putting money in the bank. It will brace the movement during hard times and fuel its continued growth and survival.

Hezbollah is also trying to counter the effects of the PLO-Israeli peace process. One of its tactics is to undermine PLO influence among the quarter-million Palestinians in southern Lebanon. Hezbollah has come a long way from protecting themselves against the PLO in the 1970s and 80s to today where they are extending their hegemony over them.

They are capitalizing on internal dissent within the PLO and extending their revolutionary social activity to Palestinian enclaves in southern Lebanon. Hezbollah's goal is to infiltrate the Palestinian enclaves on all levels: politically, economically, socially and by controlling their security.

They are opening clinics and religious schools using the same techniques that have stood them well in the Shi'ite communities in southern Lebanon.

Using Iranian-supplied money, they are underwriting the construction and operation of small 35-bed hospitals which will offer free medical service to Palestinian refugees. Hezbollah is also building roads and other public works in a determined "winning the hearts and minds" program among the Palestinians.

Nor is Hezbollah reluctant to resort to the old Middle East custom of *baksheesh,* greasing a few palms to buy influence. It bought the services of one of Yassir Arafat's armed units in southern Lebanon when Iran agreed to pay the salaries of the army commander's 1,500 men. Hezbollah also arranged for a $100 per month subsidy to Palestinian families who have lost family members either fighting the Israelis or in the intercine fighting against Arafat.

• • •

Hezbollah is flexing its muscles, solidifying its base among the Shi'ite community in southern Lebanon and preparing itself for the coming radical Islamic fundamentalist assault on the West. It sees itself as the spear-carrier for spreading Khomeini-style Islamic revolution throughout the globe. The world, unfortunately, hasn't seen the last of Hezbollah's terrorist attacks.

Chapter 9
Palestine Revolution

They told me about martyrdom, about death in the name of God.
They told me that as a Shoheed *(witness) I will ensure a place for*
my family in Paradise and that I will marry seventy-two virgins
in Paradise. I will be God's holy martyr...
Rachid Sakher, captured Islamic *Jihad* suicide bomber

Of all the Muslim revolutionary terror groups, the Palestine
Liberation Organization (PLO) is unique; it has passed through all of
the classic stages of Mao's revolutionary war strategy.

The PLO emerged from the Palestinian diaspora which occurred in the wake of the founding of the state of Israel and the
subsequent Arab-Israeli wars. Over a million Palestinians ended up in
squalid, ramshackle refugee camps in Jordan, Lebanon, Egypt and
Syria. These camps were a financial and political burden on the host
countries, and strained their limited social welfare resources. The camps
were also viewed as possible hostile centers of subversion against the
host countries' governments.

Nevertheless, most of the Palestinian diaspora looked to the
various Arab governments to go to war on their behalf against Israel,
crush them and enable the Palestinians to return to their homeland.
Many Palestinians actually joined the various Arab armies confronting
Israel and participated in battle against their foes alongside their Arab
hosts.

The crushing defeat of the Arabs in the 1967 Six day war was a wake-up call for the Palestinians. They realized if they were going to return to their homeland it would have to be largely by their own effort.

However, a small group of Palestinians, living in Kuwait, had reached the same conclusion well before the Six Day War. Convinced in 1965, they decided the only way to liberate their homeland was through a protracted revolutionary armed struggle. This close-knit group, headed by Yassir Arafat, had several things in common. They had grown up in Gaza and had attended college in Cairo, where they became active members of the Moslem Brotherhood. All had served in the Egyptian army and received Egyptian military or intelligence training.

In October 1959, Arafat and three of his friends had founded their own Palestinian nationalist organization, "Fatah," meaning conquest. After its founding in Kuwait, Arafat travelled widely recruiting funds and supporters.

A 1962 visit to Algeria convinced Arafat to carefully consider the effectiveness of revolutionary guerrilla warfare as the vehicle to expel the hated Israelis from Palestine. After all, he reasoned, the Algerians had just won independence from the French with such a campaign. He and his Fatah followers would use guerrilla tactics to liberate Palestine.

Inspired by the success of the Algerian revolution against the French, Fatah, and eventually the PLO, eagerly adopted the revolutionary protracted terror war strategy to establish a Palestinian state on the ashes of the state of Israel. It was easy for the PLO to sell the concept to other Arab backers, and cash poured into the PLO coffers.

This enabled them to organize politically and militarily and their organizational skills were to sustain them through the many crises that beset both Fatah and the PLO throughout their long history.

The PLO evolved from the 1964 Arab summit meeting when Egypt's President Nasser became their patron. He urged the Arabs to embrace the cause of the Palestinians by establishing and supporting both a liberation organization and a Palestinian army. This event launched the PLO.

The infant group set up a Palestine National Council (PNC) to be its governing body and, in 1968, formed the Palestine Liberation Army (PLA). The PLO became an umbrella group consisting of a variety of Palestinian groups, including Arafat's Fatah. Because of Fatah's active small-scale hit-and-run military attacks on Israel, Arafat demanded at the 1968 meeting of the PNC that Fatah be allocated half the seats on the Council.

The PLO gave in to Arafat's demand and, with Egypt's support, within a year, Yassir Arafat formally became head of the PLO. From that point on until today, he has been the undisputed leader of the organization.

The PLO's organizational structure is nominally centered around the PNC. Composed of over 400 members, however, the PNC serves mainly as widow-dressing to present a democratic veneer to the West. The real power of the PLO resides in the fifteen-man executive committee which oversees the daily routine operations of the PLO. Since the Executive Committee meets infrequently—only every month or two—the real power was, and still is, held by its chairman, Yassir Arafat.

Arafat runs the PLO as his personal fiefdom but he doesn't have the total control he would like to have.

Because the PLO is an umbrella organization composed of

many different Palestinian component groups, those disagreeing with his policy can, and frequently have, voted with their feet. Arafat can give orders to Fatah, but not to the other component groups. He can only attempt to coordinate their activities and his disciplinary actions are limited to persuasion and control of PLO funds, (even this isn't effective as many of the groups are funded separately by various Arab intelligence agencies, and Arafat has no control over those).

The PLO can be visualized as a floating crap game, with different players in the game at any one time. The group's factions move in and out as a result of disagreements with Arafat. Some kiss and make up, rejoining the game only to leave in a huff over another argument with Arafat.

To succeed, the PLO needed money and lots of it. Their ambitious programs require a strong financial base to ensure their stake in Palestinian and Middle East politics. Arafat's need for cash was twofold: he needed the continued support of the Palestinians by using the PLO as a massive civic action humanitarian organization and, at the same time, maintain the PLO's military ability. Achieving these goals would keep the PLO in the forefront of the Palestinian struggle.

The PLO was extremely successful in finding the cash, becoming in the process the richest revolutionary movement in the world. They became so flushed with cash that, at times, their annual revenues often exceeded the revenues of some Third World countries. Up until the signing of the Oslo Accords, they operated far more like a multinational "murder incorporated." The PLO had to recruit accountants and lawyers as much as guerrillas and terrorists.

In 1970, the PLO created an organization directly under Fatah's control. Its goal was to set up various Palestinian businesses that would eventual enable it to become financially independent, and not be held hostage to the whims of on-again-off-again financial contributions from Arab states.

Called Samed—"standing firm" in Arabic—it became the PLO's holding company—the economic arm of the military forces. As a result, the terror organization became self-funding and no longer had to depend on outside donations for its survival. Through excellent management and astute investments, Samed evolved into a huge multinational conglomerate and is made up of over a hundred different businesses, ranging from light manufacturing plants, to film studios, farms, and stores.

With ample cash in the bank, the PLO could afford a healthy "hearts and minds" campaign in the various refugee camps throughout the Middle East. It established free schools and provided medical care in the camps, and also provided compensation to the families of Palestinians killed or injured fighting against Israel.

The PLO was also able to fund newspapers, universities, and underwrite basic social services in both Gaza and the West Bank. Through such activities, it has retained the loyalties of most Palestinians even though the group's political fortunes suffered many setbacks; and they have yet to achieve their goal—the destruction of Israel. The base of support for the PLO among the Palestinians is a direct result of its wise civic action program made possible by its financial deep pockets.

The PLO has been extremely successful at making money. The CIA estimates the total value of PLO assets is somewhere between eight and fourteen billion dollars. This financial power has enabled Arafat to become a powerful revolutionary political player on the world stage.

Through Samed, their enterprises extend worldwide, having branches in more than thirty countries, employing thousands, and giving legitimacy to PLO activities in those countries.

Other cash producers for the PLO are the Arab Bank Ltd., the world's largest commercial Arab bank; the Palestinian Liberation Tax Fund (PLTF), an income tax imposed on every Palestinian worker residing in the Islamic world; contributions from Islamic states; and revenues from various criminal activities such as drug dealings, protection rackets and blackmail schemes, (pay us and we won't blow up your airliners, for example,) and terrorist-for-hire activities.

The funds enabled the leaders to live lavish lifestyles—Arafat gave $100,000 to a member of the PLO Executive Committee for his son's wedding. In spite of this opulence, they still managed to be viewed as the champion of the downtrodden Palestinians throughout the world. The PLO maintains a huge foreign policy establishment consisting of nearly a hundred foreign missions with fifty-five enjoying full diplomatic status, amply funded for salaries and the costs of related propaganda efforts.

The success of this ability to raise funds and become self-sufficient, coupled with its "hearts and minds" campaigns among the Palestinian diaspora has enabled the PLO to survive and thrive as a long-standing revolutionary organization. In the long run, the organization's survivability has accomplished more than its over two decades of guerrilla and terror operations.

Through this organizational resiliency, the PLO was able "to make peace" with the late Israeli Prime Minister Yitzhak Rabin, and has become the government of a mini-Palestinian state composed of the West Bank and Gaza occupied territories.

It was organizational skills, the key to any successful protracted war strategy, that brought the PLO to this point. The rest of their protracted war strategy has been less successful.

The initial creation of the PLO in 1965 led many Palestinians to believe their Arab allies would be committed to the cause of the liberation of their homeland from the Israelis. Their added commitment to build the Palestine Liberation Army was seen as proof of such dedication. Battlefield results soon dashed that hope.

Militarily the PLO's success lagged far behind their organizational skills, but it wasn't for lack of effort. Their main problem was PLO arrogance and a strong propensity to meddle in the internal politics of whatever host country their forces were based—Palestine refugee camps primarily in Jordan and Lebanon.

There was some justification for this meddling as they were at the complete mercy of the host country where their camps lay. Those host countries viewed the refugee problem in different ways: Jordan opposed the refugee's nationalism while Egypt and Syria viewed them as pawns in their intrigues against each other. In short, the Palestinians were not masters of their own destiny and felt they had to influence each of their patrons by dabbling in local affairs. That meddling was often done with a heavy hand.

The Palestinians were convinced the situation would change with their liberation and that goal came first. With the Arabs preparing for the coming battle with Israel, the Palestinians had no choice but to join their Arab brothers and prepare for the coming struggle.

The refugee camps provided the PLO with a vast manpower pool and recruits flocked to their banners. These recruits provided the cannon fodder which enabled the PLO to mount hit-and-run guerrilla raids across the border into Israel.

As the training progressed, the PLO formed regular conventional military units. These would march, with their Arab allies to invade and destroy Israel. Instead, Israel launched a preemptive strike, and routed the armies of Egypt, Jordan and Syria in six days. Not only were the Arabs completely defeated, but the Israelis captured the West Bank, Gaza, the Sinai peninsula, and the Syrian Golan Heights.

In addition, another 250,000 Palestinian refugees were added to the refugee camps in Jordan. The embryonic Palestinian army didn't leave the safety of their camps and played no role in the fighting. The disastrous Six Day War dashed the idea of a conventional military conquest of Israel. The units languished in their main camps in Jordan where they became a thorn in the side of the Jordanian government.

By 1970, some 55 PLO terrorist bases had formed a virtual mini-state within Jordan. The PLO often set up roadblocks throughout the country and extracted "fees" and "donations" from traveling businessmen. Hundreds of lawless acts of murder, brutality, robbery and rape were committed by PLO forces against Jordanian citizens. Their depredations finally became too unbearable for Jordan's King Hussein. He unleashed his loyal Bedouin troops against the PLO.

After several weeks of bloody fighting, the Jordanian military forcefully expelled the PLO from Jordan. Arafat's organization moved to Lebanon and their dream of elevating their revolutionary war to the mobile war stage was put on hold. Instead, PLO activity against Israel consisted of acts of terror, with an occasional guerrilla raid.

In Israel, the Palestinians were facing a determined foe with well defended borders and a competent military that dealt mercilessly with any guerrilla activity that threatened them. PLO guerrilla activity proved to be only a minor irritant to Israel, who was the unquestioned military power in the region.

The PLO returned to the classic revolutionary war strategy, using Mao Tse Tung's people's war concept. Their plan was to begin with small hit and run raids, gradually escalating them as bigger and better trained units became available; establish liberated zones inside the occupied territories, and finally attack and destroy their enemy. It was a grand scheme, but they lacked the military capacity to carry it out. The best they could settle for was terrorism.

The PLO, however, didn't give up. It licked its wounds and the group's organizational resiliency enabled it to rebuild shattered forces while it waged an escalating war of terror against Israel and her allies. From bases among Palestine refugee camps in Lebanon, Arafat was once again ready to launch an invasion into Israel, but the Yom Kippur defeat canceled that idea.

The military failures of the Arabs against Israel convinced the PLO a conventional mobile war against Israel would be futile. Nor were the prospects of guerrilla war any better. Guerrillas trying to infiltrate Israel were captured or killed and the efficient Israeli security forces broke up underground cells in the West Bank and Gaza.

Unable to drive Israel from the occupied territories or inflict significant military damage on them, the PLO had to change tactics. The Israeli military was too tough for them so they switched to attacking softer civilian targets. They ceased trying to be guerrillas and became terrorists.

Terrorism was chosen out of PLO weakness. It was the only way they could punish Israel and keep the cause of Palestine before an indifferent world.

PLO terrorism was not only directed at Israel and its allies, but also against Arab regimes it felt had betrayed the Palestinian cause. The more barbaric the terror incident, the more the PLO felt the incident not only brought attention to their cause, but also punished Israel, the West and hostile or back-sliding Arab governments.

The Palestinians were particularly incensed at Jordan because of Jordanian attacks on the refugee camps and the expulsion of the PLO from the country in 1970. Arafat wanted revenge.

PLO assassins killed the Jordanian Prime Minister in February 1971 in the lobby of a Cairo hotel. To add a touch of barbarism and guarantee macabre publicity in the Middle East, one of the killers bent over the dead man and lapped his blood.

Airline hijackings, bombings, assassinations and other terrorist acts followed: the 1972 Israeli Olympic massacres in Munich; the 1972 Lod Airport massacre in Israel; the hostage taking and murder of the American Ambassador in Khartoum, are just three examples of barbaric terrorist acts carried out by the PLO.

By the mid-1970s, international terrorism was becoming the PLO's most infamous trademark.

The PLO's terrorism campaign enabled it to gain the support of the Soviets and its surrogates. Arafat became a Soviet client and arms and training were provided to the group in order to undermine U.S. influence in the Middle East.

Soviet surrogates also pitched in: PLO soldiers were trained in Vietnam; Romania provided training on running disinformation and influence-buying campaigns in the West, and also provided false documents and support for PLO operatives; East Germany provided intelligence on the U.S. and Israel in addition to its other training and support activities.

Arafat considered terrorism as only a temporary stage. In true Maoist fashion, he viewed it as a means of inflicting damage on his opponents while building up his forces and bases in Lebanon. From these he could advance to the mobile war stage and launch direct attacks on Israel.

The PLO presence in Lebanon was a disaster, as a weakened Lebanon now found a growing lion cub in their midst. The young lion began pushing the Lebanese around and became involved in the escalating Lebanese civil war.

Once again, PLO meddling in internal affairs of those countries giving them sanctuary almost did it in. It arrogantly ill-treated the Lebanese Shi'ites, Maronite Christians and Druze living near Palestinian refugee camps. Such treatment led to civil war in Lebanon involving the PLO and all the other factions. Even in the midst of all this, the PLO still continued its terror attacks on Israel.

Armed by the Soviets, the PLO had transformed most of its forces in Lebanon into regular units. They had a small army of several thousand men armed with Soviet-made artillery, tanks, antiaircraft batteries, and multiple-rocket launchers.

In the spring of 1981, they launched a new type of attack on Israel: stand-off bombardments with rocket launchers. These attacks did little physical damage and inflicted few casualties. They did cause large numbers of Israeli civilians to flee away from the border area.

Matters came to a head in 1982 when Israel invaded southern Lebanon and forced the PLO north from their camps there. Arafat's forces retreated to Beirut where they were besieged by the Israeli army. Receiving no help from other Arab states or the Soviet Union, the PLO bowed to pressure from Lebanese politicians to leave Beirut in order to save the city from destruction. The PLO agreed and dispersed throughout the Arab world. The PLO leadership was forced to make their headquarters in Tunis, a thousand miles from their area of operations.

It was only the group's organization, which had weathered earlier calamities, that was strong enough to keep the PLO from totally disintegrating during this particularly dark period of its history. For all practical purposes, their protracted war strategy had been crushed.

The scattering of the PLO throughout the Arab world brought anguish and despair to Palestinians living in Gaza and the West Bank. Their hopes of an Israeli defeat by victorious Arab forces had been dealt a severe blow and their champions, the PLO, had turned out to be a paper tiger.

The Palestinians in the occupied territories decided to take matters in their own hands. They couldn't sit around and twiddle their thumbs waiting for Arafat and his forces to win their freedom. If they were going to be free, they'd have to do it themselves.

Venting their frustration and anger, on December 9, 1987, thousands of Palestinian rock-throwing youths started riots and demonstrations against Israeli rule in Gaza.

Leading this outbreak of violence, or *intifada* as the Palestinians called it, was an organization of militant Palestinian Islamic fundamentalists, Hamas, an acronym for Islamic Resistance Movement.

Militant Muslim extremists played a dominant role in these early riots and confrontations with Israel's security forces. In a few days the disorders spread from Gaza to Palestine refugee camps on the West Bank. Again, it was militant fundamentalists that were stirring up the trouble: invoking the ancient religious themes of a conquering Islam, brandishing the green flag of Islam, and calling for a holy war against their occupiers.

In what appears to be a standard blueprint for militant Islamic fundamentalists, mosques were central to the spread of the *intifada* both as makeshift headquarters for the militants and as propaganda forums to rally crowds to revolt in the name of Allah.

The PLO was taken by surprise by the uprising but quickly tried to take over its leadership by setting up an umbrella group, the Unified National Command (UNC). The UNC consisted mainly of PLO elements, other radical secular Palestinian organizations, and the Palestine Communist Party. The militant Islamic extremists, however, refused to join the UNC and continued on their own.

Hamas ran its own military and propaganda activities without any coordination with the UNC. It stressed the religious nature of the struggle, and one of its propaganda pieces, a handbill, was the first to apply the term *intifada*—tremor—to the revolt. It was more than a tremor, as far as Hamas was concerned. It was a full-blown deadly religious war between Islam and Judaism, an Islamic holy war, a *jihad* in their eyes.

Hamas considers the Jews as interlopers who stole lands that were eternally consecrated for Islam and the Muslims. The fight with Israel, therefore is a fight to the finish; there is no room for compromise by partition or otherwise, only a fight to the death. Any Palestinian group, such as the PLO, who seeks a compromise, such as the Middle East Peace Accord, are traitors to the cause of Muslim Palestine.

Hamas also took issue with the PLO over the PLO's vision of a secular instead of an Islamic state for the new Palestine. This is a major Hamas bone of contention in its opposition to the PLO. They weren't afraid to challenge the older organization for the leadership of the Palestinian struggle. On August 8, 1988, Hamas threw down the gauntlet by publishing a Hamas Covenant which laid out the Islamist's position on Palestine, and claimed for Hamas the role of spearhead of the struggle against Israel's occupation. By determining that *jihad* was the only way to liberate all of Palestine, Hamas also challenged the PLO's claimed exclusive right to determine the path of the Palestine struggle.

Shortly after publicizing their Covenant, Hamas began using classic guerrilla tactics of terror and intimidation to enforce its will in Gaza and the West Bank. Their tactics became routine scenes on the evening TV news—rock throwing youths rampaging and confronting armed Israeli forces in Gaza and the occupied territories.

Using force, they began compelling Arabs in the occupied territories to take part in strikes and riots planned and organized by Hamas. Its cadres burned cars and threatened to torch businesses that didn't cooperate with them. The action cowed into line those Arabs who might have questioned Hamas' confrontation policies.

Hamas also attacked the PLO and Yassir Arafat, accusing them of deviating from their own principles. Since both Hamas and the PLO declared that all of Palestine must be liberated and the only way to do it was an armed struggle, the PLO's willingness to compromise with Israel and accept Palestinian autonomy in Gaza and the West Bank, left it open to Hamas' charge of betrayal. Hamas' position was "no compromise" and the PLO's accommodation with Israel was seen as traitorous to the Palestinian cause. Only Hamas was following the true path—the total destruction of Israel.

Hamas' course is clear: violence and subversion against both the Israelis and the PLO. Most of the violence, at present, will be directed at Israel, trying to goad them into breaking the peace accords. But Hamas will continue its bloody struggle with the PLO and the militant's patience is wearing thin. On November 2, 1994, PLO leader Yassir Arafat and his bodyguards were chased out of a mosque in Gaza by Hamas supporters after he had attempted to pay his respects during a memorial service for slain Hamas militants. The Palestinians had been killed by Israeli security forces in a raid to free an Israeli soldier kidnapped by Hamas.

The *intifada* was a propaganda coup for the Palestinians. News telecasts showed stone-throwing youths facing the armed Israel soldier. Hundreds of Palestinians were killed and their deaths won them considerable sympathy from the international community. The *intifada* soon shifted the debate of the Palestinian-Israeli struggle from the question of the PLO and terrorism to the question of Israel's occupation of the Palestinian territory. Almost overnight the perception of Palestinians changed from being barbaric terrorists to victims.

From that point on all the Palestinians had to do was to continue their media campaign of victimhood, while using the violent revolt to make the occupied territories ungovernable for the Israelis. This put the Israelis in a bind: in order to crush the *intifada* it would have to resort to excessive draconian measures involving thousands of Palestinian casualties—all under the gaze of CNN television cameras. Or, they could try to contain the situation at or near its current level which would bleed Israel dry.

The Israelis couldn't take the first option and the second also bore too high a price. The only answer lay in a negotiated political settlement with their long hated enemy, the PLO.

Given the rise of Hamas and its virulent brand of Islamic extremism, the Israel government decided upon dealing with the devil they knew—Yassir Arafat and the PLO.

The Israeli-PLO peace accord in September 1993 and the Israel-Jordanian accords in the summer of 1994 are the first steps in trying to resolve the long-standing Arab-Israeli conflict.

After long years of failed revolutionary struggle, the PLO appeared to be ready to achieve part of its goal when the Israel government moved to undercut the revolutionary situation by addressing Palestinian grievances.

The signing of the Israeli-PLO Accord unleashed a wave of euphoria that was to prove self-delusionary. The Israelis kept building settlements and Arafat and his terrorists kept telling his Arab allies: "Everything you see and hear today is for tactical and strategic reasons. We have not given up the rifle." In other words the destruction of Israel remains their ultimate goal.

Recent events bear this out. There were over 90 terrorist attacks against Israelis in the immediate 31 weeks following the signing of the Peace Accord in September 1993. Of these, 37 were known to have been carried out by Arafat's Fatah terrorists. Three were "initiation rites" murders to join Fatah, which included the ax-murder of a 70-year old man and beating to death a 65-year old with iron pipes. One of the murders was carried out by two members of the new Palestinian Police Force.

In 1994, with Jericho and Gaza under PLO rule, Israel suffered more terrorism than in any year since the founding of the state in 1948.

The PLO has not renounced its goal to destroy Israel. The commander of the Palestinian Police, in demanding that Jerusalem become the capital of the new Palestinian state, added: "This is the final step toward the restoration of Jerusalem and the entire occupied land to their owners...The door is open to (those)...who wish to escalate the armed struggle."

The PLO hasn't renounced its goal of a Palestinian state at the expense of the existence of Israel. And decades-long distrust between the two parties continues to be an obstacle to be overcome if the peace process is to succeed. But, hovering like a storm cloud, there is still the problem of Hamas and the militant fundamentalists.

Hamas, along with other Islamic fundamentalist extremists in the Middle East, are determined to wreck the Israel-PLO peace process. The accord is extremely fragile and it wouldn't take much to jeopardize it. Consider the effect of the kidnapping and murder of an Israeli solder in early October 1994: it brought a temporary halt to the transfer of authority from Israel to the Palestinians in Gaza and the West Bank. Israeli Prime Minister Rabin threatened not to implement the limited self-rule over the incident.

If one kidnapping caused such a reaction from Israel, just imagine what it would be if, and when, Hamas raises the stakes with a well-coordinated campaign of terrorist attacks against Israel, as they say they have every intention of doing.

A few days later, that campaign got under way with the suicide bombing of a commuter bus in Tel Aviv. A suspension of the peace process followed and caused the Israelis to issue warnings to Arafat to eliminate Hamas, or the Israeli army would come in and sort them out. The situation inside Israel is still tense to this day.

That tactic was used again in eight days of terror in the last week of February and the first week of March 1996 with suicide bombings in Jerusalem and Tel Aviv. Those bombing cast doubts on the ability of the peace process to survive. Similar bombings occurred in 1997.

Continued terror bombings created a backlash against the peace process in Israel and the May 1996 elections narrowly brought to power the Likud Party, which had opposed the Labor government's peace initiatives.

The peace process is on a razor's edge and could evaporate at any moment. Tension continues to rise between Israel and the PLO and its Arab allies.

The bombings are a stark reminder to the world the PLO is not the only player in Gaza or the West Bank. If Arafat expects to be the undisputed leader of the Palestinians he must squarely face the Hamas challenge.

That may be easier said than done for Hamas has a lot of support and their clandestine terror network makes counter-measures difficult. Organized in small underground cells of two or three individuals, they can draw on a large support network in Gaza and the West Bank. This network includes mosques and private homes where Hamas terrorists can stash their weapons and hide from the authorities.

Given Arafat's reluctance to try and stamp out Hamas, a task he might not be able to accomplish, the world and the Israelis can brace themselves for more, not fewer, terror attacks.

It is not out of the realm of possibility to imagine, sometime in the future, Israeli security forces invading the area to punish Hamas, with much loss of Palestinian life. Such action would represent a propaganda coup for Hamas. They would exploit it to the fullest to advance their militant Islamic fundamentalist agenda at the expense of both Israel and other Palestinian political interests.

The emerging Arab-Israeli detente is running into staunch opposition from Islamic militants throughout the Muslim world. Despite their differences over a wide range of issues, these activists share a common belief: Israel, as a state, must be destroyed.

It is this common belief which succors and sustains Hamas in its war of terror against Israel and, at the same time, discredits the

PLO. From Hamas' point of view, it is an ideal situation: they can attack the universal Islamic militant's common enemy, the state of Israel, and expose the hypocrisy of the PLO in dealing with the sworn enemy of Islam.

By hewing to this goal, Hamas is guaranteed the world wide support of militant Islam, a point brought home to the United States by a recent PBS documentary, *Jihad* in America, which detailed Hamas' wide-ranging support network in the United States. At the same time, Hamas can continue its attacks on the PLO in an effort to discredit Arafat's attempted political settlement of the Palestinian-Israel problem.

We have an emerging eternal triangle involving Hamas, the PLO, and Israel. Each will react to the other's actions, their ultimate destinies intertwined in a drama that threatens to be long, violent, and bloody.

The various peace treaties made in the Middle East between the world's most ancient enemies are fragile at best. Jordan's King Hussein, who seems to be the only Arab ruler in the region who sincerely desires peace, signed a separate agreement with Israel. He may not live long enough to enjoy it. He will either die from cancer or from an assassin's bullet. In time, his kingdom will fall to militant Islamic fundamentalists who reject both the Jordanian-Israeli peace accord and Israel's right to exist.

Egypt's attitude is lukewarm at best. It too rejects the Israeli-Jordanian accord and the country's secret police state "there is no peace between Israel and Egypt." Egypt's huge military is designed to confront Israel, and Egyptian military leaders feel that war with Israel is inevitable.

Egypt is building up its military and, after Israel, has the strongest and most modern armed forces in the Middle East after Israel. It still considers Israel as its main enemy and is preparing itself for a possible war.

Senior Egyptian officials are strongly hinting that they will back Yassir Arafat's May 1999 deadline for the creation of a Palestinian state. Arafat has threatened to unilaterally declare a Palestinian state if peace talks with Israel haven't produced one by that time.

Egypt's President Mubarak in 1996 assured Syria that it would "not stand idly by" in the event of a war between Israel and Syria.

Arafat and the PLO also reject the Israeli- Jordanian peace treaty, and Arafat continues to declare to his Muslim brethren that the PLO's war against Israel will continue. He told a Cairo audience in January 1995 the PLO intends "to continue...the revolution."

While the West may delude itself as to the PLO's commitment to a lasting peace, Arabs in the area are not fooled. In what was the most comprehensive, thorough, far-reaching survey taken among Arabs—Lebanese, Syrians and ex-patriot Palestinians—a 1994 poll conducted by the American University of Beirut provides a vivid look at the Arab attitude towards a lasting peace with Israel.

To begin with, "not one respondent who favored the peace process gave positive justification for peace with Israel." According to the respondents: "It is a chance to recover territory occupied by Israel since the Six Day War. The great majority of those interviewed saw the peace "as an interim measure for Arabs to reorganize and strike later." More than 90 percent of those who support the peace process would support a war if Israel became weaker. Such widespread attitudes doesn't bode well for a permanent peace between Israel and its Arab neighbors.

Israeli concessions will not satisfy the demands of the Palestinians and, given the determined opposition of Hamas and other militant Islamic extremists, the final peace is not at hand. The bloodshed will continue. Given the United States' support for Israel, we can expect PLO and Hamas anger to result in increased terror campaigns against U.S. citizens and property both here and abroad.

Chapter 10
Freelancers: Islam's Foreign Legion

Shall the sword devour forever? do you not know that the end will be bitter?
II Samuel 2:36

The Soviet Union's 1979 invasion of Afghanistan had enormous influence on militant Islamic fundamentalism. The heroic resistance of the lightly-armed *mujahedin,* the anti-Soviet guerrilla fighters, against the mighty Soviet army inspired millions of Muslims throughout the world. The Soviet army, according to Moscow propaganda, was the most powerful in the world, and was considered invincible. Yet it was unable to overcome the determined resistance of poorly armed bands whose weapons were often those of the trenches of World War I—bolt-action Lee-Enfield rifles.

Afghanistan proved to all that the Soviet military was far from an invincible juggernaut.

During the 1980s thousands of Muslims rallied to the Afghan call of *jihad* against the infidel Soviet invaders. Volunteers from every corner of the Muslim world flocked to the cause of the *mujahedin.*

Most of the volunteers worked in the support groups laboring to sustain the Afghanistan resistance effort. They worked in the relief organizations which collected funds, equipment and supplies for the resistance fighters or for the two to four million Afghanistan refugees housed in the refugee camps in Pakistan and Iran. Most of the volunteers worked in clinics, hospitals, and schools set up in the camps.

Militant Islamic fundamentalist groups were quick to take advantage of the opportunity offered in Afghanistan. By turning Afghanistan into "us versus them"— Muslims everywhere against the evil Soviet invaders—militant Islam gained two advantages.

The militant extremists could now use the plea of "assisting our brothers in Afghanistan" as a smoke screen to cover militant subversive activity throughout the Muslim world.

The Afghan cause also enabled militant Islamic fundamentalists to send volunteers to Afghanistan to get valuable guerrilla training and military experience. This would come in handy for future use to advance the militant's struggle throughout the Muslim world.

Afghanistan became a valuable laboratory for militant Islam. It convinced the fundamentalists that they could stand up to a non-believing superpower like the Soviet Union. They also got valuable hands-on experience in revolutionary guerrilla tactics and enabled militant Islam to network with like-minded zealots fighting the faithful's struggle in Afghanistan.

These tactics and contacts would subsequently be used against radical Islam's enemies throughout the world.

As aid poured in to help the Afghans fight the Soviets, it was coordinated through Pakistan's Inter-Service Intelligence (ISI). Pakistan controlled the distribution of aid, both humanitarian and military, with a tight fist.

The Pakistan government tread gently because it didn't want to anger the Soviets to the point where Russia would strike out against Pakistan. Nor did the Pakistanis wish to see the resistance movement establish an Afghan state in exile among the refugees.

Pakistan was well aware of the destabilizing effect the PLO

and Palestinian refugees had on the unraveling of Lebanon. The Zia government was determined not to allow anything like that to happen with the Afghanistan refugees in Pakistan. As a result, they kept a tight rein on resistance activity in Pakistan.

Pakistan also saw opportunity in the situation. By allowing the resistance to operate from their soil, they would enhance their status and influence in the Muslim world as defenders of the faith.

This was not an inconsiderate action. Pakistan was one of the world's so-called pariah states because of its tireless pursuit of nuclear weapons, often in concert with the likes of Libya's Quadaffi. By championing the cause of the Afghans, it would divert world attention from the effort to build a Pakistani atomic bomb.

The expansion and the internationalization of the Afghan struggle put Pakistan in a new light at the center of the world stage—helping a people fighting for their freedom.

Muslim volunteers were encouraged to come and join their religious brothers in the fight against the ruthless atheistic Soviet invaders. They came in droves to the refugee camps where they were screened and sent to military training camps run by the ISI. After receiving their training, the volunteers fought inside Afghanistan with the *mujahedin.*

Many of the volunteers who survived the bitter fighting returned to their homelands, bringing with them the valuable military skills of the seasoned guerilla fighter. These skills would be welcomed when the local *jihad* was launched by militant Islamic fundamentalists.

Outside Muslim aid was normally channeled into Pakistan through two Islamic pipelines: the Muslim Brotherhood and the Saudi-financed World Islamic League. Volunteers, relief workers, and money were sent through this largely private effort, though under the scrutiny of the Pakistan ISI. The Brotherhood and the World Muslim League were the conduit for the huge efforts throughout the word where individuals or small groups raised money, collected food, clothing, or medical supplies for use in Afghanistan.

One of these groups was the Alikifar Refugee Center in Brooklyn, New York, run by an Egyptian, Mustafa Shalabi. The center, known as the *jihad* office, recruited funds and volunteers from the Muslim community in the New York-New Jersey area.

One of the center's volunteer workers, who eventually volunteered to fight in Afghanistan, was Mahmud Abouhalima, one of the convicted World Trade Center bombers. Abouhalima received military training in a CIA-supported training camp near Peshawar in Pakistan and fought inside Afghanistan. The World Trade Center bomber was one of the more than 20,000 Muslims who flocked to Islam's banner in Afghanistan during the 1980s.

War changes those who fight it. Living on the razor's edge between life and death effects each participant differently. Some suffer permanent damage to both body and soul. Many escape bodily harm but are scarred in their psyches. But all emerge from the experience as a different individual than the one he was before going off to war.

Abouhalima was no different. He, as well as other American Muslims, were changed men because of their Afghanistan experience. Most of them left America as ordinary men and came back different and proud. The war reminded them of the glorious old days, many hundreds of years ago, when Muslims were fighting the infidels.

Many, such as Abouhalima, couldn't let go—they are still fighting the infidel or heretical Muslim.

Because of this attitude, Afghan veterans were not always

welcomed with open arms when they returned to their native lands. Indeed, they have become a source of trouble for many of the Muslim regimes upon their return home.

The plight of the non-integrated Afghan vet was nothing new. Europe had seen it often in its past before the rise of modern professional armies. Disbanded armies spread disease—especially syphilis—and murderous criminal activity across the continent during the wars of the 16th century. The Thirty Years War of the 17th century was fought largely by mobs of Protestant and Catholic zealots, not professional soldiers. At its conclusion, having acquired a taste for bloodletting, its warriors wreaked havoc for years until they died in wars, were killed by local peasant vigilantes, or by the authorities in the emerging nation states of Europe.

Over three centuries later, the world was seeing a repeat, although on a smaller scale, in the Afghanistan aftermath.

The returning vets may have been outcasts and poison to the various Muslim regimes, but they were valued warriors for the cause of militant Islamic fundamentalism.

The Afghan vets are highly prized by militant Islamic fundamentalist organizations because of the military skills they learned in the crucible of war in Afghanistan. With the demise of the Soviet Union's terrorist schools, the avenue for the would-be Muslim terrorist to acquire subversive military skills became somewhat restricted.

The training camps of the Iranians, Libyans, Syrians and the PLO had their own agendas and graduates from these schools were expected to support their hosts' agendas. The Soviets had been more flexible.

Afghanistan was different. Volunteers were welcomed with open arms, given training and an opportunity to fight and die along side their Muslim brothers while fighting Islam's enemy. The long war against the Soviets produced a pool of Muslim foreign legion fanatics anxious to fight for the cause of the faith.

The skills acquired in Afghanistan were tailor-made for the cause of militant Islamic extremism: a revolutionary guerrilla war of terror and subversion. This type of combat requires small groups of highly dedicated, well-trained individuals who have mastered the art of hit-and-run tactics, assassinations, use of explosives, clandestine channels of communication and logistic support, and the gathering of intelligence.

These skills were honed to a keen edge in Afghanistan and service with the *mujahedin* demonstrated one's zealous commitment to Islam. The lessons learned in Afghanistan are now being put in practice by militant Islamic fundamentalism in places as varied as Egypt and Bosnia.

Fanatical members of this loose-knit Muslim foreign legion are active in all the current Muslim fundamentalist hot spots.

In Algeria many of the field commanders of the militant Armed Islamic Group (GIA) are Algerian veterans of the Afghan-Soviet war. None of these vets were part of the outlawed fundamentalist Islamic Salvation Front political party which was on the verge of winning national elections before being banned by the Algerian government.

The Afghan vets were fighters, not political activists. They, along with their other GIA comrades, chose bullets instead of ballots. Today, the GIA controls large chunks of the Algerian countryside as a result of its guerrilla war of terror.

In August 1993, Nazih Rached detonated the bomb on his parked motorcycle as Egyptian Interior Minister, Hassan al-Alfi's car drove past. The bomb, a homemade claymore mine, blasted ball-bearings at the minister's car and peppered pedestrians on the crowded sidewalks in downtown Cairo. The bomb killed four, but only wounded its intended victim. It turned out Rached had learned his explosive skills while he had fought with the *mujahedin* in Afghanistan.

Egyptian President Mubarak claims Egyptian Afghan veterans are the main terrorist threats to the Egyptian government. There is a large discrepancy as to the number of Afghan vets allegedly involved in anti-government revolutionary terrorist activity in Egypt. A Cairo lawyer who represents Islamic fundamentalists claims 20,000 Egyptians fought in Afghanistan. The Egyptian government's figure are considerably less, around 2,500, with only half of those returning to Egypt.

Whatever the number, the Egyptian government considers the Afghanistan veteran such a potential menace that Egypt passed a law allowing execution for any Egyptian who had undergone foreign military training.

Sudan has become a staging area for many of the Islamic foreign legionnaires. Intelligence sources indicate that, as of 1993, the Sudan was preparing for an influx of over 10,000 Afghan vets enroute from Iran and Pakistan.

These seasoned fighters were being shipped to the Sudan for further deployment to Algeria, Egypt, Bosnia and the Maghreb. These fighters would play a vital role in militant Islamic fundamentalism's efforts to install radical Islamic republics throughout the Muslim world.

Many of these Afghan vets have surfaced in Bosnia where they fought alongside Bosnian Muslims. In spite of the 1995 Dayton Peace Accord. They come from all over the Muslim world: Iran, Algeria, Egypt, Sudan, Persian Gulf Arab states, Pakistan, Afghanistan,

Syria, Turkey, and even Muslims from Great Britain.

The Bosnian situation demonstrates a new and very danger-ous situation for the non-Muslim world. The militant Islamic world of the 1990s and 2000s is a far more cohesive one than that of the 1980s involvement in Afghanistan. There is both a jointness of pur-poses and a working operational command and control between Iran, Sudan, and numerous fundamentalist terror groups.

The "Afghans" fight the Serbs, train the Bosnian militia, and are active throughout Bosnia. By early 1993, over one-thousand mem-bers of militant Islam's foreign legion were active in Bosnia. They were joined by a contingent of four-hundred Iranian revolutionary Guards. Militant Islam was flocking to Bosnia to assist their belea-guered Muslim brothers fight the infidel and have shown little inclina-tion to leave.

U.S. troops are under the gun from these fanatic who have not left Bosnia, in spite of assertions of UN officials in New York. They pose a continuing threat to the NATO troops in Bosnia.

In addition to their fighting skills, the members of this Is-lamic foreign legion also carry out an Islamic civic action program. They teach the Bosnians, especially the children, the message of the Islamic fundamentalist.

The fundamentalist's propaganda efforts appear to be bearing fruit as Islamic fundamentalism is making inroads in Bosnian society. There are growing signs that intolerance towards non-Muslims is in-creasing and the Bosnian government is encouraging this growing hostility.

Bosnian Muslims are ethnic Europeans and were never, until now, known for their Islamic radicalism. They share origins with the Serbs and Croats and converted to Islam when the Ottomans ruled the Balkans. Their brand of Islam, until recently, was rather subdued.

The war with Serbia changed this and the preaching of militant Islamic fundamentalism has struck a responsive chord in Bosnia.

Current peace plans envision establishing semi-autonomous regions in Bosnia based on religion. All three groups involved in the civil strife, Bosnians, Croats and Serbs, are all ethnic Slavs. The Serbs and the Croats are Christians while the Bosnians are Muslims. As part of the peace plan, the Bosnian areas would become mini-Muslim states. The growing influence of Islamic fundamentalism in Bosnia could well transform these into tiny, radical Islamic republics in the heart of Europe's southern regions, the soft underbelly of Europe.

Militant Islamic extremists will then have a valuable foot-hold for exporting and supporting Islamic terrorism throughout Europe. This real possibility is causing a lot of concern among security agencies in Europe.

This nebulous Islamic foreign legion, made tough and resourceful by fighting in Afghanistan—both against the Soviets and the continuing internal civil war—see themselves as part of an international Islamic movement. They envision a world in which the Muslim holy law will stand once again knocking on the gates of Europe. "Our religion," says a commander of an Islamic training camp in Afghanistan, "requires us to retrieve all our land up to Sicily and to the border with France."

It won't happen overnight, claims the commander, but it will happen because "youth in the Islamic world is coming out of its stupor," and hundreds of them are travelling to his camp for training.

From these camps in Afghanistan and the mountainous border area of Pakistan, militant Muslims are learning the arts of subversion, terror and guerrilla war from seasoned Afghan veterans. They are using these skills, bolstered by their radical Islamic zeal, to stir up trouble back home, or to join their Muslim brothers in combat in faraway places like Bosnia, Chechyna, or Kashmir.

These fanatics are ready to fight and die for the cause of militant Islam. They stand available, awaiting only the call to arms from their various spiritual leaders, such as Sheik Omar Rahman, one of the convicted plotters of the World Trade Center bombing in New York.

Although the Soviet Union withdrew its troops from Afghanistan in 1989, it left behind a puppet government headed by the late President Najibullah. From the Soviet's view, his government was reasonably secure: there was great disunity in his enemies, the *mujahedin* forces, and the Soviet-trained Afghan army was stronger than the guerrilla forces.

The various *mujahedin* guerrilla groups represented different religious interpretations of Islam, held differing ideological views. were ethnically based and often very hostile towards each other. For example, Gulbuddin Hekmatyar, head of the Pushtan-based militant Islamic fundamentalist Afghan resistance group, *Hezb-i-Islami,* waged war on his rivals as much as he did on the Soviets. He enjoyed the personal backing of Pakistan President Zia. It didn't hurt that *Hezb-i-Islami* members had ethnic ties to the Pushtans of Pakistan. As a result, Hekmatyar's group got the bulk of Western aid passing through Pakistan to the Afghan resistance groups fighting the Soviets.

Hekmatyar used this aid to battle his rivals. His affiliated guerrilla bands were ordered to: eliminate any rival resistance groups; inform the Soviets, if necessary, of where the rival groups were located; inform the Soviets in advance of rival's planned guerrilla operations; counter rival group's propaganda; and, in essence, destroy the influence of the other Afghan resistance groups.

With his rivals gone, reasoned Hekmatyar, only his group would remain to seize power when the Soviet's Kabul puppet regime fell.

Such treachery, added to ethnic animosity, guaranteed that a post-Soviet peace throughout Afghanistan would be an illusion.

There was little unity within most of the guerrilla groups in Afghanistan and internal dissension was widespread. Often it was over nothing more than a clash of volatile stubborn personalities. But underlying it all were long-standing ethnic disputes.

These antagonistic groups only combined and made a unified Afghan action because they faced a foreign invader, and an infidel one at that. Without the foreign devil, unified action and cooperation among the resistance groups, meager as it may have been, would have been out of the question.

The Soviet pullout deprived the resistance of their common foreign enemy, and left the Soviet puppet government in Kabul as just another factional tribal player in the age-old Afghanistan game of intercine ethnic-based tribal warfare.

For a time, the Najibullah regime, by virtue of its Soviet-trained and lavishly equipped army, was the most powerful of the new fighting Afghan factions. Given this, the Soviets were reasonably sure their client government would stay in power. They were wrong.

After the Soviet withdrawal, the Najibullah government seemed to have the upper hand. The *mujahedin* were fighting among themselves and were no longer getting huge amounts of outside aid. The Afghan army, imitating its Soviet trainers, was prepared to defend the centers of power—the cities and strategic strongholds.

It would, so the Soviets thought, require different tactics for the guerrillas to overcome their puppet's forces. It would require conventional set-piece battles to overcome these well-defended, fortified positions, something a guerrilla force is notoriously ill-prepared to do.

The *mujahedin,* however, kept on fighting, (each other as well as the Kabul government.) Islamic militants from the outside Muslim world still travelled to Afghanistan to fight Islam's enemy and to get valuable military experience. In their eyes, the Najibullah regime was still atheistic communist and thus not Islamic. The faithful hadn't fought and died to replace one atheist Soviet regime for one of its corrupt, blasphemous Muslim offspring.

Although the number of volunteers was not as large as when the Soviets were the common enemy, Islamic zeal, combined with the pragmatic need to acquire military skills, kept the training camps in Afghanistan busy.

The collapse of the Soviet Union cut off Soviet aid to the beleaguered Najibullah government and, finally, 1992, the communist government in Kabul was overthrown. Even though the non-Muslim atheists were ousted, replaced by a series of ruling coalitions which imposed a mild form of Islamic law, the intercine fighting continued. Nine main Islamic groups backed by a variety of Muslim states— Pakistan, Iran, Saudi Arabia, Uzbekistan and Tajikistan—battled each other for control of Kabul.

From among the tangled web of tribal, ethnic and political alliances, three main umbrella guerrilla factions emerged: those supporting Afghan President Rabbani, the second supporting the former Afghan army general Dostum, and the last, the current faction ensconced in Kabul, the Pakistan-supported Taliban.

As civil wars show, the internal fighting is deadly, costly and brutal with all sides using indiscriminate rocket attacks on each other's supporters, civilian as well as military.

By the early fall of 1996, the Taliban had defeated its rivals and seized Kabul. They immediately proclaimed a fundamentalist Islamic republic, with all the repression and brutality associated with such despotism.

Taliban's grip on power isn't complete. Two tribal-based groups in northern Afghanistan have successfully resisted Taliban's efforts to conquer all of Afghanistan. A Tajiki-based group is led by the legendary guerrilla leader Ahmad Masood. He has joined forces with the predominantly Uzbek force of Abdul Rashid Dostum.

Even though Taliban controls three-fourths of the country, the issue is far from settled as the Masood-Dostum forces have counterattacked and Taliban has responded in kind—and Afghanistan's agony continues.

Militant Islamic fundamentalist groups are taking advantage of the civil war. They are using the strife, and the training facilities supporting the strife, as a vast proving ground to develop future warriors for the coming *jihad* against militant Islam's enemies. The training and experience these zealot warriors get in Afghanistan are skills not readily available elsewhere.

In addition to the training and combat experience, these fighters and the leaders who sent them to Afghanistan are networking and forming a deadly international Islamic resource bank to draw upon for supporting militant Islam's future campaigns. Little by little, militant Islamic fundamentalism is building up an increasing number of seasoned guerrilla fighters who know only war, death and destruction. They are tough, zealous soldiers of Islam ready to kill in the name of Allah. Islamic revolution is their game and these militant Islamic fanatics are anxious to spread death and destruction wherever their services are needed by the holy war of Islamic fundamentalism.

Islam's foreign legion is a classic example of a growing world phenomenon: the proliferation of warlord gangs. These groups have been able to deploy anything from a score of well-armed fighters, to the hordes resembling an army with sophisticated weapons such as the Taliban or the Bosnian Muslims. These armed bands will become increasing instruments of instability throughout the world in the future.

They are already wreaking havoc with the Russians along their southern border with the Muslim Central Asian republics, especially those close to Afghanistan.

The Soviet invasion galvanized the Muslims in Afghanistan and advanced a militant form of Islamic political ideology. All of the Afghanistan resistance movements advocated a future political entity based on Islam, not secularism.

This attitude also spread across the border north from Afghanistan into the former Soviet Muslim republics. Ideology wasn't the only thing that crossed the border. Violence and a low intensity war of terror came with it.

The collapse of the Soviet Union has brought unrest and conflict to the area, especially in Tajikistan, along the old Soviet-Afghanistan border.

After declaring its independence, a six-month Tajiki civil war broke out in 1992. It ended only when ex-communists, aided by Russia, ousted an Islamic alliance. The ousted Islamists, and thousands of refugees fled across the Pabj River into Afghanistan, where the Tajiki rebels are now based.

From these bases, the Islamists launch cross-border raids into Tajikistan to harass and kill Russian troops propping up the Tajiki regime.

Afghan resistance groups are providing aid to the rebels. Both Hekmatyar and Masood are sending weapons and to help the Tajikistan rebels and extending their political and religious influence in the region.

These raids reinforce the Russian belief that Tajikistan is the last bastion guarding Mother Russia from a wave of militant Islamic extremism sweeping north from Afghanistan and Iran.

It is the Russian version of the domino theory, which posits that, if not checked, violence spreads from one epicenter and proceeds from one neighboring country to another in a contagious sequence. If Tajikistan comes under Iranian or Afghan influence, goes Moscow's reasoning, the remaining four former Soviet Muslim republics will be next, one after another.

In order to prevent this, Russia is determined to keep Tajikistan as a buffer zone to check the spread of militant Islamic fundamentalism.

To accomplish this dubious goal, it is requiring a sizeable Russian military presence. More than 25,000 troops, the largest Russian troop presence than in any other former Soviet republic outside of Russia itself, are trying to stop a determined effort by the Tajiki rebels.

In July 1993, for example, a force of several hundred Tajiki rebels attacked a remote Russian border post, killing twenty-five Russian soldiers. Similar pin-prick, hit-and-run raids continue to this day.

The bands of militant Tajiki terrorists and other assorted maverick warlords that have sprung up to take advantage of the chaos have extracted a bloody toll. At the height of the widespread fighting in 1992-93 between 20,000 and 50,000 people were killed. The fighting is still going on with no end in sight.

The militant Islamic fundamentalist's foreign legion is active on the side of their Tajiki rebel brethren. The rebels are assisted by Muslim volunteers, money and weapons from Afghanistan, Iran, Saudi Arabia, Pakistan, and Algeria.

Their on-going low-level guerrilla war in Tajikistan has wrecked the country's economy. Russia's aid efforts, covering half the Tajiki government's budget, are doing little to improve the situation. Many in Moscow feel the Russian presence in Tajikistan is nothing but a quagmire that threatens to drain scarce Russian resources.

But, given the deep and long-standing reservoir of mutual hatred between the Russians and the Muslims in these Central Asian Republics, a Russian pullout in Tajikistan would encourage Islamic extremists in all of these republics.

The Russians are terrified with the thought of this scenario becoming reality. The thought of five militant Islamic regimes on their southern doorstep strikes fear in Moscow's heart.

There are thousands of members of Islam's foreign legion who are welcoming the opportunity to turn Russia's nightmare into reality.

Americans should not adapt a smug attitude that is it Russia's problem, not ours for we are far away from Afghanistan and its bloodthirsty expatriate warriors. One of this war's veterans is now serving a life sentence for his part in the World Trade Center bombing. And that isn't the end of it.

The Islamic foreign legion have links with militant Islamic groups in the United States. These groups, many of whom are non-profit, claim they are established to protect the rights of Muslims and to provide economic, humanitarian, and educational assistance to needy Muslims. Many of these are front groups for Islamic fundamentalism terror groups.

In February 24, 1998 testimony before the Senate Judiciary Subcommittee on Terrorism, Technology and Government Information, Steve Emmerson, producer of the PBS documentary *Jihad* in America told the Senate: "...these groups are actual political wings of radical Islamic fundamentalist organizations. They have defended terrorist groups, terrorist leaders including Hamas chieftain Musa Marzook and World Trade Center conspiracy ringleader Sheik Omar Abdul Rahman, and the Sudanese terrorist regime currently engaged in a genocidal war against the Christian minority...Militant Islamic fundamentalist groups continue to propagate their views throughout the United States...In the end, these radical groups are helping to solidify the political foundations of an extremist ideological belief system that sanctions savage suicide attacks in Israel, wanton murder of foreigners in Egypt, decapitation of young Algerian women who refuse to wear the Islamic veil, and death sentences against intellectuals and writers such as Taslima Nasreen and Salman Rushdie for writing things deemed 'offensive.'"

One of these groups, the American Islamic Group (AIG), based in San Diego, California sees as its mission the establishment of Islamic fundamentalist states around the world. It has close ties with Islamic terror groups world wide and is a major supporter of the Afghan *mujahidin*. AIG also collects money and provides support to the families of the *mujahidin* foreign legionnaires who die in battle.

Through such groups as AIG, Islamic fundamentalist groups, and their foreign legion, are sinking deep roots into the fertile American soil.

Militant Islamic extremism, seasoned by its Afghanistan experience, is spreading and Islam's foreign legion will play a growing role in its expansion.

Chapter 11
Mafias, Drug Lords, and Street Gangs

The land is full of bloody crimes, and the city is full of violence.
Ezekiel 7:23

Is it possible, asks California State University, San Bernadino professor, Robert J. Bunker, that street gangs will be engaging in terrorism in the near future?

One only has to look at places like Somalia, Liberia, Colombia and the former Soviet Union to realize the world is entering a new period where armed gangs of thugs are challenging existing political structures. Nations all over the globe are being subjected to pillage, rape and murder at the hands of marauding gangs.

In much of the world traditional governmental structures co-exist nervously with gangs, mafias and warlord organizations ranging from technologically sophisticated crime networks to machete-wielding bands of Rwandan warlords.

The explosive growth of street gangs in the U.S. can be considered part of this world wide trend. Today, the most reliable estimates are that over 5,000 gangs, with over a quarter of a million members, exist in the major cities of the nation. Many of these gangs are engaging in activities that are equivalent to low-grade terrorism.

An Oklahoma City police sergeant told the 1995 Gang Violence Seminar in Anaheim, California, the U.S. is "hip deep" right now in domestic terrorism created by gangs.

The gang wars erupting in our inner cities are noted for their savagery and utter disregard for the innocent victims often caught in the cross fire. Foreigners gleefuly excoriate the U.S. for being a violent society, smugly convinced the gang wars waged on our streets are another sign of American pathology. Or is the problem more widespread?

The violent gang phenomenon is not an American monopoly. Violent youth gangs are becoming a growing presence in many European cities as well. In much of the Third World gangs are either operating in open defiance of the existing authority, or leading governments they have overthrown. The world wide gang phenomenon has grown to the point the U.S. Army has included them in its perception of early 21st-century Army operations. There is growing concern within the military that gang-type warrior sects plaguing parts of the world may be developing within the United States.

Today, with the declining efficiency of formal governments, criminal organizations and gangs are becoming the "government," for lack of a better term, in more and more areas of the world. In Afghanistan, the Taliban gang controls much of the country. In Georgia an ex-convict has become a king maker, and an Azerbaijani warlord marched on the capital, seized power and set himself up as prime minister. Chechyna has become the first gangster state. It is run by black marketeers, murders, drug dealers and pimps. Russia itself is rapidly becoming another Chechyna.

The collapse of the Soviet Union ended the threat of continental war in Europe. This supposedly made the world a safer place, no longer threatened by atomic annihilation. The retreat of Soviet power did, however, expose other threats. Ethnic and nationalist conflicts, unstable governments, escalating crime and terrorism within the former Soviet Union, threaten to spill over into areas outside the collapsed Soviet Empire's borders.

More and more of Russia is falling under the control of organized crime. Russian Security Council Secretary Ivan P. Rybkin estimates half of the national economy has fallen under criminal gangs' control. Other Russian sources claim 40 percent of the gross domestic product is in the hands of organized crime, often in cahoots with corrupt officials and businessmen. Former CIA Director Robert Gates estimates two-thirds of all commercial institutions, some 400 banks (those in Moscow control 80 percent of the country's finances), several dozen stock exchanges, and 150 large government enterprises are controlled by Russian criminal gangs.

There are at least 3,000 gangs in Russia. Over 200 operate in Moscow alone, and 365 function on an international basis. These gangs have a total membership of over 600,000 members—the equivalent of ten Russian armies. The influence of these crooks on all aspects of Russian society is immense. The Russian Internal Affairs Ministry announced in 1995 almost 1,600 connections between criminals and high ranking government officials were currently under investigation. The corruption reaches the highest levels of the Russian government.

Former Russian Prime Minister Viktor S. Chernomydrin, who was the temporary head of state during Boris Yeltsin's heart bypass surgery, became one of Russia's riches citizens when he received 12 percent of the privatized state enterprise he formerly headed. The total stock of the enterprise was valued at $100 billion, making his 12 percent golden parachute one of the biggest on record.

The interconnectedness between Russian criminals and politicians has its roots in the former communist Soviet Union. During the Brezhnev regime it was becoming apparent communism was a dead-end street for the economy. Russian criminal enterprises, (especially the so-called Uzbek mafia, centered in Uzbekistan in Central Asia,) for a fee, supplied the Soviet Union with most of its consumer goods. Other criminal gangs got into the act and a division of labor evolved. There was a "petroleum mafia," a "fishing mafia," a "fruit and vegetable mafia," a "railroad mafia," to name just a few. All had their contacts in the Soviet government and some were even members of the Soviet Politburo. Through faked statistics, these gangs extracted billions of rubles from the state for nonexistent goods and services.

In spite of all this corruption, the mafias kept the comatose Soviet economy on life-support by using the black market to move consumer goods to the Soviet people, something the official state Soviet-run sector was incapable of accomplishing. Brezhnev was ecstatic. The Russian economy suddenly seemed awash in a miraculous supply of consumer goods. Officials in the Kremlin patted each other on the backs over the apparent glowing production figures, not to mention the gifts and outright bribes they were collecting.

The illusion of prosperity clashed with reality. Russia's communist system disintegrated and finally collapsed. The collapse provided a great opportunity for the various criminal groups. Today their predatory activities control almost half the Russian economy.

Now, in the chaotic post-Cold War world, post-Soviet gangs and mafias are forming alliances with criminal gangs throughout the world. They have links with the Sicilian and American mobs, the Colombian drug cartels, the Japanese Yakuza, and the Chinese Triads. This enables them to operate with impunity across the porous borders of the world.

The criminal gangs' influence is gained through an increase in lawlessness throughout Russia. America, long taunted by the former Soviet Union for its murder rate, now takes a back seat to Russia. By 1993, murders in the Russian Republic alone were exceeding the U.S. rate by over a third—and that didn't count the other ex-Soviet Republics. Russia was now the growing murder capital of the world.

The criminal gangs thrive on the lawlessness and individual corruption in Russia where everything has its price. The country has immense resources and a huge military arsenal, and criminal gangs have their fingers in all of them.

The scope of the corruption and its related criminal activity in resources alone is immense: twenty billion dollars worth of raw-materials were illegally exported from Russia in 1992. Resources such as petroleum, timber, titanium, and even plutonium and uranium passed through the gangs' hands to eager customers. Military hardware is leaving Russia in torrents: from small-fry articles like AK-47 assault rifles and RPG-7 rocket grenade launchers, to tanks, planes, missiles, night vision devices, to a reported three atomic devices thought to have been purchased by Iran.

The corruption is so pervasive that officials of the Defense Ministry were caught stealing entire ammunition depots without fear of being caught. They were selling military equipment, ostensively because the military pay was in arrears, but, in reality, they were lining their own pockets.

Russian organized crime groups, flush with dollars, are forming alliances with Colombian drug traffickers in the Caribbean, acquiring cocaine for delivery to Europe and providing weapons to Latin American criminal gangs.

Russian gangs have even tried to sell Colombian drug lords a submarine, helicopters and surface-to-surface missiles. Law enforcement officials say that at least two helicopters, along with small arms, have been sold to Colombian drug cartels.

Surface-to-air missiles would provide the drug gangs an effective weapon to attack anti-drug law enforcement helicopters. Law enforcement efforts rely on the helicopter to move troops quickly to attack cocaine and heroin facilities in remote jungle areas. If the drug lords have effective air defense with the missiles, it adds more difficulty to counter-drug efforts. And, with the drug lords possessing armed helicopters, it gives them a more secure means of transporting drugs and thwarting raids.

From June to September 1997, several Russian ships were reported to have off-loaded shipments of weapons at the northern Colombian port of Turbo in exchange for drugs.

Russian gangsters were even negotiating with the Cali drug cartel to sell the drug lords a Tango-class diesel-powered submarine. The sub would be used to ship drugs from Colombia to the coast of California. The submarine in question was part of those based at Kronshadt, a large Russian submarine base on the Gulf of Finland.

The price of the sub, which included a crew of 20 for a year, was ridiculously low—dropping from $9 million to $5 million. The deal fell through only because the Colombians didn't think they had the necessary naval expertise to carry on after the departure of the Russian crew.

For years the Soviet Union supplied terrorist groups with the deadly weapons of their trade. Now these same weapons are being sold by the criminal gangs to anybody who has the cash to buy them. It won't be long before these weapons find their way into the hands of gangs, awash with money from their drug activity, throughout the world.

Triumph of Disorder

The explanation is simple: a market exists for these deadly commodities and, due to the world wide cooperation of criminal gangs, it is easy to get these purchases across national boundaries into the hands of the buyers.

The Italian Parliamentary Anti-Mafia Commission warned the UN in 1990 on the growing inter-cooperation of criminal gangs throughout the world and the danger they represent. This cooperation, the commission said, was "taking on the characterization of an extremely dangerous world calamity."

Murder, extortion, gambling, drugs and prostitution operate freely in Russia in a manner that makes America's prohibition era seem like child's play. The Russian government is incapable of stopping the depredations and Russian gangs are a law unto themselves.

To make matters worse, and to add emphasis to the Anti-Mafia Commission's prediction of a coming "world calamity," the Russian gangs are expanding their influence outside the Russian borders. They seem to be targeting the West, and the West doesn't realize what is going to hit them. According to Russian security officials, the Iron Curtain was a shield to the West. Now it is gone, and Russian criminals are free to leave the country. This is a very dangerous situation for the rest of the world. America is getting Russian criminals; Europe is getting Russian criminals. The criminals are especially brutal and vicious and they'll steal everything. The West has yet to feel the full fury of the Russian mafia, but they soon will.

• • •

The Liberian civil war provides a frightening example of the fruits of gang-inspired warlordism. It is an especially horrible conflict in which acts of cannibalism, torture, and random violence have been carried out by armed gangs, some bizarrely attired in women's wigs and shower caps.

The comic appearance of it "soldiers" cannot hide their depraved acts. The most widely publicized act of brutality was the videotaped torture murder of former Liberian President Samuel Doe. Doe had the unfortunate fate to fall into the hands of a gang of thugs, led by a minor rebel warlord named Prince Johnson. He was certainly no prince of a fellow in his sadistic execution of Doe. The unfortunate former Liberian President was skinned alive and the video of the execution, distributed throughout Africa, shows a Budweiser-sipping Johnson singing a Jim Reeves gospel tune while he chops off Doe's ears.

Liberia has plunged into what journalist Robert Kaplan calls a "zone of anarchy." The political order has collapsed and gangs of armed thugs have coalesced around leaders and are fighting each other over the few remaining spoils.

Looting has become a major factor in strife-ridden Africa. Unrest, civil war, or a coup inevitably brings out the looters who use "affirmative shopping" to redress perceived imbalances in the distribution of wealth. This looting phenomenon has destructive consequences. It is a major factor in discouraging foreign investment in Africa and has begun to convince relief and humanitarian organizations not to bother operating in Africa as their facilities will only be looted.

Although all the rebel factions in Liberia engaged in a general orgy of looting immediately after the fall of Doe, their current efforts are directed at looting their rivals' commercial allies, while protecting their own in order to maintain their existence.

Triumph of Disorder

The warlords are cutting deals with foreign firms and officials of the UN-sanctioned Economic Community of West African States Military Monitoring Group (ECOMOG). ECOMOG was supposed to be a peacekeeper whose job is to separate the rebel faction so a hoped for process of "nation building" could resurrect Liberia.

Charles Taylor, warlord in charge of the National Patriotic Front of Liberia (NPFL), has for years exercised exclusive control on parts of Liberia. He has cut deals with foreign commercial firms and benefits from a healthy trade in timber, mineral, and agriculture products. The cash from these ventures finance his NPFL gang and buys weapons for his fighters. Firms receive special treatment or are allowed to do business in the areas under his control in return for use of the firms' communications facilities, and basic military training for his gang of thugs.

The areas under control of the gangs are operated as personal fiefdoms of their leaders. They think of themselves as rulers and try to act the part. For example, Taylor even has a rudimentary foreign policy. He has provided backing to Sierra Leone's Revolutionary Unity Front (RUF), led by former Sierra Leone army corporal Faday Sankoh. Taylor extended diplomatic recognition to the RUF leader as the "governor" of Sierra Leone. The NPFL leader's action was simply a ploy to extend his control over cross-border trade.

Many ECOMOG commanders have turned a blind eye to the activities of the gangs they are suppose to police. In fact, several Nigerian ECOMOG commanders have provided military support to one or more of the factions in their squabbles with rivals. This support had a price: a cut of the loot.

This form of ECOMOG extortion has spread from the officers to the troops. Seeking their piece of the action, many ECOMOG troops have acted like swarms of locusts, stripping the country of fixed assets and selling them abroad. ECOMOG has followed suit and jumped into the looting game in competition with the Liberian warlord gangs. That has had two consequences.

It has put a crimp in the expansion plans of gangs in their dealings with foreign firms to exploit much of the capital-intensive mining opportunities in Liberia unless ECOMOG became a partner. ECOMOG then slowly squeezes the gangs out and become the dominant "partner", thus depriving the gangs of much potential cash. This makes it vital for each gang to more strictly control the "assets" in their areas of operations. This strict control is meant to discourage anybody from challenging their rule and to maintain vigilance over the designs of their rivals.

Such a situation doesn't hold out much promise to halt the continuing breakdown in Liberia. None of the warlords and their factions trust ECOMOG. Why should they since the peacekeeping officers and their troops have personal stakes in their business deals with the various gangs. But each gang sees an ECOMOG deal with a rival as a sell-out. As a spiralling climate of distrust keeps growing, how can ECOMOG be the unbiased mediator between the factions when it is heavily involved in the corruption itself?

The 1995 peace agreement signed by the factions is doomed. It's nothing more than a truce, and it will flounder on the shoals of distrust and corruption. The gang-driven violence will resume, if not escalate, as Liberia and other parts of West Africa plunge deeper into a state of anarchy.

In July 1997, an election was held in Liberia to see which warlord could lay claim to the country's shaky job of president. The winner of the election, which was conducted under the auspices, funding and scrutiny of international observers, was declared reasonably free and fair by the United Nations and a host of observers, including former President Jimmy Carter.

The winner in a landslide was Charles Taylor, whose gang of thugs had destroyed Liberia in an orgy of violence, killing over 200,000 and making homeless refugees of 1 million—out of a total population of 2.3 million people.

Taylor's objective and political philosophy in the election was simple: seize power and keep it whatever it takes. Why was such a bloodthirsty thug elected so overwhelmingly? Perhaps a market woman in Monrovia, the ravaged capital, had the best answer: "If Charles Taylor loses, he make more war. So the people vote for Charles Taylor."

Her answer was like a voice out of the past described by a Russian friend of the late Russell Kirk. Kirk related an experience of this friend who had been a moderate socialist Menshevik at the time of the 1917 Russian Revolution. When Lenin and the Bolsheviks seized power, Kirk's friend fled to Odessa on the Black Sea. Unfortunately, the friend found Odessa not a refuge, but a sea of violence and anarchy. "Then I learned that before we can know justice and freedom, we must have order," the Russian told Kirk. "Much though I hated the communists, I saw then that even the grim order of communism is better than no order at all. Many might survive under communism; no one could survive in general disorder."

Monrovia's market woman was echoing Kirk's friend some eighty years later. But it is unlikely that will lead to any lasting peace.

Unfortunately, this attitude will become more and more prevalent in the new world disorder, and the bloodiest of thugs will have the advantage.

• • •

The expanding presence and viciousness of street gangs in the United States also reflects the trends typified by the proliferation of gangs in Russia and West Africa. Gangs are becoming a festering sore in our failed inner cities, where poverty and crime run rampant and family social structures have often been destroyed. In such circumstances, it should surprise nobody that violent street gangs are a growing menace.

Currently, as many as 57 percent of children in America do not have full-time parental supervision. They are either living with a single parent who works full-time or are in a two-parent household with both parents working full-time. Increasingly, children are being raised in homes disrupted by divorce or economic stress. Growing numbers of children are spending too little time engaged in structural activities such as homework and far too much time just "hanging out." These rootless kids, especially the males, are good potential recruits for gangs.

It is not difficult to understand the reason children join gangs. They want to be accepted, have no feelings of love at home, and wish to belong to something bigger than themselves. Gangs in this country have a long and bloody tradition, dating back to Jesse James and his cohorts, up through the heyday of the Maffia in the 1920s through the 1960s and the ultra-violent drug posses of today. However, none of these predecessors practiced violence for violence sake, as do the major youth gangs of today.

The gang, in many instances, has become the surrogate family. It offers camaraderie and mutual affection missing in the broken family structure most gang members came from. The gang also provides the discipline lacking in the shattered family environment. This discipline, often harsh with execution as its severest form of punishment for disobedience, imposes abnormal social norms on the members that project abject hatred towards the existing social norms. This shows up in the pathological behavior of gang members such as an often total disregard for human life, and a propensity for stealing and looting.

Most gangs are formed around a strong-man type leader—a classic warlord if you will. They look up to this leader and follow his directives, almost with slavish obedience. The members bond with one another and pride themselves on being society's outlaws. Society's disdain and disgust are badges of honor for the gang. The gang members draw closer together and commit atrocious acts which further bond the members more tightly to the group, and alienate themselves more from the public at large.

Their vicious acts prevent society from offering the gang member any alternative to gang life. Unless the individual gang member can break out of this vicious cycle, his roots to society will have been torn out. His only talent will be violence and lawlessness. His loyalty will focus on his gang leader, his gang, or simply himself. These rootless Americans are becoming increasingly dangerous.

"In south central Los Angeles, in much of Newark, in and around the housing projects of Chicago, in the South Bronx and Bedford-Stuyvesant sections of New York, and in parts of Washington, D.C.," observed James Q. Wilson and John J. Dilulio Jr. in *The New Republic*, "conditions are not much better than they are in Beirut on a bad day."

To the American mind, Lebanon has become the symbol of a

lawless society run by terrorists. It is a picture of Lebanon as a Hobbesian state of nature, where each man's hand is raised against the other in perpetuity. The comparison is not one in which we can take any pride.

Criminal gangs, both the local street variety and international gang associations, are heavily involved in the drug trade. It has become one of the most important sources of revenue for gangs.

Many experts feel the U.S. drug problem has gotten out of hand. Former San Jose, California, chief of police, Joseph McNamara surveyed 488 judges, defense attorneys, prosecutors, police chiefs, and police officers in 1992 on their attitude towards drugs and various attempts to curb or ameliorate their usage. Nearly all those surveyed said the United States was losing the war on drugs (96 percent of judges, 95 percent of police officers, 85 percent of police chiefs). Drugs generate billions of dollars of hard cash for drug gangs.

The world wide drug trade is over $500 billion a year. Crooks can do a lot of mischief with that kind of financial resource. Given that fact, plus the weakening of the nation state, it is no coincidence drug cartels, gangs, mafias and triads of all shapes and sizes are proliferating around the world. Their criminal activities are inflaming the economy and internal affairs of many existing nation states.

For example, drug profits in Mexico are estimated at $15 billion annually, 5% of Mexico's gross domestic product. Some economic experts predict Mexico's economy would stagnate without the infusion of drug money.

European police officials report international crime syndicates are playing a "dominant role" in financing the genocidal wars racking the Balkans. Such activity has caused both NATO and the U.S. to make policy decisions in response to the wars financed by the drug mafias. American treasure, and possibly blood, is being expended in response to the gangs activities.

Drug traffickers have financed civil wars and insurgencies in other parts of the globe. According to Spanish police officials, from 1986 to 1988, 80 percent of the heroin in Spain was smuggled into the country by Tamil Tiger guerrillas working with Pakistani residents in Barcelona or Madrid. As soon as the Spanish police destroyed that network with arrests,it was replaced with Kurds from Turkey who completely dominated it for the next two years.

Syria uses profits from its involvement in the drug trade to finance its terrorist activities. A 1992 report by the United States House of Representatives Subcommittee on Crime and Criminal Justice detailed the Syrian involvement. Under Syrian military rule, the area in the Lebanese Bekaa Valley devoted to drug cultivation has risen from 10 percent to 90 percent. Almost 20 percent of the heroin consumed in America originates in Lebanon. Cocaine and heroin paste are shipped through the Damascus airport to the Bekaa valley, where refineries have cropped up like toadstools. Tons of heroin and large quantities of cocaine find their way from these refineries to Europe, adding billions of dollars of revenues to support terrorism.

Syrian President Assad's own brother, Rifaat, is intimately connected with drug traffickers, as is Assad's Defense Minister Mustafa Tlass, and General Ghazi Kenaan, Commander of Syrian Military Intelligence in Lebanon. Assad's drug production directly kills over 35,000 young Americans every year, (over a 1,000 times as many as died in combat during the Gulf War.)

Chances are, whenever a new civil war or insurgency erupts, the desperately poor combatants will finance their military and terrorist activities by drug trafficking. Narco-terrorism is a growing world wide plague. It is a win-win situation for those who use its funds to finance their terror activities. The largest consumer of drugs conveniently happens to be the main enemy of the militant Islamic terrorists. Getting their enemies in the West, especially the United States, to buy and consume drugs, contributes to the destabilization of their enemy.

It is a situation ripe with irony. Marxist guerrillas in Colombia are becoming more and more involved in a most capitalistic-like enterprise—the multibillion dollar drug trade. Drugs have now replaced the old Soviet Union as the financial sugar-daddy of Colombia's Marxist guerrillas.

How dependent are the guerrillas on the drug trade for their funding? Consider the group, the Revolutionary Armed Forces of Colombia (FARC), Colombia's largest guerrilla group. FARC's 1995 earnings from criminal activities (drug trafficking, kidnapping, and extortion) was $395 million. The guerrillas have raised hundreds of millions of dollars through the drug trade. The funds are used to bribe politicians, buy weapons, and pay their terrorists more than the soldiers in the Colombian army ($300-400 per month versus the $200 per month for a Colombian soldier).

Guerrilla involvement in the drug trade is a many faceted endeavor. They impose a 10% tax on drug shipments travelling through areas under their control. For an additional fee, the guerrillas will provide security for the private drug lords processing laboratories. The guerrillas aren't above getting into the actual growing and processing activities. They supervise coca cultivation and distribution in remote parts of the country under their control. Guerrillas are also playing a major role in opium cultivation, which is becoming a growing commodity in Colombia's drug trade. Colombia now has the dubious distinction of being one of the world's top three heroin producing centers.

Thanks to their drug financing and the corrupting influence of the trade, Colombia's guerrillas now exert their influence in over half the country. "In certain areas they are the law and authority," states a sociology professor at Colombia's National University in Bogota.

Drugs are providing the funding for the escalation of guerrilla activity designed to destabilize and seize power in Colombia.

Other guerrilla groups throughout the world are scrutinizing the Colombian marriage of drugs and subversion with keen analytical eyes. If it works in Colombia, why won't it work elsewhere? That attitude is a sure sign of trouble brewing in other parts of the world.

Participating in the drug trade also corrupts the societies engaging in the trade. It weakens such countries like Pakistan, Afghanistan, what's left of Lebanon, and Syria, making them fertile ground for future militant Islamic mischief. The frosting on the cake for this situation is that results come at no cost to the terrorists, since the whole business is paid for by their American and European drug customers, who happen to be their enemies.

The drug trade fosters an environment of lawlessness and corruption that makes their sordid business easier to conduct. Terrorists seek to sow fear and uncertainty in order to create a sense of chaos and disorder so they can eventually seize political power for themselves.

The marriage of terrorism with drug trafficking benefits both partners. Terrorists are often clothed with a semblance of respectability because their cause is often deemed political. No such patina of respectability accrues for the drug trafficker. He is considered nothing more than a common criminal. When the two combine, however, the terrorist derives benefits from the drug trade without losing his political status. The drug trafficker in cahoots with the terrorist has become more formidable because he has gained a measure of political clout. It is a marriage made in Hell.

The drug trade is a vicious assault on any society. It is wise to remember drugs and drug-related violence have killed more Americans, wrecked more lives, and cost us more in real-dollar terms than did the Vietnam War. Our cities have been raped, and generations of the poor have been lost forever. Drug traffickers have done that on their own.

Imagine how much more deadly the narco-terrorist partnership can become? They will have the cash and the attitude to really wreak havoc. An alarming trend can already be seen in our cities. Awash with cash from their drug business, many U.S. street gangs have acquired, or are acquiring, armaments that will enable them to outgun the local police.

Far-fetched? In May 1996, a Customs Service sting (code named "Operation Dragon Fire") uncovered a Chinese arms-smuggling ring that had supplied at least 2,000 Chinese-manufactured AK -47 assault rifles to street gangs in Northern California.

According to arms broker Hammon Ku, who figured prominently in the ring, the Chinese government was completely supportive of the arms shipments to American gangs. Ku also offered U.S. government agents posing as arms buyers for American crime groups a variety of high-tech weapons including tanks, anti-tank rockets, 57-millimeter recoilless rifles, various types of machine guns, and Chinese-made copies of Uzis and M-16s.

Most chilling was Ku's suggestion to the undercover agents

the Chinese arms network could provide criminal groups and domestic terrorists with hand-held rocket-launchers and surface-to-air missiles. The May 24, 1996 *Los Angeles Times* reported that "Ku boasted to (Customs) agents that the surface-to-air missiles, known as 'Red Parakeets,' were so powerful they could bring down a jumbo jet..." According to a criminal complaint filed with the Customs Service, "Ku said that they could take out a 747, that they were very effective."

Just because that attempt failed doesn't mean such weapons are not available to gangs. After all, if it is possible to smuggle tons of illegal drugs into the United States, weapons won't be that much of a problem either. There is also a lively traffic of arms stolen from military bases or National guard armories. And who knows, the next time the Chinese will likely be more circumspect in their smuggling efforts.

The saving grace, so far, for America is her street gangs lack the necessary discipline and military training exhibited by many of their foreign cousins.

Street gang members with military training would add a new and difficult dimension to law enforcement's struggle with these criminal gangs. If gangs start getting serious military training they would become more and more like those paramilitary groups raising Hell all over the world in places like Northern Ireland, Bosnia, Somalia, West and Central Africa, and Russia, to name just a few.

If, or perhaps the better term is when, gangs become more versed in military skills, traditional law enforcement may prove unable to cope with them. Contending with them will raise ugly issues, challenging many of the assumptions upon which our democratic values are based. Attempts to use comfortable, humane, laws and rules against gangs increasingly drunk with blood and anarchy will have dismal results. Suspending these rules and laws will effect the law-abiding as much, or more, than it will the outlaws, but it may come to that—the rule of the iron fist.

There are disturbing signs some gangs are becoming interested in the military. A July 1995 *Newsweek* article mentioned that street gangs from Los Angeles (the Crips and Bloods) and Chicago (the Gangster Disciples) are active within all four branches of the armed services. Gang activity has been reported on at least 50 military bases. A November 1994 Department of Justice report on street gangs said some gangs already have access to highly sophisticated personal weapons such as grenades, rocket launchers and military explosives. Street gang members who are or have been in the military are teaching other gang members the skills they learned in the military. With arms, weapon proficiency and tactics, some street gangs now have the ability to effectively engage in terrorist activities within the United States.

Many people will dismiss the growing danger of criminals, gangs, drugs and Islamic terrorist groups. They will contemptuously ask, in condescending terms, does one really expects a bunch of militant Islamic fundamentalist to invade Virginia or Wall Street, knowing the question begs the answer.

It *was* fringe Islamic militants that *did* bomb the World Trade Center and crack cocaine haunts the streets of Richmond and other Virginia cities. It is well to keep in mind the threat issued by Aaron Michaels, the New Black Panther Party gang leader. "There will be more uprisings like the one in L.A.," he predicts. "It's coming and you had better get ready for it."

Michaels' warning is echoed by Tony McGee, former Milwaukee, Wisconsin city councilman and head of the Black Militia. He boasted on the May 4, 1992 edition of CNN's Larry King Live program, that America had riots in 1929, 1930, 1960, the '90s. And, he predicted a full-blown insurrection in the U.S. by the year 2000.

Is this nothing more than boastful, inflammatory rhetoric, or is it a prophetic warning of future events? Only time will tell, but Americans should know better than any other country that gangs dealing drugs and carrying out mindless acts of violence not only create a climate of urban fear, but also corrupt ever-growing sectors of society. At stake is not just the survival of democratic systems, but, more fundamentally, the well-being of societies represented by those systems, in which more criminals, more broken homes, more doped no-hopers are being bred.

We continue to ignore threats like these at our peril.

Chapter 12
Hidden *Jihad*

With God's help, I shall defeat my enemies through my brave Ansar,
and the Prophet.
The *Mahdi,* as he moved on Khartoum, 1884

The world is familiar with the murderous acts of Islamic fundamentalism on Jews in Israel, and on their fellow believers in the
Muslim world.

The attacks by the PLO and Hamas grace the airwaves of the
nightly TV news whenever they launch a new atrocity against the Jews.
The viewers see the gory details of their latest terrorist incident. But
the daily and weekly massacres of innocent villagers in Algeria are
becoming so commonplace that it doesn't warrant mention on the
front pages of the newspapers.

And the scene of Iranian militants parading American hostages through the streets of Tehran occurred almost twenty-years
ago—lost in the memory of most. After the hostages were freed, it
seemed Iranian revolutionary zeal and violence was directed at their
fellow Muslims. Yet, as shown earlier, Iran still uses deniable acts of
terrorism against its main enemy the non-Muslim West—especially
the United States.

However, there is a continuing decades-long Islamic fundamentalist campaign of genocide against Christians. This savage *jihad*
has been going on off the beaten track of the world's consciousness

and out of range of CNN cameras.

"Out of sight, out of mind" is, unfortunately, a truism of today's shallow media-guided world. The agony of Christians being slaughtered, enslaved and persecuted for their beliefs are muffled amidst the chatter of a nation titillated by the latest sex scandal of the American president.

Ignoring the on-going genocide against black Christians in the Sudan won't make the atrocities go away. Sudanese Christians are under attack by militant Islamic fundamentalism and it is important that we examine their agony. It is important because it provides a graphic example of Islamic fundamentalism in action and a preview of what others may expect who are unfortunate enough to fall under their not so tender mercies.

The Sudan is an on-going example of the dark side of Islamic fundamentalism. It is a brutal nasty force which isn't bothered in the slightest by the nature and scope of the violence carried out in its name.

Remember, the World Trade Center bombing was envisioned as a series of simultaneous bombings of the United Nations complex and the Lincoln and Holland Tunnels.

The prosecutor of the bombers, Andrew C. McCarthy, wrote of the plot's mastermind Sheik Omar Abdul Rahman: "...At the 1995 trial where he and eleven followers were convicted of various charges including conspiracies to levy war against the United States, to bomb, and to Murder Mubarak, an American courtroom was mesmerized by the Sheik's chilling recorded exhortations—e.g., directions to bomb an American army base, calls for bombings to drive the U.S. military out of the Persian Gulf, and adjurations on each Muslim's purported religious duty to be a 'terrorist' (his word)..."

All of this was part and parcel of the Sheik's call for *jihad* against the United States, with the hoped for result of thousands and thousands of deaths.

The Sheik made it clear as his words echoed in the courtroom: "*Jihad* means do *jihad* with the sword, with the cannon, with grenades, and with the missile. This is *jihad. Jihad* against God's enemies for God's cause and His word."

God's cause and his word, according to the Islamic fundamentalist, requires the extermination of Christians in the Sudan.

A December 1997 interview, cited in February 24, 1998 testimony before the U.S. Senate, sheds more chilling light on the thinking of those directing Islamic fundamentalism's assault on the world. The interviewer was from the Cairo publication "Rose al-Yusuf" and he was interviewing Sheik Omar Bakri, leader of a Hamas front. Bakri was questioned about the Egyptian Islamic fundamentalist attack on foreign tourists a few weeks earlier at Luxor, Egypt.

Asked his position on the killing of tourists at that popular and historic site of Ancient Egypt, Bakri answered: "...the tourists went to Egypt with manners and conduct that conflict with those of Islam, the manners of alcoholism, indecency, and gambling. Those people are out of line with Islam and I cannot discuss their business. We believe in the principle of establishing *shari'ah* (Islamic law) even if this means the death of all human beings."

The interviewer reported: "Alarmed, I asked him: Even if this leads to the death of all humans? He confidentially replied: Even if this leads to the death of all mankind."

Given this attitude, the killing of a few million Christians in the Sudan is no problem.

But it is a problem. It is particularly a problem for the Sudanese

Christians who are on the receiving end of this genocidal activity. It is also a problem of Christians everywhere. By turning a blind-eye to the plight of their religious brothers and sisters undergoing deadly persecution by militant Islamic fundamentalism, they have made themselves accomplices of genocide.

It is also a vivid warning of what could happen to them.

The Sudan experience is the future for those societies possessing a significant minority of Christians that happen to fall under the rule of militant Islamic fundamentalism.

Let us turn our attention to the agony of the Sudan.

Chapter 13
Sudan: Islam's Proving Ground

The Islamic military government of Khartoum has been persecuting the African Christians of the south by destroying their church buildings, burning their crops, massacring their people, denying them aid, banning the Bible, and waging a war of terror against them.
Peter Hammond, Frontline Fellowship

The Sudan, the scene of one of the longest and most violent bloody conflicts of the twentieth century, is a land of huge size and contrasts. Stretching from latitude 22 degrees north to latitude 4 degrees near the equator, it is the largest country in Africa. It is as large as the United States east of the Mississippi River, containing within its borders a variety of geographical features.

The vast dry and arid Sahara Desert occupies the northern part. Below this extending southward, is a vast plain of some of the richest agricultural and grazing land in the Sudan. This includes the "Gezira" Island—located between the White and Blue Niles, traditionally the granary of the Sudan.

To the south the grasslands are replaced by thickly forested and intensely humid bush and equatorial rain forests and swamps— the infamous Sudd. The heat in this region is so intense that the White Nile loses about 60 percent of its water in evaporation as it flows through the Sudd. During the rainy season, the Sudd, an area larger than the state of Pennsylvania, is flooded by the rains and becomes almost impassable.

The stark desolate Nuba, Jebel Morra and Red Sea mountains lie north of the equatorial belt and are home to many of Sudanese who are resisting the extermination campaign of the Islamic fundamentalist regime in Khartoum.

This vast land has a population of 28 million people composed of over 140 different ethnic groups, speaking 117 different languages. Many of these groups are ancient enemies. Given this diversity and old animosities, the Sudan has been, and still is, rife with intercultural violence.

It is a microcosm of the new world order postulated by Harvard University Professor, Samuel Huntington in his book, *The Clash of Civilizations and the Remaking of World Order,* (Simon & Schuster, 1996). His thesis is that clashes between what he terms civilizations will be the greatest threat to world peace.

"Spurred by modernization," he says, "global politics is being reconfigured along cultural lines. Peoples and countries with different cultures are coming apart...Cultural communities are replacing Cold War blocs, and the fault lines between civilizations are becoming the central lines of conflict in global politics."

One of these cultural fault lines runs through the Sudan pitting the northern Islamic Arabic culture against the African cultures of the south. This culture is grounded upon Christianity and, in some areas, the pagan worship of animals. The Islamic government in Khartoum is determined to wipe them out.

To the ancient Egyptians, the Sudan was known as the land of Cush. It was a source of ivory incense, gold, and slaves. Sudan was subjected to numerous trading and raiding expeditions by the Egyptians until the 8th Century BC. Cush then became a great power and turned the tables on the Egyptians. Under their King Pianhki, Cush conquered Egypt in 721 BC and established the 25th Dynasty.

Cush's rule over ancient Egypt was short-lived. In 671 BC, the Assyrians invaded Egypt and seized control from Cush.

In 23 BC a Roman force dispatched by the Emperor Nero marched up the Nile Valley, swept into the Sudan and annexed a large part of Nubia. The Romans remained for over three centuries, departing in 297 AD. After their departure, the Ethiopian Christian Axumite kingdom invaded and insured the fall of the Cushites. Over the ensuing centuries Christianity spread northward until the three northern kingdoms of northern Sudan—Nubia, Maqarra and Alwa— were converted to Christianity. This band of Sudanese Christian kingdoms blunted the first wave of Islamic invaders in the 7th century. Subsequent efforts by the Muslims to conquer or convert the Sudanese Nubian Christian kingdoms also failed. Internal squabbling among the Christian kingdoms so weakened them that, by the 13th century, they collapsed. With the fall of Alwa in 1504, Islam finally was imposed in the Northern Sudan.

From the 7th century onward, the Sahara Desert has been a barrier between the Islamic Arab peoples of the North Sudan and the Christian south. The Sudan stands at the crossroads of Islam and Christianity in East Africa. The great Nile River has historically served as a channel for the expansion of Islam into the heart of Africa.

In the early 19th century, the Sudan fell under the control of the Ottoman Turks. The Turks were not interested in developing the Sudan. Instead, they considered it a territorial acquisition to be plundered and a hell-hole to which wayward and incompetent officials were banished.

The Ottoman conquest, however, had religious consequences

for the Sudan. The Ottoman Sultan in Turkey claimed for himself the title of lawful ruler of the Islamic world. Travelling with the conquering Ottoman were Egyptian *ulama* (learned ones or Islamic religious teachers). Their goal was to convert the infidels and establish an Islamic state in the southern Sudan. The Islamic *shari'a* law and court systems was imposed upon a recalcitrant population.

From the beginning, the Ottoman rule was deeply resented by the Sudanese. They considered the government officials, even those Sudanese who worked with the Ottomans, as Turks and outsiders. Despite the introduction of the telegraph and steam-driven ships on the Nile, the Ottoman rule bought few benefits to the Sudan. International pressure to abolish the slave trade had economic consequences for the Ottoman rulers in Cairo. It decreased their lucrative revenue from the slave trade. In an effort to recoup these diminishing funds, officials became more oppressive in raising funds for the government. This meant higher and higher taxes and relations between ruler and ruled worsened.

A smoldering hatred between the Muslims in the Sudan for their overlords simmered and grew. Near the end of the century, this resentment would explode in violence and it would be led by a precursor to today's Islamic fundamentalist.

Caught in the middle were British imperialists who had tried to reduce the oppression and neglect of the ottoman rulers. Years earlier the Ottoman ruler in Cairo went into debt building the Suez Canal and living an extravagant lifestyle. That debt finally caught up with him and drove Egypt into bankruptcy. Protecting the European Suez Canal bond-holders, Great Britain became the de facto ruler of Egypt and its southern possession the Sudan, when it took over the administration of the Egyptian government.

During this same period of history, England was spearheading the attempt to outlaw slavery throughout the world, and slavery was rampant in the Sudan.

Responding to pressure by anti-slavery groups in England, the mystical British Major General Charles G. "Chinese " Gordon, was appointed governor, first of Equatoria province, then later of all of the Sudan. Gordon embarked upon a crusade to rid the Sudan of slavery. His efforts enraged the Muslim community who claimed the suppression of slavery was against the principles and traditions of Islam.

A change in the financially strapped Egyptian government led to Gordon's replacement as Governor General of the Sudan and the halting of his anti-slavery crusade in the Sudan. Gordon returned to England.

While Gordon was leaving the Sudan, a man living as a hermit on the island of Aba, 200 miles up the White Nile from Khartoum, was about to step on the stage of Sudanese history and plunge the Sudan into violent, religious-inspired conflict. He would fulfill the prophecy of the great Islamic historian, Ibn Khaldun who wrote in his *Muqqaddama:* "It is a universal belief amongst the Muslim masses throughout the ages that at the End of Time a man of the family of the Prophet must manifest himself to confirm the faith and proclaim justice. The Muslims will follow him and he will establish his rule over the Islamic Kingdoms. He will be called the *Mahdi.*"

Chaffing at being under the control of infidels, and incensed at the efforts to suppress the slave trade, a wave of fundamentalist Islamic fanaticism, led by Mahomet Achmet, swept the Sudan.

After years spent in prayer, fasting, Koranic study and contemplation of his perceived decay of Islam, Achmet, the son of an obscure boat builder from Dongala, proclaimed himself the *Mahdi*— the Expected One—and launched a *jihad*, or Holy War. It was to challenge Christianity and the foreign penetration of the Nile Valley. His forces inflicted an appalling series of defeats on Britain, including the death of Gordon who had returned to the Sudan as its Governor General. Gordon's death was such a calamity it led to the downfall of the Gladstone government in England. By November 1883, the whole of the Sudan was at the *Mahdi's* feet.

A million square miles or more of the Sudan became *Mahdi* territory, and for 13 years the *Mahdi* and his successors were to rule a purely Islamic state by Islamic methods. That meant absolute despotism.

The *Mahdi's* state was belligerent and aggressive everywhere and his black flag and lieutenants inspired fear and terror in the region. Before his death, the *Mahdi* even claimed he would soon carry his fiery crusade to other corrupt Islamic states—to Cairo, Mecca, and beyond. Mahdism was a real menace to Africa.

The *Mahdi's* successor, his chief disciple Khalia Abdulla continued the *jihad* of his mentor in order to bring Islam to the infidels. He even dispatched telegrams to Queen Victoria, the Ottoman Sultan in Turkey, and the Khedive in Egypt demanding that they submit to his rule. The *Mahdist* rule ended in 1898 when their forces were crushed by the British army under Kitchener.

The British rule halted the campaign of forced Islam upon the southern Sudan and opened and encouraged Christian missionary activity in the country.

But Islamic fanaticism didn't disappear with the demise of the *Mahdi* at the end of the 19th century. It is alive and well today in the Sudan.

Ever since independence in 1956, the Sudan has been torn by intractable civil strife based on ethnic, economic, tribal, regional and religious considerations, with the religious factor looming larger and larger in importance.

Events in the Sudan have always seemed chaotic. They have a tendency to go from bad to worse. Disillusionment quickly settles in with discredited regimes and often leads the Sudanese to recreate the political nightmare of the past in order to get rid of their latest saviors.

Since independence, the Sudan has lurched from civilian multiparty rule, to military dictatorship, to one-party rule, back to civilian multiparty rule, overthrown by another military coup which has metamorphosed into a fundamentalist Islamic regime. In its short history since independence, instability has been the norm in the Sudan.

Islamic fundamentalism has been a key factor in this instability. The reason for this is the fundamentalist's drive to impose Islam on a multi-cultural non-Islamic segment of its population. The Sudanese are a mixture of Muslims, Christians and Animists—those who worship animals. The integration of these communities has been one of the biggest problems facing the Sudan, and is exacerbated by militant Islamic extremism.

From 1898 until independence the Sudan was a British colony. During British rule, and immediately after independence, a western-educated class of Sudanese vied with traditional Muslims, whose political roots were grounded in the *Mahdi* revolt for power in the early 1880s. The Western-educated Sudanese may have been the favorites of their former colonial masters, but it was the traditional Muslims and their fundamentalist ideas who were the force to be reckoned with.

Triumph of Disorder

The Sudanese had a valuable friend, the fundamentalist Egyptian organization the Muslim Brotherhood. They soon made their influence felt. Brought into the Sudan by Egyptian school teachers, the Brotherhood established cells in secondary schools and at the University of Khartoum.

At first, their political purpose seemed to consist of fighting the Sudanese Communist Party and supporting the Nimeiri military dictatorship. Its influence in Sudanese politics seemed small. However, in 1985, it merged with other extreme fundamentalist elements in the Sudan and became the National Islamic Front (NIF). Its goal was the transformation of the Sudan into a militant Islamic republic.

In 1987, the NIF asserted that historically, Muslims are not familiar with secularism and have a legitimate right, by virtue of the tenets of their faith, the fact they are the majority, and the rightness and purity of Islam, to impose their will throughout the country. The guiding light of the NIF was its leader Dr. Hassan Turabi. His policy is that Islamic jurisprudence shall be the general source of law in all of the Sudan. It is an expression of the will of the democratic majority, no matter what non-Muslim's may feel. This idea has been fanned from a spark at independence to the full-blown fiery Islamic extremism of the Sudanese government today.

From independence down to the present, Islamic chauvinism and intolerance have failed to peaceably integrate the different communities within the Sudan into a harmonious state. In a perversion of democracy, Sudan's fundamentalists claim that since Muslims are the majority of Sudanese, Islam should be the official religion. The fact that non-Muslim southern Christians and Animists disagree just means they will have to have the faith of Allah crammed down their throats.

The fundamentalists in the Sudan have always felt that way

but couldn't do anything about it as long as the British were ruling the country. After independence, it has been a consistent policy of theirs even if they lacked the political power to impose their will early in post-independent Sudan.

Islamic fundamentalism's fortunes took a giant step forward during the Nimeiri regime. Nimeiri, a power-hungry army officer, seized power in a coup d'etat in 1969. At first, he brutally suppressed the fundamentalists, then quickly reversed himself and began playing them off against other groups in the time-tested manner of divide and rule. He roused the fundamentalist ire, however, when he made a 1972 truce ending the on-going civil war between the Muslim north and non-Muslim south.

Dominating, Islamizing, and Arabizing the Christian southern Sudanese were policies pursued by all the dominant political groups in Khartoum before and after Nimeieri's coup. They were clearly expressed by the leaders of those groups. For example, the Minister of Education, Sayed Zinda Arbab, asserted in a January 1962 speech at Juba that national unity implied the universal adoption of Arabic as the national language and Islam as the national religion.

In his maiden address to the Constituent Assembly on October 1964, Sayed Saddiq El Mahdi, the Prime Minister, said, "The dominant feature of our nation is an Islamic one and its overpowering expression is Arab, and this nation will not have its entity identified and its prestige and pride preserved except under an Islamic revival."

Dr. Hassan El Turabi, the leader of the Islamic Front, expressed himself in a similar vein. He argued the people in southern Sudan had no culture, so this vacuum would necessarily be filled by Arab culture in the course of an Islamic revival.

The 1972 agreement provided for a degree of autonomy for

the south and recognized their religious convictions, which further angered the Islamic fundamentalists.

The fundamentalists wanted revenge. They struck back by infiltrating the military and attempted a coup of their own against Nimeiri. With Egyptian help, he defeated the coup attempt but it served as a warning—he had a serious problem on his hands with the fundamentalists. The dictator had to do something about them in order to stay in power. A survivalist at heart, he solved the problem by inviting them into his government.

Nimeiri moved closer and closer to the fundamentalist's position with blatant attempts to buy their support by promising to make his government more Islamic. His catering to them just increased the fundamentalist's demands. He made more concessions. Matters came to a head in 1983 and, by presidential decree, the so-called September Laws became the law of the Sudan.

The September Laws replaced secular laws and the post-colonial legal system with the Islamic *shari'a,* or holy law. By imposing the holy law, Nimeiri claimed to have seen the light, underwent a moral conversion, and claimed it was his duty as a Muslim ruler to found an Islamic order.

It was a clever political move on his part. With the help of the September Laws he pandered to the Islamic fundamentalists, undercut the secular leaders, and could claim that he alone had achieved what no other Sudanese politician had done since the *Mahdi* in the 1880s: establish God's Kingdom on Earth—at least in the Sudan.

Nimeiri's Islamization was initially popular in Muslim Sudan: public floggings and amputations drew large supportive crowds, and were seen as measures fighting the growing lawlessness in the country. However, Nimeiri's regime grew increasingly repressive. The indiscriminate use of flogging, and the imposition of Islamic laws on non-Muslims quickly undermined his support at home and abroad.

The result was chaos. The south erupted into open rebellion and the truce signed at Addis Abba eleven years earlier was shattered. The civil war resumed as Khartoum brutally tried to impose its intolerant rule by the sword.

Famine broke out and added to Nimeiri's problems of growing corruption and dictatorial abuses of power. Riots and demonstrations erupted. There were widespread strikes and a general breakdown in economic life in the country. The boiling point was reached in 1985 and a bloodless coup ousted Nimeiri while he was on a visit to the United States.

It was only a temporary respite. The famine and the civil war continued and political turmoil increased. The coup leaders ruled through the Traditional Military Council (TMC), a collection of high-ranking military officers. The TMC was ineffectual, prepared to do little more than preserve the status quo and divert the people's attention from the misery in their midst and the civil war in the south by staging public show trials of former Nimeiri supporters. It was not a policy that promised a long reign.

It was quickly replaced in 1986 by a coalition government. This regime, the first democratic government in seventeen years, proved incapable of governing. It dithered and did nothing on the major issues: the *shari'a,* negotiating a solution to the civil war in the south. It didn't take any action to improve the worsening economy.

One of the members of the coalition was the fundamentalist NIF party. Dr. Hassan Turabi, the party leader, had demanded, as a condition of NIF participation in the government, that more new Islamic laws be enacted. This demand and the resulting creeping Islamization was a fact of life for the five various coalition governments between 1986 and the latest coup d'etat in 1989. The question of Islamic law had become a destructive bone of contention in Sudanese politics since Nimeiri's September Laws. It poisoned the atmosphere and its corrosive effects added to the growing chaos in the Sudan. With the twenty-first century looming just ahead, and while two million Sudanese were facing starvation, the coup leaders seemed more concerned with how to amputate hands rather than how to feed the hungry in their midst.

This attitude was summed up by Turabi who proclaimed in the official Sudan Democrat Gazette that all those starving to death in the Sudan was a "small price to pay" for upholding the Islamic revolution in the Sudan. Crucial to that revolution was the imposition of Islamic law on all Sudanese—Muslim as well as non-Muslim.

The question would be settled, according to General Omar Bashir, the 1989 coup leader, by submitting it to a national referendum. This proposal was a sham as the 60-79 percent Muslim majority in the north had more votes than the non-Muslim south. But the fundamentalists were taking no chances. They opposed the idea of a referendum under the claim the September Laws cannot be repealed by man since man cannot tamper with the Word of God.

Bashir caved in. On December 31, 1990, his regime promised to implement the Islamic law. In partnership with the NIF, an Islamic republic was established in the Sudan.

The new Islamic republic was no improvement on prior Sudan governments. It, like its predecessors, seemed incapable of solving the almost insurmountable problems in the Sudan. Nor did it have many friends in the Sunni Muslim world. But help was on the way from an unlikely ally—Shi'ite Iran.

Iran was expanding its good relations with Sunni fundamentalist movements in the Muslim world by down-playing religious differences between Sunnis and Shi'ites in the common crusade of Islam against the infidel—especially the West. So it was not surprising that Iran has become a chief supporter and ally of the Sudan's radical Sunni fundamentalist state.

In December 1991, Iranian President Rafsanjani made an official state visit to Khartoum. He promised to help the beleaguered government by giving $17 million worth of financial aid, underwriting $300 million worth of weapons purchases from China and promised them an annual subsidy of a million tons of free Iranian oil.

But there was also a quid pro quo. After Rafsanjani's visit, at least 2,000 Iranian Revolutionary Guards were sent to the Sudan to train the Sudan army and help it in its genocidal campaign in the south.

All of this is done in the name of Allah as the Khartoum regime has imposed the Islamic religious law upon the nation. Public debate in the Sudan has been silenced and political parties have been banned. The Sudanese Supreme Court has even upheld the right of authorities to extract confessions under torture, and legitimized cruel punishments as being compatible with Islamic law. The enforcement of that code is particularly barbaric for Sudanese: floggings, amputations, death by stoning, and even the reported death and crucifixion of children as young as seven.

Crucifixion was the barbaric method of execution used by the Romans. Its cruel use caused the death of Jesus Christ and the cross is still the symbol of Christianity. Muslim Sudanese executioners use six-inch long nails to crucify their Christian victims. "There is no clear reason," said a Sudanese Anglican bishop, "except that they are Christians. The government is persecuting those who are Christian leaders, because they want the people to all become Muslims."

These on-going atrocities in the Sudan are reminiscent of the death camp policies of Hitler, Stalin, Mao and Pol Pot. What is different about the tragedy in the Sudan is that its atrocities are driven by a crusading religious creed—militant Islamic extremism.

Chapter 14
Sudan: Tears in the Sand

So 'ere's to you, Fuzzy-Wuzzy, at you 'ome in the Sowdan;
You're a pore benighted 'eathen but a first class fightn' man,
An' 'ere's to you, Fuzzy-Wuzzy, with your 'agrich 'ead of hair—
You big black boundin' bugger—for you brok a British square.
Rudyard Kipling, Fuzzy-Wuzzy

In the early 1820s, the Ottoman governor of Egypt, Mahomet Ali, launched a series of attacks on the Sudan. His goals were two-fold: expand Egypt's border southward, and secure a steady source of slaves. Ali sent his 25-year old son, Ishmail, at the head of a 10,000 man army to secure both objectives. 30,000 slaves were collected and sent back to Cairo in the first slave caravan, but only half survived the journey. Unfortunately for Ishmail, he was killed in a Sudanese counterattack, but by 1823, after the deaths of over 50,000 Sudanese, the Sudan was under Egyptian control.

The Sudan quickly became the favorite hunting ground for slave raiders. They pursued their trade with a grim, determined fervor. An early European explorer spoke of "those vile ruffian traders on the White Nile...The atrocities committed by these traders are beyond civilized belief. They are constantly fighting, robbing, and capturing slaves and cattle. No honest man can either trade or travel in the country; for the natives have been bullied to such an extent that they either fight or run away, according to their strength or circumstances."

Those words were written in the middle of the 19th century. They are just as valid in the Sudan today, almost one hundred and fifty years later.

As we approach the Third Millennium, one can take no comfort from conditions in the southern Sudan today. They are appalling and none of its inhabitants enjoy a decent quality of life. Such a time has now become only a memory of the aged, a fleeting moment in time when it was British imperialism that imposed security of life in the southern Sudan.

• • •

The river curves in a great horseshoe band of blue and green between banks of golden sand. The villagers fish from dugout canoes, swim and wash, their gossipy chatter floating up on a soft breeze. Children are playing in the village of thatched *turkals,* the traditional round houses of the southern Sudan.

The sights and sounds are idyllic and give no hint of the orgy of destruction about to engulf the village near the end of the twentieth century.

The thunderous sound of horses makes the villagers drop their hoes and scatter into the surrounding bush. Gunfire erupts around the village as 300 men on horseback, camels and on foot, charged through the fields of maize clustered around the huts. Within minutes the attackers have killed almost a hundred villagers.

The raiders are members of the Muslim militia, the Sudan government's Popular Defense Force (PDF) from the north. They're on a slave raid.

The survivors are herded together outside the village and, under guard, watch their village being looted and destroyed. First the raiders seize the cattle, then they move from hut to hut gathering food, blankets and people who have tried to hide inside.

The fearful survivors, mostly old men, women and children, watch in horror as a raider takes a match from his pocket and lites the tinder-dry thatch of the hut. As it flares into flames, the slaver goes behind the hut and sets fire to the family's annual harvest, a few bags of sorghum. Then he returns and burns the few jars containing sesame seeds saved to be pressed for oil.

His task finished, the Arab slave raider moves methodically through the village systematically torching everything that remains.

The village is a scene of total destruction, the acrid smell of smoke from the burning huts and crops hangs thick in the air, mingling with settling dust kicked up by the hoofs of the horses and camels. Swarms of black flies are already landing on the dead, turning reddish wounds into pulsating, humming carpets of black. Vultures are gathering in the trees, patiently awaiting their feast.

A dejected sense of despair fills the surviving villagers as they await their fate. Life at the moment is pretty bleak. It will soon get worse.

The raiders quickly separate the old, ill and injured and are ready to march the rest off into a life of slavery. But, there is one more task to perform and the PDF leader holds up his hand halting the preparations for the march.

In order to make an example of those opposing the government who fled into the bush, the leader of the raid prepares to add another atrocity to those already committed. The village is some twenty miles inside an area of the Sudan under the nominal control of the rebel Sudanese People's Liberation Army (SPLA) and most of them are Christians.

The leader sweeps his eyes over those chosen for a life of bondage and stops on a young girl holding a baby in her arms. The young mother, no older than sixteen, with the neck of a swan and the legs skinny as antennae, turns her head, avoiding the stare.

The leader quickly orders three of his men to grab the girl and her baby. As her arms are pinned to her side by two of the raiders, he takes his razor-sharp knife out of its sheath and slices off the girl's breasts. Turning to the man holding the baby, he takes it and thrusts the terrified, crying infant back to its mother.

Unable to suckle her child, both mother and child would soon perish, a warning of what to expect for daring to resist the Islamization efforts of fundamentalist Sudan.

After this act of barbarism, the leader mounts his horse and leads the raiders and their captives north. The raiders will sell their human booty to Muslim masters for between $15 and $95 a person. These slaves will be outfitted in a standard slave uniform, a red *jallabia,* which is easy to recognize if the slaves attempt to escape.

Finally, the slave caravan reaches the village which serves as the base for the PDF slave raiders. It is located next to a bush garrison of the Sudan army. The time to divide the booty is at hand. The stories of escapees from this and other raids give a consistent account of what usually happens next.

First, the slavers celebrate the success of their recent raid and report its success to the local Sudan military leader. Then the military and the PDF divide the loot: half to the army garrison, half to the PDF.

Everyone takes whatever kind of person they want. Anyone

who wants a small boy takes him, or a older man who the captor thinks may make a good man-servant. Women, however, are the most sought after prizes.

Rank has its privileges and the officers get the first choice. They select the prettiest girls to be their "wives" or concubines. Other women are taken to so-called "peace camps" which are little more than brothels for the soldiers. The troops come at night and take the women to their barracks or private quarters for a series of rapes.

Every captive women who has been in a "peace camp" has either been raped or threatened with rape. Girls as young as nine years old have been raped—with the rapers justifying it by the Hadith of Islam. The Hadith is a record of the words and deeds of the Prophet and are viewed by Muslims as divinely inspired. Next to the Koran, it is the most important source of Islamic law and its teachings are regarded as binding on all Muslims. Having sex with a nine year-old is justified because Muhammad had married one of his wives, Aisha, when she was nine.

Women have been raped when they were captured by the raiders, gang-raped upon arrival at garrisons, and repeatedly raped in the "peace camps." Through this crime, the government hopes to create a generation of children who do not belong to their mother's culture, bringing shame on the women as well as the children they bear.

In addition to being holding areas for slaves, the "peace camps" serve other functions as well. At present about 1.2 million Sudanese are in these concentration camps. They are concentration camps in the truest sense of the word: Muslim opponents of the government are held there; many of the rural population of the south has been collected in the camps under the government's infamous "tamshits" or "combing" plan.

Triumph of Disorder

The "combing" program is a facelift given to the government's prior ethnic cleansing campaign which generated too much adverse publicity.

The policy—draining the sea to catch the fish as one put it—involves depopulating the southern rebel areas by a combination of a scorched earth and forced removal policy. PDF slave raids are a key element in "combing."

Unlimited power is given to the PDF and military. Aerial bombardments and deliberate attacks on villages leave the people defenseless. Soldiers shoot at random, gunning down anyone they find. Grass huts are set ablaze, often with the inhabitants forced to remain inside.

Once a village is raided by either the army or PDF, torture and torment quickly become the norm. Women and children are abducted, taken into a life of slavery. The boys are sent to Muslim religious schools for "re-education" before being sold as workers or servants. Should they refuse to adapt to their new life, they are repeatedly beaten and often put in heavy chains.

Collecting and concentrating people from the rebel areas into camps enables the government to control their movement, and to provide a captive population for indoctrination, forced Islamization, forced labor and conscription into the army or PDF.

Hundreds of thousands of people are forced at gunpoint to abandon their traditional villages, which are then burned to the ground, and marched to the "peace camps." These unfortunate souls suffer appalling hardships during the long forced death marches. Denied adequate food or medical aid while on the march or in the camps, they die by the thousands. Since the Khartoum regime has been fought to a military stalemate by the SPLA, the government is concentrating the bulk of its efforts on defenseless villages and unarmed civilians.

Both the Sudan army and the PDF are engaged in the systematic destruction of all villages. Whatever can't be carried away is destroyed. The soldiers and militia members can kill with complete impunity. Old or disabled people who cannot run away are generally killed, or left behind after torture to instill fear in others.

An aggressive program of Islamization and Arab acculturation is carried out, seeking to force "peace camp" inmates to convert to Islam.

In particular, food is being used as a weapon to impoverish and subjugate the Christian and animist Sudanese. Without exception, both secular and Christian relief agencies from the West working throughout the Sudan testify that the Sudan government discriminates against non-Muslims in its distribution of food aid. Although some local leaders of Islamic relief agencies cooperate in distributing food to Muslims, food is frequently withheld from Christians and Animists, including small children, until they convert to Islam.

Food distribution is controlled by the Commissioner of the Displaced (COD) who is a member of the Muslim Brotherhood, which wields power in the Sudan through the National Islamic Front (NIF), the ruling party in the Sudan.

The COD tightly controls refugee food distribution, authorizing only three Islamic relief agencies to distribute food in refugee camps in accordance with the government's stated policy of Islamization and Arabization. The Sudanese Council of Churches (SCC) is also permitted to carry out limited food relief and only in designated camps.

In December 1991, the COD ruled that food relief can only be distributed in new camps being created by the government as part of their "combing" policy.

Triumph of Disorder

The construction of these new camps was preceded by a so-called government "land survey" in the areas where refugees had built squatter camps. They told the refugees they were on the land "illegally" and the government would have to move them to new camps which were more sanitary. Then the authorities began bulldozing acre after acre of the crude shelters.

According to refugees who managed to escape, the new camps were not an improvement. "They took us on transport trucks in the middle of nowhere," one escapee said. "We didn't want to get down...There was no sign of life anywhere."

Conditions in the camps, according to SCC sources, is appalling. The church official elaborated on the winter move to one of the camps, as-Salaam: "In November, it was freezing and the people in as-Salaam had no covers. Parents dug holes and buried their babies in the sand, leaving only their faces uncovered, to keep them from freezing to death."

In the camps, the Islamic relief organizations have established *khalwas* (Islamic schools) which teach only Arabic and the Koran. They require the children to memorize the Islamic creed and verses from the Koran. Rosters are then drawn up which determine who will receive food.

According to Roman Catholic officials, some clerics have encouraged small children to say the Islamic expressions so they will not starve. In the food lines, adults are asked their names to determine if they are Muslims. "If he says *Allahu akbar* (God is great), he receives his corn flour," reports the SCC. Many convert so that they can feed their families.

The same thing happens to children. Inside the refugee camps, they line up with cups to receive their milk ration and are asked to give their name. A response with a Muslim name earns the child his ration. And if they say the Muslim creed extra loud, they get an extra portion, while children who give a Christian name are turned away.

The cost of the human suffering in the Sudan staggers the imagination: since 1983 more than 1.5 million people have been killed and more than 5 million displaced out of a southern Sudan population of 8 million.

Slavery is another tool the Sudanese government uses in its campaign to crush the rebellion in the southern Sudan and impose Islam on the Christian inhabitants. The southern non-Muslims have little desire to switch religions. Few are doing so willingly.

A captured PDF officer, Farjellah Wada Mather, confirmed the existence of the government's sponsorship of slavery: "We were armed by the Government of the Sudan to fight; we were asked to collect children, sheep, goats and cattle and we used to burn some houses. Whatever was taken belonged to the PDF and was our income." Other captured Sudanese army soldiers and officers confirmed Mather's statement.

The Islamic fundamentalist regime of Sudan was grotesquely clever in its means of encouraging slavery. They arm the PDF militia but don't pay them. The government points them in the right direction, and they collect their pay with whatever booty they can loot, (property or human beings). In this manner, the Sudan government can blame the existence of slavery on rogue elements in the PDF.

It is a flimsy charade and even the United Nations sees through it. In a February 1996 report titled the "Situation of human rights in the Sudan," the UN blasted the Sudan government's policy on slavery. The U.N couldn't find any action taken by the Government of the Sudan to investigate cases brought to its attention or to bring an end to the practice of the sale of and traffic of children. The only conclusion the U.N. could come up with was the practice of slavery and traffic in children meets with the tacit approval of the government of the Sudan.

The fact that slavery exists today as the world approaches the twenty-first century is morally reprehensible. Our bloodiest conflict, the Civil War, was fought over slavery and our civil rights legislation reflects efforts to eradicate the aftereffects of that shameful period of our history.

Yet, now, at the dawn of the 21st century, slavery goes unchecked in the Sudan. America, along with the U.N. sees it. But its presence is greeted with silence. There are no Garrisons or Emersons today thundering against the evils of Sudanese slavery. Nor has Jesse Jackson or other civil rights leaders spoken out on it, although they aren't hesitant to voice an opinion on other matters.

If it isn't on the evening news it apparently doesn't exist. That seems to be the attitude of our coach potato society.

Well it does exist and it is killing and dehumanizing hundreds of thousands of our fellow human beings in the Sudan. Their agony demands both spokesmen and action. To turn a blind eye to it not only diminishes us as individuals living in a free society, but makes a mockery of those values and freedoms we are so willing to trumpet to others.

This silence will not eradicate the evil of slavery from the Sudan. It just encourages the leaders in Khartoum to continue their heinous crimes against humanity. And the poor southern Sudanese continue to be the prey of vicious slave raiding Muslims from the north.

Unfortunately, the chaotic conditions facing the world in the coming new world disorder may see the crime of slavery reappear in other parts of the world. That, however, doesn't make the evil any less tolerable.

The re-birth of slavery, despicable enough in itself, is just part of the Khartoum regime's campaign of forced Islamization of the non-Muslim southern Sudan.

The Sudan air force indiscriminately and deliberately bombs villages in non-Muslim areas of the southern Sudan and even attempts to shoot down planes carrying refugee relief aid supplies. Helicopter gunships, MIG-23 fighter bombers and Antonov aircraft bomb market places and villages with impunity because the SPLA lacks adequate air defense weapons. They have no more shoulder launched "Red Eye" missiles, and the Sudan government know this. So their bombers fly and bomb at will throughout the southern Sudan.

Cluster bombs are now routinely used by the Sudan government to spread even more destruction on their bombing raids against the infidel southern Sudanese. The aim is to destroy and depopulate the area.

Reports of humanitarian agencies underscore the ruthlessness of Sudan's Islamic regime's genocidal campaign against its non-Muslim citizens. Humanitarian aid is failing to reach hundreds of thousands of victims of war and famine. The Government of Sudan continues to refuse to give access to SPLA administered areas in the Nuba Mountains and to other areas. The denial of access means that thousands of people are dying from lack of food and medicines.

The Government of Sudan continues to try to transform, by force, the ethnically and religiously diverse country into an Arab, Islamic state, against the wishes of the vast majority of its non-Muslim population. The devastating effects of this policy are nothing more than ill-disguised genocide.

Genocide is the goal of the Sudan leaders in Khartoum. They don't refer to it as a civil war between the state and a group of dissenting citizens, but as a holy war by Muslims against infidels. Every non-Muslim and non-Arab is an enemy of the state.

Church officials in the West have received reports that hundreds of thousands of rural Sudanese have been executed under the pretext they are "rebels" or just *kafir* (the Arabic term for infidels, i.e. non-Muslims).

"They gain merit by killing so many *kafir*," said one church official. "Before they shoot, they say *bismallah* (in the name of God), and then afterwards they say *Allahu akbar* (God is great)."

The Islamic republic in the Sudan is systematically trying to destroy the fabric of southern Sudanese society by means of terror and mass starvation. In short, it is following a policy of extermination.

Khartoum's holy war of genocide has created catastrophic conditions in the southern Sudan. The war has wreaked havoc on the southern Sudan infrastructure, deliberately destroying the economic, health care, education and communications systems. The southern Sudan has become a wasteland where food production and distribution is minimal and disease threatens to spread beyond its borders.

Genghis Khan skillfully used terror as his Golden Horde swept aside his opponents. Those who resisted or rebelled against his authority were ruthlessly dealt with. More than one rebellious city in his empire was wiped out, the severed heads of its citizens piled in heaps outside the city walls as an example to others. Such gruesome acts caused many would-be enemies to tremble in fear and submit without a fight.

His use of terror worked because he had both the will and the ability to carry it out.

The terror campaign of the Sudan government is failing because of its lack of success against the southern Sudanese. Like Genghis, the Islamic fundamentalists in the Sudan have no qualms against using terror and slaughtering innocents. Unlike the Great Khan, their efforts haven't paralyzed their opponents with fear. Instead, they've only encouraged a fatalistic "what have we got to lose" resistance on the part of the southern Sudanese.

Even though the Sudan government has the preponderance of military power, the war is not winnable for the Sudan Army. Over 90% of the southern Sudan is now in the hands of rebel forces. The Sudan military and governmental presence is limited to a few besieged garrison towns which require resupply either by air or massively guarded convoys, protected by tanks and helicopter gunships—convoys that are susceptible to devastating ambushes by hit and run rebel bands.

The harsh terrain, vast swamps, wide rivers, dense vegetation and rolling hills of the southern Sudan are ideal for unconventional war.

The southern Sudanese people are uncompromisingly opposed to the attempt to cram Islamic fundamentalism down their throats. The war is also a huge financial drain on the government and is further impoverishing an already heavily indebted regime. Neither is the war popular with the army soldiers and they lack the will and the means to win.

It is a war that amply fulfills the Van Creveld prophecy on the conduct of war in the future.

The Islamic fundamentalists, however, show no desire to reverse their goal of Islamizing the whole Sudan. The war will not end peacefully as long as the regime insists on an Islamic republic. The non-Muslim Sudanese are certainly not interested in any so-called Islamic "benevolence." The bombs, bullets and mass starvation are already enough Muslim "charity."

Without seeking the consent of those to be governed, without a ratification of their leaders' proposals, without a determination of their status within the existing constitutional framework, the current policies of the Sudan government will surely fail. This fundamental condition of democracy and the rule of the people, for the people and by the people is usually decided by self-determination. But self-determination as a precondition for any resolution to "The Problem of the Southern Sudan," has appeared so threatening that every Sudanese government in Khartoum has refused to even consider it.

The present fundamentalist government has never seriously contemplated self-determination for the peoples of the southern Sudan. Self-determination is feared because those Sudanese who insist upon a united Sudan fear the southerners will vote to go their separate way.

The choice for the Sudan is simple: either a just, democratic Sudan which is inclusive for all its racial, cultural and religious diversities—an almost insurmountable task given the centuries-old hatreds between Muslims and non-Muslims; or consign the present Sudan state to the dustbin of history and allow the non-Muslim south to separate and become independent from the Arab north.

Separation is a logical move but, in the current international climate, is unlikely to occur. The Organization of African Unity (OAU) considers *all* existing borders sacred and written in stone. To allow succession in one African country will, in their view, open the floodgates to change the artificial boundaries drawn up in colonial times. Nor will the current government of the Sudan be keen on losing "their" southern regions.

As the collapse of nation states increases, separation and secession will become more and more common, especially on the African continent.

Separation, while most logical and desirable, will not ensure a stable independent South Sudan. They are now somewhat united because they have a common enemy, the Islamic invaders from the north. Remove that threat and age-old ethnic, tribal and cultural animosities will resurface. Instead of fighting the Arabs from the north they will fight among themselves—as they have for centuries.

In this, even though others may view them as backward cultures, they will be quite at home in the violence of the new world disorder.

Even separation from the Arab north won't end the danger from Islam. Given the messianic nature of Islamic fundamentalism, a separate south will always face the danger of an Islamic invasion from the north. It has been a fact of life for centuries, and shows no sign of stopping.

The Sudanese government is making some halfhearted attempts to dispel Western apprehension of Sudan's role in carrying Islamic fundamentalism throughout the world. In one such bid in 1992, Hassan al-Turabi, the de facto power in the Sudan spoke of a benign "Islamic renaissance."

"I'm trying to tell my audiences," he told *Newsweek* in June 1992, "that the values which are dear to them are also common to Islam: Free government, a human being's freedom and dignity, a free economic system with an emphasis on justice."

But the government's campaign of Islamization in the Sudan appears to be proceeding more along the lines spelled out by Ibn Khaldun, the 14th Century North African historian and Islamic jurist. Non-Muslims, especially Christians, he said, have three choices: conversion to Islam, payment of the *jizya* (poll tax), or death.

The Sudan Minister of State, Ghazi Salah el Din told a meeting of the Foreign Ministers of Uganda, Kenya, Ethiopia and Eritrea on September 6, 1994 in Nairobi that the Sudan state has a "divine mission of Islamizing Africa."

With an attitude like that war, chaos and desolation will be a predicable Hobbsean-Van Creveld nightmarish future.

In January 1997, an alliance of opponents of the Khartoum regime launched coordinated attacks against Sudan government forces in the Blue Nile province. The attacks were launched from rebel bases in Ethiopia and Eritrea. The "United Opposition Forces of North and Southern Sudan" under the overall military command of Colonel John Garang launched an offensive into the Eastern Sudan along its borders with Eritrea and Ethiopia.

Although the major thrust of the United Forces has been undertaken by Garang's SPLA down the Blue Nile from Kurmuk on the Ethiopian border, armed units of the National Democratic Alliance have been engaged in piecemeal guerrilla attacks against government forces throughout the Eastern Sudan. In the Red Sea hills are the redoubtable Fuzzy-Wuzzies of Kipling fame operating as the Beja Congress and reminiscent of the feared Blemmyes who forced the Romans to withdraw from Nubia to Aswan and contributed to the collapse of the Kingdom of Kush in the fourth century. Further south along the Eritrean frontier near Kassala numerous firefights have been reported between the government militia and deserters from the

Sudanese army, who call themselves the New Sudan Brigade and the Sudanese Allied Forces supported by units of the SPLA.

Nevertheless, except for the important line of communications between Khartoum and Port Sudan which passes through Kassala, the seizure of territory by the rebels has little strategic value except for the Roseires Dam 300 miles southeast of Khartoum on the Blue Nile at Damazin. This dam supplies 80% of the electricity for the three towns, Khartoum, Khartoum North, and Omdurman.

The military capabilities of the SPLA and its new allies are uncertain. After the fall of Menghistu in Ethiopia, the SPLA's main source of support, schisms appeared within the ranks of the SPLA. Thus, there is doubt the SPLA forces under John Garang are any stronger than when they first advanced down the Blue Nile from Kurmak in 1987. But neither are the forces of the Sudan government capable of imposing its will by force of arms. The reputation and effectiveness of the Sudan People's Armed Forces has dramatically declined during the past ten years. The officers corps has been purged, the enlisted ranks have been replaced with Islamic militias who have suffered heavy casualties while winning no victories, Morale among the remaining regular officers and men has plummeted as gauged by the large number of desertions to the rebels.

At the same time, efforts to enlist students from the University of Khartoum into "Jihad Units" of the Popular Defense Force militia to seek martyrdom is a vivid example of panic triumphing over patriotism. The unpopularity of the regime and the grievances flowing deep within the Sudanese promise stormy days ahead for the government.

Immediately after the fall of Kurmak on January 13, 1997, Sudan Vice-President al-Zubayr Muhammad Salih was sent to scour the Arab capitals in search of support against the invaders only to be rebuffed with the rejoinder that the dispute was strictly an internal affair.

The response from Iran was, however, more encouraging and within a week Russian tanks, aircraft, and heavy weapons were arriving in Khartoum. Whether the Revolutionary Guards advisors who accompanied the equipment can repair the damage and disarray in the Sudan army appears doubtful.

Even less effective is the determination of the Bashir government to open a second front in SPLA heartland in southern Equatoria Province by using surrogates in Acholiland, and the Lord's Resistance Army as well as his Kakwa collaborators of the West Nile Bank Front under Juma Oris, former foreign minister to Idi Amin, to increase the tempo of bandit depredations along the Sudan-Uganda border.

The situation appears headed to a long, bloody stalemate.

The rebel attacks took on added significant by coming just a few weeks after Saddiq Mahdi, the former leader of the Sudan, ousted in a coup in 1989 by the current Islamic fundamentalist government, fled Khartoum and received asylum in Asmara, Eritrea.

The use of external bases by the Sudanese rebels indicates some of Sudan's neighbors are becoming more and more concerned with the specter of a second Iran on their doorstep. The attempted assassination of Egyptian President Mubarak in June 1995 when gunmen ambushed his motor cavalcade in Addis Abba, Ethiopia opened a lot of eyes to the growing menace in their midst.

Cairo charged the Sudan government with responsibility for the attempt and the United Nations imposed diplomatic and travel sanctions against the Sudanese regime for failing to extradite three suspects to Ethiopia to stand trial for the attack.

Under these circumstances, some of Sudan's neighbors, chiefly Eritrea, Ethiopia and Uganda began cooperating with one another and Sudanese rebel groups to take action against the Khartoum government. The January offensive was an example of this cooperation.

The Sudan government responded to the attacks by calling for "a general mobilization" to wage a "holy war" against the enemies of the Islamic republic, and requested a meeting of the U.N. Security Council to consider the threat.

One of the objectives of the rebel attacks was the city of Damazin on the southern Blue Nile. The city is the site of a hydro-electric power station that supplies power to Khartoum.

The attacks also showed the SPLA was opening a new front in its campaign to defeat the government forces. The SPLA has claimed the capture of a substantial swath of the eastern Sudan. The rebels will now attempt to use this territory to take further offensive action against the Islamic government in the capital, some 350 miles away.

SPLA officials believe this is where they can win the war. The war can only be won, they feel, by capturing Khartoum—a highly dubious prospect.

The government's response was a scorched earth policy similar to the one it used in the southern Sudan. The government has bombed and burned villages suspected of harboring rebels. Over 50,000 eastern Sudanese have become refugees as a result. The government has also made the territory held by the rebels off limits to aid and humanitarian groups, adding to the misery in the Sudan.

The SPLA's dream of a final offensive on Khartoum may be wishful thinking. Guerrilla forces are notorious for their lack of ability to defeat conventional forces in conventional battles. As long as the Sudan government has the will to keep fighting and doesn't collapse on its own accord, it can rally sufficient support by playing the Islam versus the infidel card and hang on, even if only by the skin of their teeth. Nevertheless, the rebel action has weakened the Sudan government's hold on more of its remote territory.

As a result of the new united opposition, something of potential significance has happened. For the first time all the opposition parties, at one time and in one place, have signed a document—the Asmara Agreement—affirming their pledge to the principle of self-determination.

In the past opposition leaders have given lip service to self-determination, but now the sincerity of their signatures is a grudging acknowledgment that no future government in Khartoum can rule without such an agreement. Such a realization may be the best guarantee that self-determination will be honored and not become just another passing political promise.

It will still be a rocky road to travel. The SPLA leader Garang has had to reconcile his belief in a new, but united Sudan, with the southerner's demand for independence. He, like his opposition allies, realize that only by a mutual alliance will the possibility of overthrowing the Islamic regime in Khartoum become a probability. The price for success will be the right of the southerners to have the choice: independence or a united Sudan.

Although the 1989 coup was carried out by army officers, their ability to remain in power would have been nonexistent without the support of the National Islamic Front whose leader Hassan al-Turabi became the most powerful individual in the Sudan. He has used his power to wreck any negotiations which appeared to grant reasonable terms to the southern Sudanese. His policies have led the government into isolation as a world pariah, facing United Nations sanctions, expulsion from the International Monetary Union, and universal condemnation for Sudan's support of world terrorism.

There is no secret within and without the Sudan that the present regime is devoid of any popular support. There is war-weariness after years of conflict without victories and only body bags, and the deterioration of the economy from which no Sudanese can escape. Crushing taxation, uncontrolled inflation, the collapse of essential services, the decline of agricultural production, collapse of the Sudanese currency, unmanageable debt, a three-million-dollar-a-day war, have all destroyed the quality of life in the Sudan.

Faced with this appalling list of conditions, it is a wonder the Khartoum regime survives. It survives because of three constituents which it relies upon to keep the Islamic Republic alive—force, Islam, and its allies.

First, the Bashir government has built a formidable security system which it is determined to use any means without restraint to ensure its survival.

Second, the Islamic Republic has no doubts as to the source of its inspiration. It has claimed responsibility for the most treasured possession of any man, his soul and its salvation, by assuming the uplifting but burdensome duties as the Defender of the Faith, the Protector of Islam. To some Sudanese the abandonment of the Islamic Republic is tantamount to disavowing one's faith.

Third, the present Sudanese government has allies. Iraq remembers the diplomatic support Khartoum gave it during the Gulf War when all its Arab brothers deserted Baghdad. Unfortunately for Sudan, Iraq's gratitude is constrained by its own international isolation and internal troubles.

Iran is a different matter. It circumstances are not as constrained as Iraq's. No sooner had Turabi given his stamp of approval to the 1989 coup than his representatives were meeting with Iranian President Rafsanjani. Iran's steadfast support for Sudan's Islamic Republic was motivated by a common cause in an unholy alliance between Shi'ite and Sunni Muslims to promote Islam in the southern Sudan as part of a larger religious mission to spread Islam into Sub-Saharan Africa.

President Rafsanjani had already declared a *jihad* against the southern Sudanese insurgents as a prelude to his state visit to the Sudan in December 1991. When he returned to Khartoum in September 1996 he reaffirmed Iran's support to the Sudan. It would continue to receive arms, oil, and Revolutionary Guard advisors in return for unlimited access to anchorage at Port Sudan for the Iranian navy and the continued support and sanctuary for Islamic terrorists.

The willingness of the Sudan government to become directly involved in terrorism has turned it into an outlaw nation.

While the SPLA may not be able to march on Khartoum and overthrow the Islamic republic, they have raised the costs to the regime to prolong its existence. The rebel offensive demonstrates the growing inability of the government to defeat the rebels. It also shows the growing capability of the SPLA to mount coordinated actions on more than one front.

The recent outbreak of hostilities between Ethiopia and Eritrea may reduce or eliminate their support of the SPLA. This will enable Khartoum to continue its genocidal policies against the southern Sudanese.

The agony of the Sudan will continue, with neither side in a position to impose its will on the other. The world's longest war of the twentieth century will likely carry over well into the Twenty-First

Century.

Chapter 15
New World Disorder

The first duty of any social entity is to protect the lives of its members. Either modern states cope with low-intensity conflict, or else they will disappear: the suspicion grows, however, that they are damned if they do and damned if they don't.

Martin Van Creveld

Sir William Osler observed that "humanity has but three great enemies: fever, famine and war." In Uganda and Zaire virulent strains of new epidemic diseases have appeared that are more deadly than the plagues of the Middle Ages. Famine has occurred in the Sahel, Sudan, Ethiopia and Somalia, and over 30 wars are being fought throughout the world.

As the new millennium approaches are we on the threshold of a golden age? Or are we standing on the edge of the abyss, facing chaos and troubled times?

The collapse of the Soviet Union was hailed by many as the dawn of a new world order. A vista of peace and prosperity was to open for the world now that fear of nuclear annihilation had been swept away.

Nowhere was this more evident than in President George Bush's address to a joint session of Congress on September 11, 1990 when he joyfully proclaimed that "a New World Order" was upon us. His prophecy was premature.

Almost a decade later, it is clear the world is becoming more unruly and dangerous. The Cold War, even with the threat of nuclear disaster, was somewhat orderly and predictable. Its demise has opened a modern-day Pandora's box of strife, crumbling societies, and a new world disorder.

The end of the Cold War swept aside the hatreds engendered by the clash of communism and capitalism. One set of hatreds is being replaced by others. Humanity faces a possibly more dangerous era of ethnic, racial, and cultural animosity.

As the United States has demonstrated, it is possible for people of different ethnic origins, religions, and cultures to live together peaceably in the same geographical area. But, as Arthur Schlesinger, Jr. points out, if there isn't a common bond or purpose uniting them together, "tribal hostilities will drive them apart."

There is ethnic, political, social, and economic chaos throughout the world as despots, would-be revolutionaries, drug barons, and terrorists, armed with increasingly lethal weapons, are taking advantage of the growing instability throughout the world.

Pollution and environmental degradation are threatening social and economic stability in parts of Africa. Deforestation, overgrazing, desertification, and overpopulation are drawing more and more people into sprawling shanty-towns surrounding the major cities.

Sub-Saharan Africa, with the exception of the continent's southern tip, is rapidly becoming a collection of colonial-imposed fictitious nations who are becoming increasingly ungovernable and are on the brink of dissolution.

The jury is still out on the future of the continent's southern tip. South Africa may go the way of its northern neighbors and join

Triumph of Disorder

them in coming apart at the seams. The collapse of Liberia into warlordism is a good example

West Africa is reverting to its 19th century status: a series of coastal enclaves serving as gateways to the outside world and an interior that is becoming virtually terra incognito. As the rural population surges into the cities on the West African coast, the entire coast from Abidjan in the Ivory Coast to Lagos in Nigeria, threatens to become one continuous megalopolis consisting of mostly poverty and disease-ridden shanty-towns.

Nigeria is a growing example of the dark future of nation states in sub-Saharan Africa. The former British colony had held out so much hope as being the model for post-colonial Africa. Nigeria consists of four principal tribal-based nations: the Hausa, Ibo, Yorbua, and Fulani.

It has already experienced a civil war which killed hundreds of thousands of people and afforded no real settlement. A series of military dictatorships has barely kept the peace and seems unlikely to hold the country together.

The growing confrontation between Islam and Christianity in Nigeria is adding fuel to the tribal conflicts. Islamic fundamentalism has reared its ugly head in the country and more religious strife lies ahead.

The U.S. State Department's assessment of Nigeria's future is pessimistic. The country is becoming increasingly ungovernable. Ethnic and regional splits are deepening and religious cleavages are becoming more serious. Muslim fundamentalism and evangelical Christian militancy are on the rise, and the will to keep Nigeria together is now very weak.

The Indian subcontinent is also seething with chaos and strife.

Both India and Pakistan are in danger of falling apart as centralized state bureaucracies struggle to govern diverse ethnic groups who have been historical enemies.

Once the unifying euphoria demonstrating the ability to build and detonate a nuclear device wears off in both countries, the underlying stresses and strains will reassert themselves. Neither country can afford the expensive costs involved in building up their nuclear arsenals. Such weapons will drain scarce, much-needed resources from other vital governmental programs. In the long run, the nuclear weapons may prevent attacks on each other, but they won't address the problems of internal disintegration.

India is torn by religious fanaticism and is trying to cope with several different armed insurgencies at the same time. Coping with this internal squabbling is a swollen, unwieldy bureaucracy in New Delhi, trying to govern almost a billion people of diverse languages, religions, and cultures.

It is well to remember that India was made up of several states and principalities who were constantly warring against each other at the time of the British arrival in India in the early 18th century. India is sliding towards a return of that pre-colonial situation as it approaches the 21st century.

India is also concerned over the instability of Pakistan and the rise of Islamic fundamentalism in Central Asia. India casts a wary eye on the sizeable number of Muslims living within its borders.

Pakistan's problems are more basic. The country is a post-World War II artificial nation set up as a homeland for the Muslims of the Indian sob-continent. The country makes little geographic or demographic sense. There are more Muslims living outside of Pakistan on the sub-continent than living within Pakistan's borders.

Triumph of Disorder

Yet most of the ethnic groups lumped together in Pakistan are long-standing enemies of one-another. Today clashes among them are frequent and increasingly violent.

Pakistan has already experienced fragmentation when East Pakistan broke away, with India's help, to form independent Bangladesh. Further fragmentation is likely in the future.

University of Toronto demographer Thomas Fraser Homer-Dixon thinks India and Pakistan will probably fall apart. Both secular governments have less and less legitimacy as well as less management ability over their people and resources.

China, touted by many as the new emerging Asian economic miracle, is also threatened by growing destabilization. It is well to remember most of China's booming economic activity is confined to coastal China, where it seems to be becoming a part of the thriving Pacific Rim.

Inland China is a different kettle of fish. Arable land in the interior is declining, deforestation, loss of top soil, and increased salinization are growing problems. Water supplies are declining, or becoming contaminated. Many Chinese irrigation systems and reservoirs are filling up with silt and China's population keeps on growing.

China, with the largest population and fastest growing economy in the 1990s, is built upon the thinnest foundation of arable land per capita of any country other than Bangladesh. More and more of this arable land is being lost as a result of Chinese development.

China's economic miracle is moving in the reverse direction in interior China. This is causing an exodus of the rural population from the interior to the coastal area of China, from villages to the cities. The resulting urbanization is bringing crime and discontent.

China's drive to modernize her economy after the disastrous

policies of Mao Tse Tung has created a conspicuous divide between rich and poor in China.

This gap is causing concern. China watchers note the ideology of egalitarianism is still very much alive. It's one of the lingering legacies of Mao. The rising disparity between rich and poor is full of irony after a revolution designed to eradicate that. If inequality increases, or is perceived as increasing, it's going to be highly incendiary because of this legacy.

Chinese officials are worried and fear more polarization if the gap continues to widen. That isn't the only concern of China. Less than a decade after the Tiananmen democracy demonstrations were put down, a new threat faces the Chinese leadership. Crime has become a threat to order in China on par with separatist challenges.

The rise in crime hits particularly hard in a society in which honesty was a ruthlessly enforced norm. The crime rate has tripled since the early 1980s.

Chinese now feel apprehensive about the growing crime wave sweeping China. In a survey taken in Beijing in October 1996 for the publication China Youth Daily, 35 percent of those polled said they or someone in their immediate family had been robbed at least once. More than 60 percent expressed the belief that China's social order has deteriorated in recent years.

The Chinese leadership, while not disputing the effects of violent crime, has focused on official corruption as the most serious threat. The Communist Party well remembers that corruption was a major factor in the rot that led to the collapse of the last Chinese imperial dynasty in 1911. The rampant corruption of Chiang Kai-Shek's Kuomintang officials helped build support for Mao Tse Tung and his supporters in the civil war that brought the communists to power.

Triumph of Disorder

The current Chinese leaders do not want history to repeat itself.

"If the support of the people is lost and corruption is rampant, then the ruling power will be lost," said Chinese President Jiang Zemin.

The Chinese crack-down on corruption is indicative of the unrest that seems to be simmering below the surface in China—a country many are predicting to be the world superpower in the 21st century.

Discontent is growing on farms and in factories. Soldiers and paramilitary police have had to maintain order in some bankrupt state factories. In the countryside, warlordism, banditry and deadly clan feuds are on the rise.

Chinese officials are also anxious over ethnic and religious separatist movements in Tibet and the western province of Xinjiang. In April 1996, a fire-fight broke out between Uighar separatists and police after authorities banned the creation of new mosques and ordered a crackdown on Muslims who, Chinese officials charged, were fomenting "holy war."

Uighar leaders claim their people are being repressed under assimilationist Chinese policies.

Oil-and uranium-rich Xinjiang borders Tibet and three ex-Soviet muslim republics in Central Asia, as well as Afghanistan and Pakistan. Beijing fears the spread of instability from hotspots such as Afghanistan and Tajikistan, areas where Islamic fundamentalists are quite active.

As regional disputes become more pronounced and the central government becomes less capable of coping with the situation, regional conflicts are a growing possibility. China could easily revert to its chaotic warlord-dominated past of the 1920s.

•••

The heartland of Islam is a powder keg of potential regional ethnic conflicts. Most current states in the Middle East are artificially created entities. They have borders enclosing land and people drawn by their colonial overlords after the First World War. Serious internal divisions exist within these states. No state is free of major ethnic divisions except Egypt. Yet even Egypt has internal conflict between Muslims and its minority Christians.

Iraq has major ethnic and cultural problems among its Kurds, Shi'ite, and Sunni Muslims. The Kurds have been engaged in a bloody, decades-long struggle to establish an independent Kurdish state. The majority Shi'ite Muslims live under the dictatorial heel of Saddam Hussein while Sunni Muslims make up the bulk of his government.

It is only the iron rule of Saddam Hussein that prevents Iraq from flying apart into separate Sunni, Shi'ite, and Kurdish enclaves.

Ethnic or religious conflict could destabilize the Gulf States. In some of the Gulf States large Shi'ite minorities are ruled by Sunni Muslims. These states are neighbors of Shi'ite Iran, which is constantly trying to stir up trouble among the Shi'ite population in the area.

Nor is Saudi Arabia free of potential ethnic strife. There are large numbers of foreign Muslims, from the Middle East, Asia, and Africa, working and living in Saudi Arabia. The principal cities of Jidda and Riyadh have large numbers of non-Saudi residents. There are also large number of Shi'ites living in Saudi's eastern province, who are a continuing source of concern to Saudi security.

Ethnic conflict in any of these Middle East countries has the possibility of spilling over into neighboring countries. It is wise to look at the example of the Kurdish struggle for an independent Kurdish state to see what this may mean to the world.

Kurds are located in Iran, Iraq, Syria, and Turkey. So far the Kurdish struggle has resulted in serious conflict in three of them. Only Syria, so far, has managed to avoid having a serious Kurdish rebellion within its borders.

Ethnic clashes are not the only factor in the looming new world disorder. Competition for scarce resources among burgeoning populations are also dashing cold water on former President Bush's idea of a new world order. The reality of more people striving for fewer resources is a sure-fire formula for conflict.

One of the resources they will be fighting over, especially in the Muslim Middle East powder keg, is water. Look at Turkey's current water policy: it has the potential of unleashing widespread conflict over water in the region. This secular Muslim state has advantages not shared by many of its Middle East neighbors. It has rich resources, extensive areas of fertile soil and surplus water.

Turkey also has problems, such as high inflation and a huge foreign debt of over $40 billion. If this foreign debt, which has tripled in ten years, continues to grow at the same rate, Turkey will have trouble servicing its debt. Turkey's ambitious water development plan will continue its rising foreign debt.

The heart and soul of this scheme is the Southeast Anatolia Project, a $25 billion plan involving dams, irrigation and hydroelectric projects. It involves building a series of twenty-two dams which will hold the waters of both the Tigris and Euphrates rivers.

Most of the future water requirements of many people throughout the Middle East will be spilling over these Turkish dams.

Water allocation policy is an important geopolitical weapon of the Turks. "We can stop the flow of water into Syria and Iraq for up to eight months without the same water overflowing our dams, in order to regulate their political behavior," said a Turkish hydroelectric official.

Turkish water politics could touch off conflict with Syria or Iraq over the water flow in the Tigris and Euphrates.

The uncertainty of adequate water for the riparian countries along the Tigris and Euphrates will cause a shift away from agriculture, and require an increase of food imports. This would further diminish hard currency reserves, or increase foreign indebtedness, and cause mass migration out of the area.

The Middle East isn't the only region facing a water crisis. Experts have long warned that Asian nations must reduce water consumption and curb wastage or face economic and social disruption.

Water experts for Worldwatch Institute in Washington, D.C., report water tables are falling, rivers are drying up and competition for dwindling supplies is increasing.

A World Bank study said water supplies are being siphoned away from farmlands surrounding Beijing in order to meet rising urban and industrial demands. With some 300 Chinese cities now short of water, this shift is bound to become more pronounced.

Most Asian countries will have severe water problems by the year 2025. The proliferation of water wells could dry up underground water sources in Bangladesh, India and Pakistan. This is a formula for mass migration and conflict. Human beings can't live without water and will fight to get it.

"I suspect in the next 50 years, we will see a shift from oil to water as the cause of great conflicts between nations and people," said Wally N'Dow, Secretary General of the U.N. at its Conference on Human Settlements held in June 1996 in Istanbul. "There is a tremendous economic and human cost involved due to inadequate supplies of water."

Water shortages will cause people to migrate to areas with water, and many will flock to the cities. The World Bank reported in September 1994, the world's big-city population is growing by a million people a week and will hold more than half the earth's population within a decade.

The urban population is growing at a rapid rate—as if another New Orleans grows from scratch every seven days. This migration is swamping the abilities of cities to absorb population increases and is turning existing cities into gigantic slums.

Facing this dismal prospect, people will try their luck on foreign shores, sometimes by desperate measures, as the Haitian and Cuban boat people now show. Migration of peoples has been a fact of life throughout human history. It would be foolish to think it would cease today.

By the start of the Third millennium, there will be almost 400 cities with more than a million residents, up from 288 in 1990. A World Bank study predicts that at least 26 of these cities will be megacities, each having more than 10 million people. Most will be in the unstable Third World.

By the turn of the century, Sao Paulo, Brazil is expected to have almost 23 million people, Bombay and Calcutta, India, 18 and 13 million respectively, Shanghai, China almost 18 million, and Mexico City, over 16 million.

All of these cities run the real risk of becoming dysfunctional centers of mass poverty and social collapse.

Other urban centers face the same problems due to migration. Right now there are 143,000 people per square mile in Lagos, Nigeria and 130,000 per square mile in Jakarta, Indonesia. To give an idea of just how dense these cities are, consider that the density of New York City's five boroughs is only 23,700 per square mile.

The rapid urbanization of the world will be accompanied by urban pollution, unhealthy water and air, little or no sanitation, open sewers as drainage, mounds of garbage and solid wastes along with poor or non-existent industrial waste management.

Whole communities, composed of poor teeming masses of people, bereft of jobs, packed together in shanty-towns, amidst deteriorating civic and social enmities, will be condemned to lives of poverty and despair.

Economic discontent will vie, or combine, with disease and malnutrition to provide a continual source of societal breakdown. Conflict, instability and violence will be the order of the day as the law of the jungle replaces the rule of law in the growing urbanized new world disorder.

This Hobbesian nightmare will come about as rural communities throughout the world, especially in the Third World, are washed away as if by a torrential flood. Whole populations will be uprooted and dumped into gigantic urban slums. The nations containing these slums will become more and more ungovernable and impoverished.

Their people will either explode in revolutionary violence or will seek refuge elsewhere. No professional revolutionary, militant Islamic included, could ask for a better revolutionary laboratory than the existence of these mass urban ghettos of the future.

Those who flee and seek refuge elsewhere may not find their presence welcomed in their new home. Magnify the growing controversy over immigration in Europe and the United States by a factor of four or five, and you can see the potential for growing xenophobia throughout the world. It could manifest itself in mindless violence against immigrants. Neo-nazi youth in Germany have already been implicated in violent attacks on Turkish workers, some resulting in death.

Every society strives to preserve its own customs and mores. Anyone who wonders what a multicultural society can become has only to turn on his, or her, television set and watch the events in Sarajevo, Chechyna, Tajikistan, or Beirut.

Numerous instances exist throughout history where immigrants and their progeny have threatened the stability of the state they moved into.

English immigrants into the Transvaal in the late 19th century brought on the Boer War and caused the destruction of the Boer Republics.

Indian immigrants and their decedents grew in numbers to the point they were able to elect a majority in the Fiji parliament. The Indian Fijian's attempt to govern was cut short when the ethnically Fijian army mounted a coup and deposed the new government.

Nor do we in the United States have to look overseas to observe this phenomenon. Texas provides us with an American home-grown example. Early American immigrants to Texas were lured there by land grants from the Mexican government. These grants, however, came with certain conditions: the American immigrants were to become Mexican citizens, obey Mexican laws, learn Spanish, and become Catholics.

The American immigrants ignored these conditions and quickly became a problem for the Mexican government. The eventual result was the Texas war of independence in 1836, and its consequences: Texan independence, becoming a new state in the United States, and, within a decade, war between the United States and Mexico.

The Texan-Americans refused to be assimilated into Mexico in 1836 and bloody conflict resulted. Today, there are ethnic enclaves of Muslims in the West that refuse to become assimilated into the society of their new homes.

The West's wealth, combined with the overpopulation of the Muslim world, creates irresistible pressures and attractions for immigration. A wave of Muslim immigrants, especially into Europe, is almost inevitable.

This tide will bring their values and problems with them to their new homes. It will be a migration of Islamic power. An influx of fifty million Moslems over the next few decades would bring into Europe and the United States many of the tensions and difficulties already sweeping the Muslim world. The potential for violence will grow as the clash of cultures in these newly multi-ethnic societies escalates.

There is a growing minority already of Muslim immigrants that refuse to become reconciled to the secular West. These irredentist Muslims are causing growing tensions in places like France and England and are supporting the cause of militant Islamic fundamentalism.

Clashes between Muslim traditions and secular authorities have already erupted in France and Great Britain.

France has a Muslim population of over 4 million, and the French discovered that Islam is not a form of personal piety, but a culture rooted in race, language, and tradition. Islamic immigrants, while looking for the legal protection of French citizenship, were not interested in assimilating the distinctive French way of life.

France looks south at the unraveling of her former colony, Algeria and fears the real prospect of millions of Muslim refugees fleeing to France, adding to France's Muslim population. France's former Minister of the Interior, Charles Pasqua, is hoping a tough crackdown on immigration will stop the feared flood in its tracks, and has even threatened to close France's borders.

In 1993, Pasqua changed 200 years of French policy of asylum by announcing that henceforth France would become a "zero immigration" country. Such a step was necessary, in Pasqua's view, because France faced a very serious immigration problem in the near future and preventative steps had to be taken in order to cope with the growing problem.

By the year 2000, Pasqua claimed, there will be 60 million people in Algeria, Morocco, and Tunisia under the age of twenty and without a future. Where will they go? Why to France, of course, claim Pasqua and his supporters, where they can live the good life, observed every night by the teeming masses of North Africa, courtesy of French television.

Not only is France concerned with a future Muslim refugee tide washing up on its shores, French officials are becoming more and more concerned with the growing militant Islamic fundamentalist activity in France. Fundamentalist groups such as the Union of Young Muslims, the National Muslim Foundation, and the *al-Da'Wa w'al Tabligh* have created potential revolutionary cells in France through these socio-religious associations. These groups, in addition to doing legitimate charity work among poor families, are also teaching the Koran, Arabic and martial arts within the Muslim community in France.

Militant fundamentalists are using these groups, willingly or not, as a smoke-screen to further the violent radical Islamic agenda. Militants levy a "revolutionary tax" on Muslim merchants. The proceeds of the "tax" are sent to the militant Islamic Salvation Front group in Algeria.

Militants also use these groups to recruit youths for guerrilla training in Afghanistan, and preach *jihad* from Muslim pulpits in France.

Some militants in France are involved in serious revolutionary activity. In November 1994, French police broke up a ring of Islamic fundamentalists, arresting 80 people and seizing a substantial arms cache in a Paris suburb. There were also several bomb attacks in Paris during 1995 and 1996.

The southern European states of Spain, Portugal, France, Italy and Greece, whose combined populations are estimated only to increase by five million between 1990 and 2025, lie across the Mediterranean Sea from a looming Islamic demographic bomb.

In the North African countries facing Europe's soft underbelly—Morocco, Algeria, Tunisia, Libya, and Egypt—populations are expected to grow by almost 110 million during the same period. Those North African Muslim economies are incapable of handling such a population rise, and Islamic migration out of these countries is inevitable.

The vast Sahara Desert lies to their south and forms a barrier to migration. The bulk of the Muslim migrants will cross the Mediterranean into Europe or across the Atlantic to the United States. These Muslim immigrants will bring their customs, values and religion with them. The waves of Muslim immigrants will be the shock troops of radical change in Europe in the early years of the 21st century.

England is seeing a resurgence of ethnic clashes within its

borders. In 1993, London recorded more than 5000 racial incidents ranging from murders to writing threatening hate mail. Almost half of the victims are from the Indian sub-continent, Muslim Pakistanis and Bangladeshis, and Hindu Indians.

The victims are fighting back and murders and fire-bombings are becoming more frequent in the ethnic neighborhoods of London, where nearly half of England's ethnic minorities live.

Relations have never been this polarized before, say those living in London's Camden borough. Revenge attacks will mean counter-revenge attacks. Nobody seems able to control it.

There is growing resentment of poor whites living near Camden borough. The whites complain the Bangladeshis exaggerate and complain in order to pressure British authorities for more benefits and preferential treatment, while Bangladeshi intimidation of whites is ignored.

The point here is not to demonstrate where the blame lies, but to show that ethnic tension and violence are escalating in societies, such as France and England, which have demonstrated tolerance for minorities in the past.

Such growing violence and tensions are not the sign of a new world order, but are further evidence of disquieting troubles ahead.

The Salman Rushdie affair also demonstrates what can happen when ethnic minorities refuse to assimilate the traditions of their new homeland. Rushdie's book, *The Satanic Verses,* is no doubt offensive to Muslims, but does that give Muslims the right to systematically violate the laws of tolerant societies where they happen to live?

Many Muslims obviously think they have that right because Muslims, in countries where they are a minority such as England, France and India, rioted, fire-bombed bookstores selling Rushdie's book, and demanded Rushdie's death.

The Islamic world was further inflamed when Iran's Ayatollah Khomeini issued a religious decree, still in effect, ordering Rushdie dead. These weren't spontaneous outbreaks either. British Muslims organized book burnings and looted bookstores well before the Ayatollah's death decree was issued.

The disturbing crux of the Rushdie affair is the fact Muslims are taking advantage of the freedoms and values of countries where Muslims are in the minority and where, therefore, they can practice their religion only thanks to the tolerance of others.

Not only do Muslims obtain the right to practice their religion in the West (whereas this right is very rarely granted to Christians and Jews in Muslim countries), but Muslims also demand the exorbitant privilege of imposing their views on the majority.

The point is not the offensive nature of the book to Muslims, but whether the Muslim response shows they are capable of blending into western liberal democracies.

When one joins a society grounded in tolerance, one is presumed to accept that society's tolerance, including the right to protest injustices. Tolerance does not give Muslim protestors the right to kill or maim in the name of Allah any more than it gives pro-life supporters in the United States the right to firebomb abortion clinics, or kill abortionists.

When the attitude "the end justifies the means" become the ruling value in a society, that is a society which is well on the way down the slippery slope towards self-destruction.

These Muslims claimed the right to impose their values and beliefs on tolerant, pluralistic societies, not by democratic processes but by violence and intimidation.

Triumph of Disorder

The fundamentalist influence is spreading to British schools where militant youths are intimidating their fellow students to toe the fundamentalist line. Young school girls are especially vulnerable to this type of intimidation. The girls are threatened not to take certain courses because they are "un-Islamic." School teachers often report the threat is real. Girls often come to them and complain of the pressure they are under to wear *hijab* (traditional dress). Students have often been fearful of taking art, history and social studies, simply because the Islamic radicals consider them anti-Islamic.

This type of intimidation is prevalent in the cities of London, Leicester, Bradford, Blackburn—indeed, any place with a sizable Muslim population in the British Isles.

The Muslim youth have their own organization, the Muslim Youth Organization dedicated to imposing the *Khilafah,* or Islamic government on Great Britain. One of the organization's branches, the Waltham Forest Islamic Bureau, issued a manifesto justifying the ongoing campaign of intimidation in the schools under the guise of protecting Islamic culture. The manifesto claimed the only guarantee of protecting their culture was to live in an Islamic state. Since the current school system is under the control of the infidel, intimidation is justified as a vehicle of change, and will be a new epoch in the history of Islam .

They will make that history, they feel, by following classic revolutionary war strategy, a strategy well-suited to the new world disorder: intimidation followed by violence. The racial violence and the campaign of intimidating fellow students to follow the militant's program are part of militant Islam's goal of establishing an Islamic regime in Great Britain, where the Islamic religion has never been stronger.

The militants have the upper hand because the authorities are afraid to respond to the growing terror campaign in the schools. If British officials take action, the militant Islamic groups will hide behind the skirts of the claim of discrimination. So the authorities turn a blind-eye to the low-level revolutionary activity going on in the schools under their noses.

This irresponsible conduct by non-assimilable Islamic residents in England and France will be the cause of future cultural clashes throughout the West.

• • •

Since the 1917 Russian revolution, the communist ideology has been driven by the urge to create and impose a classless society on all of humanity. As this classless society spread over the world, a new type of universal human being will emerge, steeped in communism's ideals, and severed forever from the past.

Communism's universal man lies on the rubbish heap of history. But the ideal of the universal man is not dead. With communism gone, capitalism, so its more zealous proponents insist, will emerge and create a sort of universal capitalistic society consisting of billions of human beings creating and trading by means of a world wide free market.

Neither the classless society promised by the Mandarins of communism nor the global village of entrepreneurial capitalism has managed to homogenize the world during the twentieth century. Although the world grows smaller and more interdependent because of air transport, modern communications and international economic activity, it is not creating the universal man. "Instead," claims Macalester

Triumph of Disorder

College anthropology professor Jack Weatherford, "ethnic and cultural identities grew stronger, everywhere from the largest cities to the remote jungle valleys. Rather than blending into a homogenized world culture shared by all, the various tribes, nations, religions, and ethnic groups accelerated their differences to become more varied than ever."

Advances in communication and transportation, claims Trinity College Political Science professor, Walker Connor in his book *Ethnonationalism: The Quest for Understanding,* tend also to increase the cultural awareness of the different groups by making their members more aware of distinctions between themselves and others. The impact is twofold. Not only does the individual become more aware of alien ethnic groups, he also becomes more aware of those who share his identity.

According to Connor, the more unlike groups come into contact with one another, the less they can abide each other's company. As long as these groups, peoples, or whatever term you wish to use, perceive themselves to be different, with different interests and loyalties, the potential for conflict among them is great.

Ethnic strife is threatening the breakup of many states. The former Soviet Union, Yugoslavia, India, and South Africa are all on the verge of widespread ethnic strife. Ethnic tensions are boiling in Sri Lanka, Burma, Ethiopia, Indonesia, Iraq, Lebanon, Israel, Cyprus, Turkey, countless countries in Africa, Guyana, Trinidad—almost everywhere you look.

Europe is not immune from ethnic tensions. Britain, France, Belgium, Spain, and Germany face growing ethnic and racial troubles.

Many of these conflicts stem from the West's colonial policy of creating states by drawing arbitrary lines on maps. This forces different peoples to live under the same created roof. The Western elites mistakenly believed different cultures and ethnic groups could be incorporated by map-makers into a given territory and, ergo, a nation would be created.

Over a period of time and given a common purpose, these different peoples might evolve into a true nation in the Western sense of the term. More often than not, given no common purpose such as surviving the Cold War, mutual hostility, intolerance and conflict will break out between the ethnic groups. It is becoming more and more of a factor in the world, as ethnically diverse peoples are finding fewer reasons to see themselves as part of the same old nation.

This problem is plaguing Eastern Europe. That region is a cauldron of unresolved territorial disputes, intense ethnic and religious rivalries; and, fragile, unstable political systems. The process of nation building in Eastern Europe today resembles the same process in Western Europe three or four centuries ago, with all the attendant brutality and intolerant forms of nationalism.

Nationalism has brought down every great empire that existed at the start of the 20th century: Austrian, German, Ottoman, British, Dutch, Portuguese, American (the Philippines) and Russian— the last, the oldest and the largest. As we prepare to step into the 21st century, nationalism is ripping apart more than old empires. Fourteen empires have disappeared already in the 20th century. The breakdown of empires is part of a process that will ultimately weaken, or dissolve, the nation state. Bosnia is not likely to be the last horror show. Similar dramas will likely erupt in Africa, Asia, Europe and South America.

Many of the nation states in the world community are feeling the pressure of ethnic and cultural desires for autonomy and may come apart. The government of the nation state is usually at odds with ethnic groups within its borders because there are intrinsic conflicts of loyalty between both.

The state demands obedience to itself and its definition of the public good, while the ethnic group often has a different idea of loyalty and that public good as applied to them. Since the state usually holds the monopolistic reins of coercive violence, it normally could impose its way on cultures and groups within its borders that dare oppose its views. This may become a thing of the past as more and more private entities seem willing to take on the state.

"As the second millennium A.D. is coming to an end," said Martin Van Creveld, "the state's attempt to monopolize violence in its own hands is faltering...Should present trends continue, then the kind of war that is based on the division between government, army and the people seems to be on its way out. The rise of low-intensity conflict may...end up destroying the state. Over the long run, the place of the state will be taken by war-making organizations of a different type."

"Present trends" are continuing, and show no signs of slowing. Non-state war is already a reality in many parts of the world, and we can expect it to soon be a factor in ours.

Chapter 16
March to the Scaffold

You may not be interested in war. But war is interested in you.
Leon Trotsky

We are facing an ominous, threatening future. Order is break-ing down, and it's going to get a lot worse. There is a connection between the rise in terrorism, the anarchy of the former Soviet Union, the riots in Los Angeles, Islamic fundamentalists taking over Muslim countries, and the local thugs who threaten your life and limb.

The nature of warfare has changed, is changing, and the United States had better understand this. The words of General Giulio Douhet, a leader in a revolution in military affairs during an earlier age are appropriate today: "Victory smiles upon those who anticipate changes in the character of war, not upon those who wait to adapt themselves after the changes occur."

The fighters, or "warriors" as retired Army Lieutenant-Colo-nel Ralph Peters terms them, are the most likely foes of America's military in the future. They will not be the traditional soldiers our military has faced in the past. Instead, they will be an erratic, vicious throwback to a more primitive age. These "warriors" will have little or no stake in peace, little education and a bleak economic future. War is their future and calling.

"With a Kalashnikov in hand and the hateful spittle of nation-

alist ideology or religious fanaticism dripping from his mouth," said
Peters, "today's new soldier murders those who once slighted him,
rapes the women who scorned him, and plunders what he can't achieve
by productive economic activity."

That certainly is *not* the way the U.S. fights its wars. Her soldiers, instead, are infused with the moral and behavioral codes of U.S.
culture which are manifestations of Western Judeo-Christian tradition. Our military, steeped in this code, practices a highly organized,
structural form of war fought within accepted and customary rules.

The "warrior-soldier" of the new world disorder won't fight
by these rules. Nor will he be reside and fight from military bases in
isolation from his fellow citizens. Instead, they will be intermingled
within the populations they spring from. The more this intermingling
takes place, the more the distinction between the "warrior" armed
forces and the civilians becomes less and less. They will blend together and it will be difficult to tell friend from foe. Remember how
difficult it was for American forces in Vietnam to identify and bring
to battle the Viet Cong guerrillas? It was only when the Viet Cong,
beefed-up by North Vietnam regulars, launched conventional attacks
on towns and cities during their 1968 Tet Offensive, that the American could fight them in a familiar battle mode. Walter Cronkite was
terribly wrong. The decision by the Viet Cong to engage American
forces in traditional forms of war, led to their destruction by superior
American firepower, not an American defeat.

The blending together of the population and the new world
disorder fighters renders useless many of our weapons systems. After
all, how can one call down artillery on a gang or bunch of guerrillas
ambushing our troops from some back-alley in some overcrowded
Third World slum without destroying the neighborhood of the poor

peasants caught in the cross fire. Such an act *may* get the bad guys, but it *will* also alienate the local population and increase the local support for the bad guys in the future.

The end of the century reveals a stark dichotomy: the apparent end of war between sovereign nation states but a marked disastrous increase in terrorism and criminality.

The advent of criminal, terrorist, and warlord para-states is a far more urgent challenge than what expensive weapons systems to adopt, fund, and the smoothing of ruffled feathers such arguments engender.

Such spats over which weapons, like the B-2 bombers or aircraft carriers, are the core of our defense thinking—and they miss the point. At present, we are preparing for the war we *want* to fight, instead of the conflicts that we *can't avoid.*

Yet promotions are to be made in the military and fortunes amassed in the civilian sector by purchasing expensive weapons systems that may never be placed in harm's way.

With the exception of Desert Storm, all of America's wars in the 20th century were wars of attrition. The American way of fighting them was, and still is, to use our overwhelming firepower to kill more of the enemy than they can kill of us. The American people put up with both World Wars because they were convinced the cause was just.

Support for committing troops in wars of attrition started to erode in the Korean War and vanished during the long Vietnam War. In Vietnam our opponents mostly refused to play by our rules. When they did confront our forces in a traditional war manner, they suffered horrendous casualties. The Chinese in Korea and the North Vietnamese had no compunction against using their soldiers as cannon fodder. Both had a vast pool of manpower to replace their casualties. It didn't bother them if they lost 10 men to every American killed. Over the long run they knew Americans would tire of the endless lists of killed and maimed on battlefields far from American shores. Their successful strategy involved incremental bleeding until the price of staying was too high and we withdrew our forces.

Our surprisingly low casualties and the swiftness of Desert Storm gave us a false sense of confidence. Somalia should have been a rude awakening. The ambush that killed 19 Army Rangers showed Americans are rightly concerned about shedding her sons' blood in perceived useless ventures. The hue and cry after that incident resulted in the withdrawal of American forces from Somalia.

What do our Somalia and Vietnam experiences show? Americans dislike war and are wary of committing our troops in ventures not directly threatening the United States' interests, (sending troops to Bosnia and Haiti was done over the vehement protests of many.) Once committed, Americans want the war over as quickly as possible and with few casualties. Our future opponents know this and their strategy will be to bog us down in a "death-by-a-thousand-cuts" war of attrition.

We must face the unpleasant fact that our future non-state opponents won't fight according to our rules of engagement.

Unfortunately, our future leadership is ill-prepared to counter Van creveld's warfare. 1992 marked the ascension of the first Vietnam War era president. He won't be the last for at least the next few presidential elections. Just like our Cold War leaders were tried and tested by their World War II and Korean War experience, Vietnam will be the defining experience for our future leaders until possibly the end of the first quarter of the next century. Reluctance to commit troops in Vietnam-type conflicts will likely form the core of their defense and foreign policy thinking. Look how fast the first Vietnam era president pulled our troops out of Somalia after the Mogadishu ambush. Our future leaders may be ill-prepared to deal with the proliferation of non-state war.

They won't have any choice. No country in history has had so many of its citizens, assets and raw materials located abroad—many of them in areas where non-state war is either underway or likely to break out. There are areas where the proliferation of non-state war would carry very serious consequences for American interests.

Look at the Middle East, and particularly Saudi Arabia, whose rulers have for years been carefully trying to balance the conflicting demands of traditionalism and modernization. If the Saudis fall to the militant Islamic fundamentalists, or simply become bogged down in a civil war similar to the one in Algeria, there would be no question vital American interests are at stake. If that were to happen, it is problematic whether U.S decision makers will be able to do more than wring their hands. To solve that dilemma may require the occupation of a land whose population both hates us and would have no compunction against killing every infidel American who was defiling their land. (Could you imagine the hue and cry from the rest of the Muslim world if their holy cities were being occupied by the hated Christians?) Such a prospective can of worms would hold little appeal to policy makers at that precipitous point in time.

As for the U.S., for anyone to claim, (after the World Trade Center and the Atlanta Olympic and abortion clinic bombings) that "it can't happen here" is simply preposterous. Non-state war can easily spill over into the U.S. One only has to look at our southern neighbor, Mexico. That country figures high on the World Bank's list of ungovernable states. The very economic takeoff which a modicum of liberalization and privitization helped to achieve in recent years also threatens to pull it apart. Faced with growing poverty as a result of being left behind as Mexico's economy grows, important parts of the rural population may turn to guerrilla war. In fact insurgencies have already broken out in parts of Mexico. If our southern neighbor goes up in flames on lines similar to those that destroyed Yugoslavia, the U.S. will have a serious problem on its hands.

We may be faced with either intervention in Mexico in an attempt to restore stability, or use our military to try and seal our porous southern border in an attempt to keep the problems from spilling across. A balkanization of Mexico will, at the least, cause large numbers of people to become refugees and flee north into the U.S.

Imagine the burden that will put on our social and welfare resources already feeling the strain of our aging population?

Some, if not all, of the Mexican non-state combatant groups will try to engage the large U.S. Hispanic population to support their cause. These groups will use the refugees in the U.S. to plot, recruit, and arm new cadres before recrossing the border to rejoin the conflict in Mexico. They will establish clandestine bases and marshal support among their Spanish-speaking brethren and will strongly resist American government attempts to dislodge them.

If Mexico collapses in waves of non-state war, the problem will not be limited to the Mexican side of the border. The consequences to the U.S., as one can imagine, are serious and frightful.

Because of the weakness of their governments (the product of enormous socioeconomic gaps between the different segments of their populations), Latin America and the Caribbean have always been, and still remain, fertile breeding grounds for non-state wars. These wars have a nasty habit of ignoring national frontiers, as the examples of France, which from 1958 to 1962 came close to civil war, and Russia, which is now obliged to fight Muslim insurgents along the border of the former USSR, clearly show.

• • •

The demise of order and growing instability throughout the world is creating a perfect environment for the spread of radical Islamic fundamentalism because it appeals to two basic human needs: the need for security and spiritual comfort.

Humans have a natural fear of disorder. They are comfortable with the known and familiar. Disorder creates a high degree of uncertainty and fear for the future. The more the fear and uncertainty, the higher the anxiety. The higher the anxiety, the more of a detrimental factor it becomes in coping with the disorder. It is a vicious cycle.

Man also has an innate sense that something "out there" exists that is higher than himself. The religiously inclined puts his faith in a transcendent spiritual being or force. The secularist puts his faith in more earthly things: the community, the Party, the state, the folk or tribe. But we all have the tendency to look to something outside our human nature to succor and comfort us in time of need.

Islamic fundamentalism satisfies both of these needs. The answer to the problems of the world, they say, are found in the religion of Islam. It has all the solutions to life's problems. "Follow the holy writings of Islam" is their message to the downtrodden. It's all there and if you accept and follow its laws, rules and strictures a new and just order will be established on earth.

The fact that the new order is also grounded in Allah's word and is religious-based also appeals to the spiritual yearning in man. Order and security—two powerful human desires rolled into one—is the appeal of Islamic fundamentalism. Its appeal is especially seductive in Muslim countries because they are already steeped in Islamic traditions, and many are beset with serious problems engendering a climate of instability and disorder. Along comes the Islamic fundamentalist with his message that only by following the true path of Islam will the growing problems cease. The true path, of course, is that outlined by the fundamentalist.

Many decision makers in the West, including American leaders, say they have no problems with Islam, only with its violent extremist elements. These officials are turning a blind eye on history. The relationship between Islam and non-Islamic societies has been tense and full of conflict for over fourteen centuries. It is well to remember that half the wars involving pairs of states with different religions between 1820 and 1929 were wars between Muslims and Christians. Since the collapse of communism removed the common enemy of both the West and Islam, each now perceives the other as its major threat. The rhetoric between the West and Islam reflects that today: it focuses less on seizing or defending territory but on broader issues such as the world view of both, weapons proliferation, human rights and democracy, control of oil, migration, terrorism, and Western meddling and intervention.

The on-going conflict between Islam and the West is war. Libya, Iran and Iraq consider themselves at war with the U.S. The United States has classified seven states as terrorist states and five of those are Muslim countries. In the eyes of the U.S., this sets them apart as enemies because they are engaging in acts of war via terrorism against the U.S. and its allies. It is well to remember that one of the charges leveled against the Islamic World Trade Center terror bombers was intending "to levy a war of urban terrorism against the United States." At the trial the prosecution argued that the bombers planned to bomb other targets in New York City and were "soldiers" in a struggle "involving a war" against the United States.

"If Muslims allege that the West wars on Islam and if Westerners allege that Islamic groups war on the West," said Harvard University's Samuel Huntington, "it seems reasonable to conclude that something very much like a war is underway."

The brutality and viciousness of Islam's war on non-Muslims in the Sudan, described in these pages, provides a vivid example of what the future may hold if more and more conflicts break out between Muslims and non-Muslims.

Evolving socioeconomic trends throughout the globe make such conflicts more probable, and will also effect our ability to mount adequate responses.

So volatile and unpredictable is the international socioeconomic system, it wouldn't take much to touch-off a crisis of global proportions. A major war in the Middle East, another India-Pakistan war, the implosion of populous states like China, India or Indonesia, could send inflation-rates soaring. Even a nonviolent event like a 1929 stock-market collapse could cause panic, depression and widespread social disorder.

With so many gloomy prospects, all hanging in the balance, much will depend upon the choices people make. Wise choice will require wise leaders and informed citizens. Unfortunately, emotion, not wisdom, seems to be the guiding criteria in capitals throughout the world and emotion is hostile to rational thought.

Triumph of Disorder

Unless our political leaders are prepared to think and act with courage and a vision that extends past the next election, coming generations are going to pay an extremely high price.

Given the current timbre of our politicians, does anybody think they'll respond in any manner other than doing what is natural for them—equivocate and make meaningless compromises?

Unfortunately, the historical forces at work in the world will easily swamp these ineffectual actions.

• • •

The U.S. and the West no longer have the economic or demographic dynamism required to impose their will on other societies, and to make any attempt would be a revival of European imperialism. There is little support for that in the West, and it would be resisted by the rest of the world.

The West's principal responsibility is not to resurrect the past glories of the age of imperialism and try to remake the world in their image. That is beyond the West's declining ability. Instead, the West must preserve, protect and renew the unique qualities and contributions of our Western civilization. These include its Judeo-Christian heritage, pluralism, individualism, and the rule of law. They are what is unique to the West. These are European ideas, not Asian, nor African, nor Middle Eastern ideas, except by adoption. We can't impose these values on others. They must adapt them to their own societies on their own.

We can still be a beacon of rationality and hope, a calm oasis in the wasteland of the new world disorder. What is desperately needed in the West is a reaffirmation of its faith in itself and its ideals. Faith, as the Islamic fundamentalist show us, is a powerful force.

Force against faith is fundamentally useless. Without arms, without an army, without generals, led by speakers and bishops, early Christians suffered three centuries of murderous persecution not only from Romans, but from adherents of other religions. In the end the Christian faith triumphed.

The Islamic fundamentalist has a faith bordering on that of the early Christians. Yet we in the West seem to be losing ours. That may change. Martin Van Creveld reminds us, "If the growing militancy of one religion continues, it almost certainly will compel others to follow suit. People will be driven to defend their ideals and way of life...Thus Muhammad's recent revival may yet bring on that of the Christian Lord, and He will not be the Lord of love but of battles."

So long as Islam remains Islam, as its militant resurgence demonstrates, and the West remains Christian, this fundamental conflict between the two world views and ways of life will be the crux of their relationship in the future as it has defined them for the past 14 centuries.

The crisis, conflicts and instabilities facing the world in the future will not put a damper on this ancient feud. If anything, it will fan the flames of mutual animosity.

• • •

If America manages to stay together as a nation, we will still face areas of the globe which will be in a state of anarchy. Our interests will require the use of force to protect our resources and citizens.

Most of these commitments of American military force will be in the Third World where anarchy will be endemic in the new world

Triumph of Disorder

disorder, and our troops had better be prepared to "get down and dirty" with the unscrupulous "warriors" infesting these areas.

The new world disorder is going to place enormous strains on those who must confront the "warriors" of the future. It is clear our most likely opponents will not fight in a manner that will expose them to our "smart" laser-guided bombs or artillery fire. To cope with the enemy, our soldiers must find, fix and bring the "warriors" under fire.

Many of our foes will be Islamic fundamentalist terror and guerrilla groups. They will be formidable enemies because of the nature of their cause. The religious-underpinning of their crusade will have demonized their enemies and that will manifest itself in an eagerness to kill all that oppose them. Calm reasoned argument will have no deterring effect on their murderous tendencies. The massacres and atrocities in Algeria preview the ugly norm of their non-sate war.

Their willingness, even eagerness, to be killed in the fight against the infidel guarantees that fighting them will cost our forces tremendous of casualties. Given the potential pool of millions to draw from, the non-state Islamic "warriors", infused with religious zeal and having nothing to lose, will require grit, determination and a corresponding ruthlessness on our part if we are to be victorious.

That job will take an individual possessing the skill of both the policeman and soldier. That is asking a lot of an individual because the jobs are vastly different.

A policeman's job is to enforce the laws and rules of society and bring violators before the bar of justice for punishment. They only use deadly force when the policeman's life is in jeopardy. A soldier's task, on the other hand, is to kill his enemy. Combining the two jobs requires a dedicated, highly motivated cross-trained individual possessing the patience required of good police work to track down the warrior-criminal before using his superior military skills to kill his enemy.

The U.S. will not have to reinvent the wheel. The U.S. military in the past has successfully used paramilitary police forces to overcome insurgents and bandits. The U.S. Marines provided the training, assigned NCOs and officers to lead the Haitian Gendarme and Nicaraguan paramilitary police forces in the various Banana Wars in the early part of the 20th century. The U.S. Army, at the turn of the century, formed, staffed, trained, and led the Philippine Constabulary which was instrumental in pacifying the Philippines.

The difference today is in the lethality of the weaponry available to the new world disorder "warriors", and the vast pool of tens of millions of potential new world disorder fighters. Our military in the past has shown the ability to adapt and successfully counter non-state war. It will have to do so again in the very near future.

America has kept her police and military functions separate, but the likely enemies we'll face will require some adjustment. It won't entail turning our infantry into cops on the beat, but some police-type training would be of value to our military. For example, a well-trained police officer practices a lot of "shoot, don't shoot" drills. These involve a series of suddenly appearing target scenarios where the trainee has to make a decision whether or not to shoot. Sometimes the target scene that pops up is an unarmed individual, other times they are bad guys in a variety of situations—one-on-ones, multiple threats, hostage situations, etc.. The shooter has a split-second to analyze the situation and make a decision to shoot or not based on that assessment.

This type of training will be valuable to the soldier engaged in operations in the murky realm of non-state war.

Like it or not, our fighters are going to have to go where the warrior-enemy is, and that will likely be in some rabbit warren maze in some Third World shantytown slum.

This type of warfare is going to require highly trained, intelligent, dedicated soldiers. It is a sergeant's and lieutenant's war, inimical to the military mind-set determined to refight another Desert Storm with expensive fancy planes, tanks and grand wide-sweeping panzer tactics. Killing our "warrior" opponents is going to put a lot of pressure and responsibility on the shoulders of these young soldiers and marines. They must have adequate training to assume the responsibility to react to the situation as they see it without being subjected to the micromanagement tendencies of higher command.

Our infantry must be trained to take the initiative because they are on the ground and time will be of the essence. Good sound training will minimize the potential mistakes and if the sergeant/lieutenant runs into problems, the company or battalion headquarters are available for assistance.

This doesn't imply that the squad leader goes off on his own, draws up his own mission plan, and then executes it without the knowledge of his superiors. That mission plan is the work of a higher headquarters. But the squad's task, derived from the higher headquarter's mission plan, should have enough flexibility where the squad leader can adapt it to the situation he faces on the ground. Too rigid a battle plan and too much micromanagement by headquarters will tie our troop's hands and our "warrior" opponents will dance rings around us.

Such flexibility is a must because our new world disorder foes will be those who have acquired a blood-lust for killing and don't react rationally as we perceive rational action to be. They are utterly ruth-less and capable of the most despicable atrocities, and will do any-thing to survive. They will not be impressed or beaten by half-hearted shows of force under restrictive rules of engagement.

Facing the international threats of the new world disorder will pose a dilemma for our defense and foreign policy elites. While most of the opponents our military are likely to face will be non-state enti-ties, our forces will still need ships and planes to get from here to there. The military will still require the immense logistical and com-munications systems to sustain our forces whether they are fighting in some backwater Third World country or somewhere else in Africa, Latin America, the Middle East or Asia. Even though the vast major-ity of our military encounters in the troubled times ahead will be against non-state groups, we can't turn our military into commandos.

Nor must we go in the other direction and prepare for the war we'd like to fight. Unfortunately, this seems to be the course our de-fense and foreign policy elites are following. It is a course given intel-lectual justification by former Secretary of Defense Casper Weinberger's book *The Next War.* The book, while justifying a strong Desert Storm-style military, gives credence to the adage that generals are busy fighting the last war instead of preparing for the next one. This, regrettably, is understandable because individuals, as well as cor-porate bodies, are comfortable with the familiar. Following Weinberger's advice translates into continuity, big bucks for defense contractors, advancement for military careerists and lucrative post-military em-ployment. To the denizens of academia and think-tanks, it offers in-tellectual certitude rather than having to face conflicting ideas requir-ing analytical thought.

Yet no ostrich has ever saved its life by sticking its head in the sand, and this attitude won't faze our future opponents one bit. If we get embroiled in these struggles, our foes will kill us with gusto in spite of the expensive, useless equipment so beloved by our defense establishment.

As Leon Trotsky reminds us: "You may not be interested in war. But war is interested in you." The troubled times ahead will bear this out. Non-state war will entangle us in its vicious tentacles and to successfully cope with it we do well to consider the advice of England's counterinsurgency expert, Sir Robert Thompson:

"Getting forces into the same element as the insurgent is rather like trying to deal with a tomcat in an alley. It is no good inserting a large, fierce dog. The dog may not find the tomcat —if he does, the tomcat will escape up a tree; the dog will then chase the female cats in the alley. The answer is to put a fiercer tomcat. The two cannot fail to meet because they are both in exactly the same element and have exactly the same purpose in life. The weaker will be eliminated."

In short, the high-tech conventional forces, with their tanks, artillery and aerial bombardment of the air forces will likely cause more harm than good in trying to destroy the "troops' of the new world disorder. Civilian casualties are likely to exceed those of the combatants by relying on the heavy weaponry of our conventional forces. Instead we will have to rely on the bloody eyeball-to-eyeball infantryman's war—with resulting moderate to heavy casualties.

Do we have the will to be Sir Robert Thompson's stronger tomcat? To date, the Somalian experience says "No."

For our sake, we had better develop that will, otherwise we face very rough days ahead in the new world disorder. The enemy must first be eliminated before civic action, nation-building, or peace-keeping can be effective. Otherwise our "warrior" enemies will simply bide their time and wait until our forces are withdrawn. He will resurface as vicious as ever.

Why is the triumph or failure of disorder so important? Stability, says former French government official Phillipe Delmas in his book *The Rosy Future of War,* is the precondition for any peace, because instability is the primary source of war.

Close examination of two centuries of conflicts reveals that totalitarian states are no more likely to start a war than are democracies. In unstable states, however, the probability of war doubles. Periods of transition to a democratic system are particularly unstable. At such times, the power-wielding class, who face being removed from power, are apt to incite the masses with nationalism and the threat of outside aggression so as to retain their power. This led Germany to start World War I and Japan to invade Manchuria. It played an important role in the Russian war in Chechyna and the Serbian war in Bosnia.

This isn't the only reason instability can lead to war. The transition to democracy—a worldwide crusade the U.S. is leading with messianic zeal—unleashes many forces that can easily generate conflicts: fear of revolt (Russia today, China and Cuba tomorrow?), fear of being denied one's due (the Serbs, the Kurds, the Berbers, the Zulus), the appearance of radical ideologies (Muslim fundamentalism), and the proliferation of criminal gangs, to name a few.

So disorder does matter because development and democracy can only ripen in stable states. As Delmas reminds us: "There exists no example of a state whose prosperity or whose justice came into being under conditions of instability. But examples of unstable states that have lost these virtues abound. Historical logic seems to be a one-way street. Economic development necessarily brings human rights along behind it...On the one hand, human rights cannot survive misery and the prosperity of nations cannot survive the instability of states."

• • •

The burdens under which we struggle in the new world disorder, the foes and dangers we face from the chaos and the collapse in the world, and the proliferation of terrorism, subversion, gangsterism and non-state war are both serious and onerous. They can be overcome if we have the will and the courage to confront, admit and repair the problems and dangers facing our fragmenting country.

The long history of the world and its cultures is one of successive civilizations, empires, glories and failures. No people in that long record ever created a civilization without a faith. And no civilization has ever outlasted the loss of its faith. Loss of faith is inextricably entwined with the loss of faith in both government and in individuals.

We are a numerous people who were once united and proud. We spoke a common language, took care of ourselves, and stood tall in the world not only because we worked hard and allowed every citizen to choose his own path with a minimum of restrictions, but because we honored our heritage.

Today our government has escaped our control: we are as cobwebbed with restrictions as was Gulliver, and hindered and smothered by a nanny-knows-best, oppressive, inefficient, and unbelievably ignorant government. A sense of hopelessness and anxiety, instead of hope and confidence, is now our growing public mood. This is not the ideal attitude to have when facing serious challenges.

We cannot return to the glory days of the past, but we can

return to what worked in the past. In other words, a re-assertion of Western Judeo-Christian values—the values that underlie America's greatness. It will take a re-awakening of this faith if we are to successfully cope with the waves of disorder, chaos and the destructive forces mentioned in these pages, which threaten to overwhelm us.

If we fail, the world faces a return of barbarism, and a new Dark Ages descending on humanity.

Epilogue

The sword without, and the terror within, shall destroy both the young man and the virgin, the suckling also with the man of gray hair.
Deuteronomy 32:25

For those who still are skeptical of the dangers described in this work, the following article from the Sept/Oct 1997 issue of *Counterterrorism & Security Reports* should dispel those doubts. The publication is the official newsletter of the International Association for Counterterrorism & Security Professionals (IACSP) and the author is a member. The article, "Recent Meanderings in Las Vegas," written by fellow IACSP member Paul Copher, demonstrates the presence and potential danger of Islamic terrorism in America: (reproduced with permission of IACSP).

"While presenting a CT/AT training course to some state investigators here in the South West, I stopped in Las Vegas with a few former military agents that I worked with in the Middle East. A taxi driver picked us up and we noticed his Middle Eastern name. At first he was very closed mouth about such questions as the spread of Islam in Nevada, but after hearing that we were familiar with the various conflicts of the region and Islam he began to open up. By the end of the ride we had made plans to meet the local Imam. The mosque was situated in a housing project and bore no outside indications of its usage.

"Upon entering we were politely searched for weapons or

recording devices then led into a front room. The first thing I noted was a map of Nellis AFB with certain areas marked such as the motor pool, gas/fuel storage and weapons/ammo dump. A large photo of Sheik Rahman was displayed as was the Ayatollah Khomeini's poster size likeness. After a few minutes of over hearing Arabic remarks in the next room, our best Arabic speaker/agent called out we were not 'on the job' and were not being properly treated as 'guests.' Tea was brought out and a young Shi'ia stereotype (several days beard, sweater under a sports coat, buttoned up collar with no tie) sat down. As we ate goat cheese and pita bread with olives and cucumbers, the man produced a gold leaf bound copy of the Koran and asked what we wanted. We said that all of us were formerly in the Middle East and two of our group had extensive duty in Egypt, Iran, and Lebanon. A few more men joined this odd scene with more food and a bottle of wine. The wine trick was familiar to us and we all turned our glasses upside down refusing the wine in this alleged semi-mosque or Koranic school. In fact, our Egyptian-born ex-USAF Captain criticized the men for offering us an alcoholic drink in such surroundings. Apparently we passed the test by accepting only tea and snacks (with the correct hand).

The individual said that all were Egyptians with a few Palestinian born members thrown in and were in this country seeking political asylum, although none had met with an INS board and were employed as limo and taxi drivers. While being polite, the men still believed us to be 'secret police' for some US agency. The far interior of the room was divided by a nice tribal rug. Behind this was a small area for prayers and many martyr photos of suicide bombers and Egyptian/Lebanese clerics. I noted

HAMAS and HEZBOLLAH logos on the photos. This was verified by the self-appointed religious leader/teacher that the others called the Imam..."

"The group said that they were studying the American way of life and found it repulsive in Las Vegas due to the life style. They also commented on the remarks about Moslems that their passengers made when working their taxi jobs. I said many American think all Moslems are hostile but there are good and bad in both countries. I also said that US students should study geography and other cultures more than they currently do. The Imam replied that this was true of the Middle Eastern students as well.

"As I became familiar with the photos and posters I noted a heavy cardboard stock poster of the design of an RPG-7 and AK-47. A map of Las Vegas was also marked just like the map of Nellis AFB. One man saw me looking and told me they were studying the layout of the city for their taxi/limo jobs. Numerous photos of the men and their families were displayed showing that a few were in cammo uniforms carrying weapons. I pointed out a Rumanian AKM with its distinctive fore grip in one photo and this seemed to impress the group. Another photo was of a group of men at the Lake Powell region of Northern Arizona, with the large dam behind them. I was told that this reminded them of Lake Nasser and they take tours of the site often on their free days.

"After about 1 1/2 hour we all got up, retrieved our shoes and said goodbye...The next day we met with a Vegas police officer and asked about Moslem presence in the town. He replied that only 'Mohammadins' (a term I had not heard in years and only by tourists in the Middle East) were in Vegas to 'drink, gamble, meet women and live it up.'

"Although this incident shows that at least one group/cell/ association is in Las Vegas, the intelligence of its existence is not being circulated to the law enforcement community. In a place that contains high level 'Great Satan' targets with little security (not to inconvenience the guests) plus military facilities that grant access to these individuals when driving taxis, I would hope that the rest of the town and military police would have knowledge of the potential threat. My fellow briefers and I had performed facility vulnerability surveys in Iran, Lebanon, and Turkey. Our thoughts on securing a hotel/casino would conflict with the whole areas life style. A bio/chem weapon in a casino would inflict severe damage. An explosive of a great size would cause a massive lateral detonation far exceeding the damage at the World Trade Center."

The article shows clearly that America is wide open to possible terror attacks. How many other terror cells are skulking around the highways and byways of the nation waiting to lash out at our cities and people? The enemy *is* among us.

Wake up America, the new world disorder is staring us in the face. We can't turn our heads and ignore it any longer.

Selected Bibliography

The material includes books, newspapers, periodicals, and numerous private sources acquired in years of research and operational experience. The books have been separated into four general categories. Obviously, many overlap, but they were assigned to the grouping they seemed most appropriate.

Books by Section
New World Disorder

Albion, Adam Smith & Lampe, John R., *Strains of Economic Transition and Ethnic Conflict*, Woodrow Wilson Center, Washington, D.C., 1994.

Anderson, Benedict, *Imagined Communities*, Verso, London, 1991.

Ardrey, Robert, *The Territorial Imperative*, Atheneum, N.Y., 1966. *The Social Contract: A Personal Inquiry into the Evolutionary Sources of Order and Disorder*, Atheneum, N.Y., 1970.

Aron, Raymond, *On War*, University Press of America, Lanham, MD., 1957.

Baechler, Jean, *Revolution*, Harper & Row, N.Y., 1975.

Barnett, Frank R., Tovar, B. Hugh, Shultz, Richard H., *Special Operations in U.S. Strategy*, National Defense University Press, Washington, D.C., 1984.

Billington, James H., *Fire in the Minds of Men: Origins of the Revolutionary Faith*, Basic Books, N.Y., 1980.

Binnendijk, Hans, 1*997 Strategic Assessment: Flashpoints and Force Structure*, National Defense University, Washington, D.C., 1997.

Black, Jim Nelson, *When Nations Die,* Tyndale House Publishers, Wheaton , IL, 1994.

Bloom, Howard, *The Lucifer Principle: A Scientific Expedition Into The Forces of History,* Atlantic Monthly Press, N.Y., 1995.

Breytenbach, Jan, *Forged in Battle,* Saayman & Weber, Cape Town, 1986. *They Live By The Sword: 32 "Buffalo" Battalion-South Africa's Foreign Legion,* Lemur, Alberton, RSA, 1990.

Bork, Robert H., *Slouching Towards Gomorrah: Modern Liberalism and American Decline,* Regan Books, N.Y., 1996.

Bozeman, Adda B., *Politics & Culture in International Relations,* Princeton University Press, N.J., 1960. *Conflict in Africa,* Princeton University Press, N.J., 1976. *Strategic Intelligence & Statecraft,* Brassey's (USA), N.Y., 1992.

Bridgland, Fred, Jonas Savimbi: *A Key to Africa,* Paragon House, NY, 1986.

Brimelow, Peter, *Alien Nation,* Random House, N.Y., 1995.

Charters, David A., *Peacekeeping and the Challenge of Conflict Resolution,* Centre for Conflict Studies, Fredericton, New Brunswick, 1994.

Colburn, Forrest D., *The Vogue of Revolution in Poor Countries,* Princeton University Press, N.J., 1994.

Cole, Barbara, *The Elite,* Three Knights, Transkei, 1984.

Connor, Walker, *Ethnonationalism:The Quest For Understanding,* Princeton University Press, N.J., 1994.

Cronin, Patrick M., *From Globalism to Regionalism: New Perspectives on U.S. Foreign and Defense Policy,* National Defense University Press, Washington, D.C., 1993.

Crozier, Brian, *The Rebels,* Beacon Press, Boston, MA., 1960.

Daly, Ron Reid, *Selous Scouts Top Secret War,* Galago, Alberton, RSA,

1982.

Davidson, James Dale & Rees-Mogg, Lord William, *The Great Reckoning,* Summit Books, N.Y., 1991. *The Sovereign Individual,* Simon & Schuster, N.Y., 1997.

Diak, Nadia & Karatnycky, Adrian, *New Nations Rising: The Fall of the Soviets and the Challenge of Independence,* John Wiley & Sons, N.Y., 1993.

Elshtain, Jean Bethke, *Just War Theory,* New York University Press, N.Y., 1992.

Enzensberger, Hans Magnus, *Civil Wars From L.A. to Bosnia,* The New Press, N.Y., 1993.

Fischer, David Hackett, *The Great Wave: Price Revolutions and the Rhythm of History,* Oxford University Press, N.Y., 1996.

Gall, Carlotta & Thomas de Waal, *Chechyna: Calamity in the Caucasus,* New York University Press, NY, 1998.

Garrett, Laurie, *The Coming Plague,* Penguin Books, N.Y., 1994.

Gray, Colin S., *The Geopolitics of Superpower,* University of Kentucky Press, Lexington, KY, 1988.

Guehenno, Jean-Marie, *The End of the Nation State,* University of Minnesota Press, Minneapolis, 1993.

Gottlieb, Gidon, *Nation Against State: A New Approach to Ethnic Conflicts and the Decline of Sovereignty,* CFR Press, N.Y., 1993.

Handel, Michael L., *Masters of War: Classical Strategic Thought,* Frank Cass, London, 1992.

Haught, James A., *Holy Hatred: Religious Conflicts of the '90s,* Prometheus Books, Amherst, N.Y., 1995.

Hoffman, F.G., *Decisive Force: The New American Way of War,* Praeger, Westport, CT, 1996.

Homer-Dixon, Thomas F., *Environmental Scarcity and Global Security,*

Foreign Policy Association, N.Y., 1995.

Hooper, Jim, *Koevoet,* Southern Book Publishers, Johannesburg, RSA, 1988.

Huband, Mark, *The Liberian Civil War,* Frank Cass Publishers, London, 1998.

Hunter, *James Davidson, Before The Shooting Starts: Searching For Democracy in America's Culture War,* Free Press, N.Y., 1994.

Huntington, Samuel P., *The Clash of Civilizations and The Remaking of World Order,* Simon & Schuster, N.Y., 1996.

Ignatieff, Michael, *Blood and Belonging,* Farrar, Straus & Giroux, N.Y., 1993. *The Warrior's Honor: Ethnic War and the Modern Conscience,* Henry Holt & Co., NY, 1997.

Johnson, Paul, *Modern Times: From The Twenties to the Nineties,* Harper Collins, N.Y., 1991.

A History of The American People, Harper Collins, NY, 1998.

Kaplan, Robert K., *The Ends of The Earth: A Journey At The Dawn of The 21st Century,* Random House, N.Y., 1996.

Kennedy, Paul, *Preparing For The Twenty-First Century,* Random House, N.Y., 1993.

Kennon, Patrick E., *The Twilight of Democracy,* Doubleday, N.Y., 1985.

Kolkin, Joel, Tribes: *How Race, Religion and Identity Determine Success in the New Global Economy,* Random House, N.Y., 1993.

Lasch, Christopher, *The Revolt of The Elites and the Betrayal of Democracy,* W.W. Norton, N.Y., 1995.

Lieven, Anatol, *Chechyna: Tombstone of Russian Power,* Yale University Press, New Haven, 1998.

Luttwak, Edward, *Coup d'Etat: A Practical Handbook,* Harvard University Press, Boston, MA., 1979.

Macgregor, Douglas A., *Breaking the Phalanx: A New Design for Landpower in the 21st Century,* Praeger, Westport, CT, 1997.

McDougall, Walter A.,*Promised Land, Crusader State: The American Encounter With the World since 1776,* Houghton Miffin Co., Boston, 1997.

Moynihan, Daniel Patrick, Pandaemonium: *Ethnicity in International Politics,* Oxford University Press, N.Y., 1993.

Ohmae, Kinichi, *The End of The Nation State: The Rise of Regional Economies,* Free Press, N.Y., 1995.

Pfaff, William, *Barbarian Sentiments: How The American Century Ends,* Hill & Wang, N.Y., 1989. *The Wrath of Nations: Civilization and The Furies of Nationalism,* Simon & Schuster, N.Y., 1993.

Quigley, Carroll, *Tragedy and Hope: A History of The World In Our Time,* GSG & Associates, San Pedro, CA, 1966.

Rappoport, Anatol, & Graham, J.J., *Carl Von Clausewitz On War,* Dorset Press, N.Y., 1991.

Revel, Jean-Francois, *How Democracies Perish,* Harper & Row, N.Y., 1983. *Democracy Against Itself: The Future of the Democratic Impulse,* Free Press, N.Y., 1993.

Schlesinger, Arthur M., Jr., *The Disuniting of America: Reflections on a Multicultural Society,* W.W. Norton, N.Y., 1991.

Strauss, William & Howe, Neil, *The Forth Turning,* Broadway Books, N.Y., 1997.

Sowell, Thomas, *Conquest & Cultures: An International History,* Basic Books, NY, 1998.

Tainter, Joseph A., *The Collapse of Complex Societies,* Cambridge University Press, London, 1988.

Tenner, Edward, *Why Things Bite Back: Technology and The Revenge of Unintended Consequences,* Alfred A. Knopf, N.Y., 1996.

Triumph of Disorder

Thomson, Janice E., *Mercenaries, Pirates & Sovereigns,* Princeton University Press, N.J., 1994.

Thompson, Leroy, *Ragged War: The Story of Unconventional and Counter-Revolutionary Warfare,* Arms & Armour Press, London, 1994.

Waltz, Kenneth N., *Man the State and War,* Columbia University Press, New York, 1959.

Watts, Barry D., *Clausewitzian Friction and Future War,* National Defense University Press, Washington, D.C., 1966.

Weatherford, Jack, *Savages and Civilization: Who Will Survive?,* Crown Publishers, N.Y., 1994.

Wolf, Eric R., *Peasant Wars of the Twentieth Century,* Harper & Row, N.Y., 1969.

Wright, Robin & McManus, Doyle, *Flash-points: Promise and Peril in a New World,* Alfred Knopf, N.Y., 1991.

Yergin, David & Gustafson, Thiane, *Russia 2010 and What It Means for The World,* Random House, N.Y., 1993.

Drugs, Gangs, Guerrillas and the Changing Nature of War

Alexander, Bevin, *The Future of Warfare,* W.W. Norton, N.Y., 1995.

Antokol, Norman & Nudell, Mayer, *No One A Neutral: Political Hostage Taking in the Modern World,* Alpha Publications of Ohio, 1990.

Asprey, Robert B., *War in The Shadows, Vols. I & II,* Doubleday, N.Y., 1975.

Barkun, Michael, *Religion and the Racist Right: The Origins of the Christian Identity Movement,* University of North Carolina Press, Chapel Hill, N.C., 1994.

Bodansky, Yossef, *Some Call It Peace: Waiting For War in the Balkans,*

ISSA Books, Alexandria, VA, 1996. *Target America: Terrorism in the U.S. Today,* SPI Books, N.Y., 1993.

Bowman, Stephen, *When The Eagle Screams: America's Vulnerability to Terrorism,* Birch Lane Press, N.Y., 1994.

Callwell, C.E., *Small Wars,* Greenhill Books, London, 1990.

Chaliand, Gerard, *Guerrilla Strategies,* University of California Press, Berkeley, CA., 1982.

Clutterbuck, Richard, *Terrorism and Guerrilla Warfare: Forecasts and Remedies,* Routledge, London, 1990.

Collins, John M., *Special Operations Forces: An Assessment,* National Defense University Press, Washington, D.C., 1994.

Dean, David L. *Low-Intensity Conflict and Modern Technology,* Air University Press, Maxwell AFB, Alabama, 1986.

Delemas, Phillippe, *The Rosy Future of War,* Free Press, N.Y., 1995.

Douglas, Joseph D., Jr., *Red Cocaine: The Drugging of America,* Clarion House, Atlanta, GA, 1990.

Dupuy, Trevor N., *Future Wars: The World's Most Dangerous Flashpoints,* Warner Books, N.Y., 1992.

Ehrenfeld, Rachel, *Narco-Terrorism and The Cuban Connection,* Cuban American Foundation, Washington, D.C., 1988. *Narco Terrorism,* Basic Books, N.Y., 1990.

Evans, Ernest, *Wars Without Splendor: The U.S. Military and Low-Level Conflict,* Greenwood Press, Westport, CT., 1987.

Flynn, John C., *Cocaine,* Birch Lane Press, N.Y., 1991.

Griffin, Samuel B., *Mao Tse-Tung on Guerrilla Warfare,* Praeger, N.Y., 1962. *Sun Tzu: The Art of War,* Oxford University Press, N.Y., 1977.

Grosscup, Beau, *The Explosion of Terrorism,* New Horizon Press, N.J., 1991.

Han, Henry H., *Terrorism & Political Violence: Limits & Possibilities,*

Oceana Publications, N.Y., 1993.

Hayden, H.T., *Shadow War: Special Operations and Low Intensity Conflict,* Pacific Aero Press, Vista, CA., 1992.

Heckler, Richard Strozzi, *In Search of The Warrior Spirit,* North Atlantic Books, Berkeley, CA., 1990.

Hoare, Mike, *The Road to Kalamata,* Lexington Books, Lexington, MA, 1989. *Congo Mercenary,* Robert Hale, London, 1967.

Horner, D.M., *SAS: Phantoms of the Jungle,* The Battery Press, Nashville, TN., 1989.

Kahane, Rabbi Meir, *The Story of the Jewish Defense League,* Chilton Book Company, Radnor, PA., 1975.

Keegan, John, *A History of Warfare,* Alfred A. Knopf, N.Y., 1993.

Keeley, Lawrewnce H., *War Before Civilization: The Myth of the Peaceful Savage,* Oxford University Press, N.Y., 1996.

Kerry, John, *The New War,* Simon & Schuster, N.Y., 1997.

Kirk, Russell, *The Roots of American Order,* Open Court Press, LaSalle, IL, 1974.

Larteguy, Jean, *The Centurions,* E.P. Dutton, N.Y., 1961. *The Praetorians,* E.P. Dutton, N.Y., 1963.

Lenin, V.I., *What Is To Be Done,* Foreign Language Press, Peking, 1971.

Lord, Carnes & Barnett, Frank R., *Political Warfare and Psychological Operations,* National Defense University Press, Washington, D.C., 1989.

Mao Tse-Tung, *Selected Works, Vols. I & II,* International Publishers, N.Y., 1954.

de Marenches, Count, *The Fourth World War: Democracy and Espionage in the Age of Terrorism,* Wm. Morrow, N.Y., 1992.

McCuen, John J., *The Art of Counter-Revolutionary War,* Stackpole

Books, Harrisburg, PA., 1966.

McKnight, Gerald, *The Terrorist Mind: Why They Hijack, Kidnap, Bomb and Kill,* Bobbs-Merrill, N.Y., 1974.

McRandle, James H., *The Antique Drums of War,* Texas A & M Press, College Station, TX, 1994.

Moorcraft, Paul I., & McLaughlin, Peter, *Chimurengha! The War in Rhodesia 1965-1980,* Sygma/Collins, Marshalltown, RSA, 1982.

Netanyahu, Benjamin, *Terrorism: How The West Can Win,* Farrar, Straus & Giroux, N.Y., 1986.

Noer, John H. & Gregory, David, *Chokepoints: Maritime Economic Concerns in Southeast Asia,* National Defense University Press, Washington, D.C., 1996.

Norval, Morgan, *Death in the Desert: The Namibian Tragedy,* Selous Foundation Press, Washington, D.C., 1989. *Inside The ANC: The Evolution of a Terrorist Organization,* Selous Foundation Press, Washington, D,C., 1990.

O'Neil, Bard E., *Insurgency & Terrorism : Inside Modern Revolutionary War,* Brassey's (USA), N.Y., 1990.

O'Neil, Bard E., Heaton, William R. & Alberts, Donald, Jr., *Insurgency in the Modern World,* Westview Press, Boulder, CO., 1980.

Porzecanski, Arturo C., *Uruguay's Tupamaros: The Urban Guerrilla,* Praeger, N.Y., 1973.

Pryce-Jones, David, *The Strange Death of the Soviet Empire,* Henry Holt &Co., NY, 1995.

Puren, Jerry, *Mercenary Commander,* Galago, Alberton, RSA, 1986.

Pustay, John S., *Counter-insurgency Warfare,* Free Press, N.Y., 1965.

Ra'anan, Uri, Pfaltzgrafp, Robert l, Jr., Shultz, Richard H., Halperin, Ernst, Lukes, Igor, *Hydra of Carnage: International Linkages of Terrorism,* Lexington Books, Lexington, MA.,   1986.

Seabury, Paul & Codevilla, Angelo, *War Ends and Means,* Basic Books, N.Y., 1989.

Schannis, Gerardo Jorge, *War and Terrorism in International Affairs,* Transaction Books, N.J., 1980.

Schwartau, Winn, *Information Warfare: Chaos on the Electronic Superhighway,* Thunder's Mouth Press, N.Y., 1994.

Shafer, D. Michael, *Deadly Paradigms: The Failure of U.S. Counterinsurgency Policy,* Princeton University Press, N.J., 1988.

Shultz, Richard H., Jr., *The Soviet Union and Revolutionary War,* Hoover Press, Stanford, CA., 1988.

Shultz, Richard H., Jr., Ra'anan, Uri, Pfaltzgrafp, Robert L., Jr., Olson, William, Jr., & Lukes, Igor, *Guerrilla Warfare & Counter-Insurgency: U.S.-Soviet Policy in the Third World,* Lexington Books, Lexington, MA., 1989.

Smith, Paul, Jr., *On Political War,* National Defense University Press, Washington, D.C., 1989.

Snow, Donald M., *Uncivil Wars: International Security and the New Internal Conflicts,* Lynne RiennerPublishers, Boulder, CO., 1996.

Steenkamp, Willem, *South Africa's Border War 1966-1989,* Ashanti Publishing, Gibraltar, 1989.

Sterling, Claire, *Thieves World: The Threat of the New Global Network of Organized Crime,* Simon & Schuster, N.Y., 1994.

Stiff, Peter, *Nine Days of War,* Lemur Books, Alberton, RSA, 1989.

Thomas, Andrew Peyton, *Crime and the Sacking of America: The Roots of Chaos,* Brassey's, Washington, 1994.

Thompson, Sir Robert, *Defeating Communist Insurgency,* Praeger, N.Y., 1966.

Toffler, Alvin & Heidi, *War And Anti-War: Survival At The Dawn of The 21st Century,* Little Brown, Boston, MA., 1993.

Trease, Geoffrey, *The Condottieri: Soldiers of Fortune,* Holt, Rinehard, Winston, N.Y., 1971.

Trinquier, Roger, *Modern Warfare: A French View of Counterinsurgency,* Praeger, N.Y., 1964.

Van Creveld, Martin, *The Transformation of War,* Free Press, N.Y., 1991. *Nuclear Proliferation and the Future of Conflict,* The Free Press, NY, 1993. *The Encyclopedia of Revolution and Revolutionaries: From Anarchism to Zhou Enlai, Facts on File,* NY, 1996.

Van Der Waals, W.S., *Portugal's War in Angola 1961-1974,* Ashanti Publishing, Rivonia, RSA, 1993.

Wardlaw, Grant, *Political Terrorism,* Cambridge University Press, London, 1982.

Wilson, Edward O., *Consilience: The Unity of Knowledge,* Alfred A. Knoff, NY, 1998.

Zabih, Sepehr, *The Iranian Military in Revolution and War,* Routledge, London, 1988.

Islam, Iran, PLO & Surrogates

Abuljobain, Ahmad, *Islam Under Siege: Radical Islamic Terrorism or Political Islam?,* United Association for Studies and Research, Annandale, VA., 1993.

Ali-Sweet, Dr. Abdulaziz L., *Saudi Arabia: A Kingdom in Transition,* Amana Publications, Beltsville,MD., 1993.

Arnold, Anthony, *Afghanistan: The Soviet Invasion in Perspective,* Hoover Institution Press, Stanford, CA, 1985.

Bull, Gerald, *The Arab World,* Brooks/Cole Publishing, Pacific Grove, CA., 1987.

Clawson, Patrick, *Iran's Challenge to the West: How, When, And Why,*

Triumph of Disorder

Washington Institute For Near East Policy, Washington, D.C., 1993.

Diehl, Wilhelm, *Holy War,* MacMillan, N.Y., 1984.

Eickelman, Dale F., *Russia's Muslim Frontiers,* Indiana University Press, Bloomington, IN., 1993.

Elst, Koenraad, *Ayodhya and After: Issues Before Hindu Society,* Voice of India, New Delhi, 1991.

Esposito, John, *The Islamic Threat: Myth or Reality?,* Oxford University Press, N.Y., 1992.

Farrakhan, Louis, *A Torchlight for America,* FLN Publishing Co., Chicago, IL., 1993.

Fullerton, John, *The Soviet Occupation of Afghanistan,* South China Morning Post, Hong Kong, n.d.

Hader, Leon T., *Quagmire: America in the Middle East,* Cato Institute, Washington, D.C., 1992.

al-Hibri, Azizah, I*slamic Constitutionalism and the Concept of Democracy,* Muslim Foundation, Washington, D.C., n.d.

Hiro, Dilip, *Holy Wars: The Rise of Islamic Fundamentalism,* Routledge, N.Y., 1989.

Hodgson, Marshall G.S., *The Venture of Islam: Conscience and History in a World Civilization,* Vols. 1, 2, & 3, Chicago University Pres, Chicago, IL., 1974.

Hopkirk, Peter, *Like Hidden Fire,* Kodansha International, N.Y., 1994. *The Great Game,* John Murray, London, 1990.

Hourani, Albert A., *A History of The Arab Peoples,* Warner Books, N.Y., 1991.

Jackson, James Turner & Kelsay, John, *Cross, Crescent and Sword: The Justification and Limitation of War in Western and Islamic Tradition,* Greenwood Press, N.Y., 1990.

Kepel, Gilles, *Muslim Extremism in Egypt,* University of California

Press, Berkeley, CA., 1985.

Khomeini, Imam, I*slam and Revolution: Writings and Declarations of Imam Khomeini,* Mizan Press, Berkeley, CA., 1981.

Klaus, Rosanne, *Afghanistan: The Great Game Revisited,* Freedom House, N.Y., 1987.

Kramer, Martin, *Hezbollah's Vision of the West,* Washington Institute For Near East Policy, Washington, D.C., 1989.

Lewis, Bernard, *The Arabs in History,* Oxford University Press, N.Y., 1993. *Islam and the West,* Oxford University Press, N.Y., 1993. *The Political Language of Islam,* Chicago University Press, Chicago, IL., 1991. *The Assassins: A Radical Sect in Islam,* Oxford University Press, N.Y., 1967.

Lincoln, C. Eric, *The Black Muslims in America,* Kaycode Publications, N.Y., 1961.

Livingston, Neil Jr., & Halevy, David, *Inside The PLO,* Wm. Morrow, N.Y., 1990.

Mansfield, Peter, *A History of the Middle East,* Viking, N.Y., 1991.

Marr, Phebe & Lewis, William, *Riding The Tiger: The Middle East Challenge After The Cold War,* Westview Press, Boulder, CO., 1993.

Mohaddessin, Mohammad, *Islamic Fundamentalism: The New Global Threat,* Seven Locks Press, Washington, D.C., 1993.

Morey, Robert, *The Islamic Invasion: Confronting The World's Fastest Growing Religion,* Harvest House, Eugene, OR., 1992.

Muhammad, Elijah, *Message To The Blackman In America,* United Brothers Communications System, Newport News, VA., 1992. *I Am The Last Messenger of Allah,* Secretarius Publications, Cleveland, OH., n.d.

Pipes, Daniel, *In The Path of God: Islam and Political Power,* Basic Books, N.Y., 1983.

Reeves, Mirou, *Female Warriors of Allah: Women and the Islamic Revolution*, E.P. Dutton, N.Y., 1992.

Roy, Olivier, *The Failure of Political Islam*, Harvard University Press, Boston, MA., 1994. *Islam and Resistance in Afghanistan*, Cambridge University Press, Cambridge, 1986.

Rubin, Barry, *Revolution Until Victory? the Politics and History of the PLO*, Harvard University Press, Boston, MA, 1994.

Sharati, Dr. Ali, *Red Shi'ism*, Free Islamic Literature, Inc., Houston, TX., n.d.

Swarup, Ram, *Understanding Islam Through Hadis: Religious Faith or Fanaticism?*, Voice of India, New Delhi, 1983.

Smith, Wilfred Cantwell, *Islam in Modern Society*, Mentor Books, N.Y., 1957.

Taheri, Amir, *Holy Terror: The Inside Story of Islamic Terrorism*, Sphere Books, London, 1987.

Taylor, Alan R., *The Islamic Question in Middle East Politics*, Westview Press, Boulder, CO., 1988.

von der Mehdin, Fred R., *Two World of Islam: Interaction Between Southeast Asia and the   Middle East*, University Press of Florida, Gainsville, 1993.

Waller, John, *Beyond The Khyber Pass*, Random House, NY, 1990.

Wright, Robin, *In The Name of God: The Khomeini Decade*, Simon & Schuster, NY, 1989.

Zakaria, Rafiq, *The Struggle Within Islam: The Conflict Between Religion and Politics*, Penguin Books, NY, 1989.

Sudan

Hammond, Peter, *Faith Under Fire In Sudan*, Frontline Fellowship, Newlands, RSA, 1996.

Hill, George Chenevix, *Colonel Gordon in Central Africa, 1874-1879,* Kraus Reprints, NY, 1969.

Khalid, Mansour, *The Government They Deserve: The Role of the Elites in Sudan's Political Evolution,* Kegan Paul International, London, 1990.

Morehead, Alan, *The White Nile,* Adventure Library, NY, 1995. *The Blue Nile,* Amerin Ltd., NY, 1976.

Nutting, Anthony, *Gordon of Khartoum,* Charles N. Potter, NY, 1966.

Packenham, Thomas, *The Scramble For Africa,* Random House, NY, 1991.

Trench, John, *The Road To Khartoum,* Dorset Press, NY, 1989.

Waller, John, *Gordon of Khartoum,* Atheneum, NY, 1988.

Newspapers and Periodicals

African Armed Forces

American Survival Guide

Armed Forces Journal International

Chalcedon Report

Christian Observer

Chronicles

Combat and Survival

Commentary

Counterterrorism & Security International

Counterterrorism & Security Reports

Cross Border Control

Current History

For Your Eyes Only

Foreign Affairs

Frontline Fellowship

Insight Magazine

Intersec: The Journal of International Security
Journal of Civil Wars
Journal of Conflict Studies
Journal of Intelligence & National Security
Journal of Slavic Military Studies
Journal of Small Wars & Insurgencies
Journal of Terrorism & Political Violence
Journal of Transnational Organized Crime
Marine Corps Gazette
National Defense
National Review
Newsweek Magazine
Otto Scott's Compass
Parameters
Salut
Soldier of Fortune
Tactical Response & Security
The American Spectator
The Atlantic Monthly
The Baltimore Sun
The Cape Times (RSA)
The Chief
The Economist
The Los Angeles Times
The New American
The New Republic
The New York Post
The New York Times
The Wall Street Journal

The Washington Post
The Washington Times
Time Magazine
Truth in Media
U.S. News & World Report
Voice of the Martyrs
West Africa
World EOD Gazette

Printed in the United States
3643